MURDER
YOUR
DARLINGS

MURDER
YOUR
DARLINGS

*And other gentle writing advice
from Aristotle to Zinsser*

Roy Peter Clark

Little, Brown Spark
New York Boston London

Little, Brown Spark
Hachette Book Group
1290 Avenue of the Americas, New York, NY 10104
littlebrownspark.com

First Edition: January 2020

Little, Brown Spark is an imprint of Little, Brown and Company, a division of Hachette Book Group, Inc. The Little, Brown Spark name and logo are trademarks of Hachette Book Group, Inc.

The publisher is not responsible for websites (or their content) that are not owned by the publisher.

The Hachette Speakers Bureau provides a wide range of authors for speaking events. To find out more, go to hachettespeakersbureau.com or call (866) 376-6591.

ISBN 978-0-316-48188-5
LCCN 2019946513

10 9 8 7 6 5 4 3 2 1

LSC-C

Printed in the United States of America

To all reading and writing teachers—
especially in public schools. To all
journalists who speak truth to power in the
public interest. You deserve medals as
champions of literacy and democracy.
Thank you for your service.

CONTENTS

Contents

Contents

MURDER
YOUR
DARLINGS

INTRODUCTION

A Writing Book about Writing Books

Fans of the TV comedy *Seinfeld* will remember the one great literary success of that slapstick lunatic Cosmo Kramer: He wrote a coffee-table book about coffee tables. The book came with little legs you could unfold to make it into a miniature coffee table. He sold the film rights.

Murder Your Darlings, an allusion to a famous bit of writing advice from a British professor nicknamed "Q," turns out to be a writing book about…writing books. I love writing guides, and they love me. They confirm things I know about the craft, teach me methods I have never heard of before, and, in rare but crucial cases, spin my head around like an owl's at an exorcism.

You are holding my sixth book on reading, writing, and language since 2006. Thank you, Little, Brown. Professors often ask me to reveal the secrets of my productivity. "It's easy," I answer, and I'm serious. "I write during faculty meetings."

"How do you get away with it?"

"Everyone thinks I am taking notes."

Introduction

The first and most popular of my Little, Brown books is *Writing Tools*. Where did I find the fifty-five writing strategies shared in that book? They came from close readings of great works of literature, a skill I learned in college and honed into a craft I call "X-ray reading." They came from writing and writing and rewriting, with the guidance of teachers, editors, and other writers. And they came from countless essays and guidebooks on the writing craft, some published well before the birth of Christ (a pretty good storyteller himself) and some published just last year.

In focusing on these important writing books, I am not trying to steal their thunder. I am trying, instead, to amplify it, to pay back my debt to the authors who shaped my craft. Read them! To those who say that you can't learn to write by reading a book on writing, I answer: "Then why are there so many of them?" Most bookstores devote a shelf or two or even a full bookcase to writing guides. I own about 1,500 books, most of them about reading, writing, grammar, rhetoric, composition, language, literature, and journalism. I understand that the writing teacher and legal scholar Bryan Garner has a space in Dallas called the Scriptorium, a Taj Mahal of lexical Know-It-All. I have a space at the Poynter Institute I call my cubby. Among its roomlike, womblike virtues, it hides ten steps from a specialized library comprising 12,000 books, most of them on my favorite topics.

So many writing books. Which ones will I choose to write about, and by what criteria? Let me explain what I am *not* trying to do. I am not choosing the *best* writing guides, or the most practical, or the most enduring, or the most anything. As a reader I happen to like those lists, the ones you find in *Rolling Stone:* the 100 greatest rock 'n' roll songs, the 100 greatest guitar solos of all time, Dylan's 100 greatest hits.

I do *not* rank the writing books, but I do appreciate them. Most of what you will read here is *why* I appreciate them, what I or others have learned from them, and what I think you, the reader, can take away and apply to your own work. As you will see, my appreciation is not without a critical edge: any advice from John McPhee should come with the knowledge that he has been a privileged *New Yorker* writer, with time and resources most of us can only dream about; Anne Lamott is way too hard on herself, running the risk of discouraging others; and, sad to say, Dorothea Brande, who wrote one of the most original writing guides of all time, turns out to have been— along with her editor hubby—a 1930s-style American fascist and anti-Semite. We teachers prefer our apples without bruises, but there you go.

Before I compiled these books, I did some crowdsourcing. On social media, I asked writers for the names of writing guides that had informed or inspired them. Suggestions arrived by the dozens, many with authors and books I had read many times, but others with introductions to strangers I was glad to meet. All of those worthy candidates made my selection process harder.

I began by listing books that were famous, popular, or influential: *The Elements of Style* by Strunk and White; *Writing Down the Bones* by Natalie Goldberg; *Bird by Bird* by Anne Lamott; *The New Journalism* by Tom Wolfe. Among the five Ws (*who, what, where, when,* and *why*), *why* is hardest to answer. I made it my mission to capture *why* such books matter.

I wanted to include writing guides that were ancient, and thus foundational, from Aristotle on the cathartic nature of tragedy to Quintilian on the influence of the spoken word. Such texts allow us to trace the long and powerful story of making meaning through reading, writing, and speaking—that is, through the essential acts of literacy.

I could not avoid the temptation to include several books written by authors and teachers whom I know personally. A teacher at Oxford (where I spent a glorious summer) is called a don, and many a great don has passed by my writing room (Don Fry, Don Murray, Don Graves, Don Hall). I repay them, when I can, by passing along their knowledge. The writing world is cozy enough for me to have worked with Bill Zinsser, Bill Howarth, and Connie Hale, to name a few. I once interviewed Stephen King. I exchanged a letter with E. B. White. On a buffet line at a literary conference in Tucson I got to meet Elmore Leonard and engaged him in a friendly argument about how many exclamation points are allowed in a text. (His take was one for every 100,000 words unless you are Tom Wolfe—then the sky's the limit.)

I drop these names not for me, but for you. When an author writes a good writing guide, that author is inviting you—in Frank Smith's good phrase—to join a club. You may aspire to become a writer, but after reading their work on writing, you can better identify as one, feeling part of a community, a tribe of scribes.

HOW THIS BOOK WAS WRITTEN,
AND HOW IT IS ORGANIZED

Murder Your Darlings is divided into six parts. I did not draft the book that way. I wrote without a structural plan, selecting books off my shelves as the muse guided me. I built momentum by writing about the books I knew best—with some side trips along the way. I wrote about book after book, chapter by chapter, until the writing train crashed through the 75,000-word barrier, and then through the 100,000-word frontier. I paused after drafting fifty chapters, with another fifty or so books nearby that I knew I wanted to write about. I panicked. Then in my ear I heard the voice of my writing coach Donald Murray with a tip I have passed along to countless other overwriters: "Brevity comes from selection, and not compression." I got down to 36 chapters, and then 33.

What would be the order of the chapters? How would I divide them into sections? I looked up to see near my desk a stack of new index cards. I thumbed through them and counted six colors: white, pink, yellow, green, violet, and blue. Hmm. Six colors. Maybe six sections? So I gave it a shot.

- Yellow stood for "Language and Craft."
- Violet for "Voice and Style."
- White for "Confidence and Identity."
- Blue for "Storytelling and Character."
- Pink for "Rhetoric and Audience."
- Green for "Mission and Purpose."

Many of the books summarized here touch on all of these themes and topics. Don't be surprised when I scoot off-topic to show you something interesting or useful being played out down a side street. Reading these books, analyzing them, appreciating them, playing with them, made me want to write. They made me want to write not just about the books themselves, but about all aspects of my creative life, personal and professional. It is my wish that they will make you want to write, too.

THE ADDED BONUS OF READING
MURDER YOUR DARLINGS

- You will get a taste of more than fifty writing guides, helping you to choose which ones you would like to read and/or own.
- There are hundreds of writing lessons in some of these books. I will focus on one or two that I have found particularly helpful in my own writing.
- Many of the books are in print and for sale. Others, of a certain vintage, are free online. Still others are rare or no longer in print. This book gives you some access to these gems.
- Citations from each book include not just writing tips, but brief excerpts that let you hear the voice of the original author.

Early in my research for *Murder Your Darlings*, I came upon the word *asymptote*. It comes from mathematics and denotes a curved line that approaches a straight one on a graph, getting closer and closer to it without ever reaching it—to infinity. I embraced *asymptote* as a metaphor for my own life and work. In my daily teaching, I tell students—of all ages—that it is my goal to learn something new about the craft every day, something I can pass along to them. If that sounds hokey to you, just kick me in the asymptote. If not, feel free to embrace the idea of a life of language learning as your own. Let *Murder Your Darlings* show you the way.

I

Language and Craft

Donald Hall, who served as America's poet laureate, writes about the English language as if it were a place you could inhabit, a life-enhancing atmosphere that lets you breathe. The love of words shines in all the works studied in *Murder Your Darlings*. Language turns out to be the raw material of meaning. It takes craft to turn words into an essay, a novel, a poem.

Writing may look like magic in the hands of an author such as John McPhee, but Bill Howarth reveals that the magic is not magic at all, but the product of a process—elaborate, yes, but one that can be learned. I should know. I used McPhee's method to write my first book. You are about to learn it, too.

Sir Arthur Quiller-Couch encouraged his students to cut their self-indulgent words and phrases. But William Zinsser was so dedicated to his craft that he was willing to reveal his work in all its imperfection, highlighting the clutter that made it feel impenetrable, and then cutting every word not doing useful work.

George Campbell, a brainy minister of the word and the Word, thought it most worthy in the eighteenth century to turn his attention to the English language in all its glory. Wordcraft could work on the page and from the pulpit. Sentences could be shaped for maximum clarity or for a desired literary effect, to express utility or beauty.

All of these authors—across generations and cultures—share a love of language that feels inspirational when you read them. Their special gift to us is not just the creative language we might find in a poem or novel. It is the use of words about words, of language about language, a meta-perspective that sharpens our own vision.

1

Murder your darlings.
Keep your eye on those fancy phrases.

On the Art of Writing
By Sir Arthur Quiller-Couch

Toolbox: *You will write things you love. That's wonderful. Enjoy that feeling. During revision, though, ask yourself a crucial question. Does that gorgeous passage or that clever thought support your main idea? If not, take it out. You do not have to "murder" that darling metaphor. You can save it for another story on another day.*

One of the most famous bits of writing advice comes to us from British author Sir Arthur Quiller-Couch, known to his mates and university students as Q. (He should not be confused with the Quartermaster, played by actor Desmond Llewelyn, who provides 007 with those wonderful gadgets in the James Bond movies.)

"Murder your darlings," Q ordered his students in 1914. When his lectures were published, he emphasized the imperative in italics: "*Murder your darlings.*" Thank you, Q, for giving me a title for this book.

In America the phrase has been misattributed (sometimes to Orwell) and misquoted as "Kill your babies." Like other short sentences, "Murder your darlings" has the ring of truth, made more shocking because Q's commandment bumps into a more famous one from Mount Sinai: "Thou shalt not kill."

The eccentric Professor Q described exactly what he meant in the lecture "On Style," the final chapter in his book *On the Art of Writing.* Before he offered his own definition of what writing style *is,* he argued for what style is *not:*

> Style...is not—can never be—extraneous Ornament. You remember, may be, the Persian lover...: how to convey his passion he sought a professional letter-writer and purchased a vocabulary charged with ornament, wherewith to attract the fair one as with a basket of jewels. Well, in this extraneous, professional, purchased ornamentation, you have something which Style is not: and if you here require a practical rule of me, I will present you with this.

Freeze frame. As I read that passage, I imagine I am a university student at Cambridge in 1914—not yet facing trench warfare in France or the Spanish flu pandemic, seeing only a world of language and letters before me, sitting on the edge of my chair in the lecture hall, a quill in my hand, waiting to record the wisdom of Professor Q:

Whenever you feel an impulse to perpetrate a piece of exceptionally fine writing, obey it—whole-heartedly—and delete it before sending your manuscript to press. *Murder your darlings.*

As Q delivered this message, the *Oxford English Dictionary* was chugging along toward completion, so it seems only right to check the OED for a definition of *darling*. Derived from Old English, it denotes a "dear one," more broadly: "A person who is very dear to another; the object of a person's love; one dearly loved. Commonly used as a term of endearing address."

For Q, then, it is not enough to murder a word, phrase, or passage that you like—or even love. His sadism requires you to commit verbicide on the words you love the most. Your darlings. In human terms, your favorite child; perhaps, your blushing bride; dare I say it, your sainted mother.

Here is where, for me, Q's metaphor met real life.

Travel back with me to March 2017. A series of phone calls informs me that my alma mater, Providence College in Rhode Island, wants to give me an honorary degree: Doctor of Journalism. More significant, the president, Father Brian Shanley, asks me to deliver the commencement address in celebration of the college's centennial. I am struck dumb.

I had read speeches in front of big crowds before, but nothing like this. My assignment was to inspire and delight 1,200 graduates and a stadium crowd numbering about 10,000. From the moment I said yes to the moment I delivered the goods on Sunday, May 21, my stomach hurt.

This felt like the greatest honor of my professional life, with deep connections to family and friends. Over the next hundred days I thought of little else but that speech. Without committing a word to paper or screen, I spent a month in bed, in the shower, over coffee, behind the wheel, rehearsing the imagined text. When friends asked, "How's it going?" I would try out the occasional theme statement or funny line, forming a kind of ad hoc focus group.

I calculated that I could deliver about 2,000 words in 15 minutes. By early May I had a first draft. It spread to 8,000 words. I did the math. I had prepared a speech that would take at least an hour to read. I knew my remarks would come near the end of the ceremony, with a huge audience butt-numb from more than two hours of sitting. I imagined I was on the stage of the Apollo Theater, where on Amateur Night bad performers might be dragged offstage with a hook. I would be like the guy who spoke for two hours at Gettysburg before Lincoln got his two minutes.

"You were selected," said a friend, "because you wrote a book on SHORT writing."

"Yes," I responded, "but it was a BOOK about short writing."

In examining my first draft, I loved everything I had written. What was I to do? A voice with a British accent invaded my thoughts: *Murder your darlings.* So that's what I did. I murdered my mother.

Before I confess the how and why of it, let me turn back to Q's directive.

"Whenever you feel an impulse to perpetrate a piece of exceptionally fine writing, obey it—whole-heartedly—and delete it before sending your manuscript to press. *Murder your darlings.*"

Notice that Q does not say "Don't write down the words you love best." He encourages us to write them down—almost as a way of purging them from our system. Draft, purge, murder. Before you murder that darling, you must create it. The murder comes through revision. That reveals Q to be a "putter-inner" rather than a "taker-outter," the type of writer who puts it all in during drafting and cuts ruthlessly during revision.

In my 8,000-word first draft, I included eight references to my mom. Two things conspired to make my early draft so Mom-heavy. The first was my misunderstanding that the commencement was scheduled for Mother's Day, when in fact it came a week later. The second was a ghostlike visit from Mom in the form of a long-saved voice-mail message. Mom died in March of 2015, closing in on the age of ninety-six. Looking for a lost message, I stumbled upon this saved one, which began, "Hello, Roy. This is your mother. Remember me? The one who created you?"

She was inquiring about someone in the family, but out of that context, this felt like a visitation, and it led me to reflect upon my favorite Shirley Clark anecdotes, some of which were pure entertainment, others that carried potential lessons for the graduate. Two examples will suffice.

- Mom was a conservative Catholic church-lady who could swear like the love child of a longshoreman and a gangsta rapper. I believe I once heard her use the f-word as four different parts of speech in a single sentence. When her assisted-living facility conducted a trivia contest and she could not quite remember the name of a famous Peter, Paul and Mary song, she blurted, "F--- the Magic Dragon."

- She learned at the age of ninety that her firstborn granddaughter was gay. The next day she phoned to assure Alison that her only concern was Alison's happiness. "We love you," she repeated. "Your family loves you."

There was much more, but you get it. I had a lot to work with. And I thought the mothers of the graduates would be pleased to hear me honor my own mom on this special day.

How do you turn an 8,000-word text into 2,000?

Maybe I did not have to murder my mom; I could just select the best of her multiple personalities. Over days and then weeks, the text grew shorter and shorter. Eight references to mom became five, became three, became one. Became none.

Why did she have to make the ultimate sacrifice? Because the speech was not *about* her. Mom was nothing more than the scaffolding for my story, the parts I had to erect until I learned what I really wanted to say, what I thought the graduates really needed to hear.

The short version of my theme derived from the meaning of the name of the college, Providence, as expressed in an old religious saying I learned in eighth grade: "God writes straight with crooked lines." I told the graduates that out of high school I did not want to attend Providence. I wanted to go to Princeton, but did not get in.

"It turns out I was never, ever accepted to the place I thought I wanted to be, but in retrospect I *always* wound up at the place I *needed* to be. Only looking over my shoulder could I see that pattern. Time after time, what I had experienced as Disappointment became transformed into Opportunity."

My brothers, Ted and Vincent, offered their opinions on what Mom would have thought about being elbowed out of the final draft in favor of a little light theology. I should mention that Shirley Clark was very theatrical and wrote and directed many community variety shows. She may never have murdered a darling, but our best guess is that in some corner of heaven she has Sir Arthur Quiller-Couch in a chokehold.

LESSONS

1. If you think of something clever, by all means write it down.

2. Ask yourself, "Am I including this because it provides the reader with a memorable and delightful piece of evidence to prove the point of my text? Or is it beside the point even though it reveals what a good wordsmith I am?"

3. If you decide to "murder" that passage, remember that you have another choice. You can save it in a file or journal. It may work well in a different context.

4. You may not be able to make these judgments on your own. Trust an editor or a writing friend to help. My editor, Tracy Behar, called attention to dozens of passages in my manuscript that were impatiently waiting for a different opportunity to appear in print.

2

Find and cut the clutter. Search for lazy words, even after several drafts.

On Writing Well: The Classic Guide to Writing Nonfiction
By William Zinsser

Toolbox: *Like William Zinsser, assume that your third draft, even your fifth draft, maybe your eleventh draft, contains too many words. But how can you cut clutter if you can't see it? Test every word. You do not have to keep the reader on the "proper path." The word* path *has the idea of "proper" built in.*

What if we polled readers to determine the most influential writing books of all time? The winner, no doubt, would be *The Elements of Style* by William Strunk Jr. and E. B. White. We'll get to those old boys later. Next on the list would be *On Writing Well* by William Zinsser, which has sold more than one million copies over the last thirty years. If I had to summarize Zinsser's advice in three words, it would be "Dump the clutter."

My appreciation for this book is marked by my affection for the man. I met him just after its publication and reunited with him by phone just before his death at the age of ninety-two. By then he was blind but still working with visiting writers in his Manhattan apartment and taking lessons from a poetry tutor. I can't get out of my head the thought of a ninety-year-old man taking poetry lessons. The idea inspires me and makes me laugh. It exemplifies the phrase *lifetime learning*. It reinforces my personal mission to try to learn something new about the craft every day. It makes me want to take trombone lessons. Maybe by ninety, I might join a jazz band.

To be honest, when I first met him in 1980 at a journalism conference in New York City, Zinsser already looked like an old man. The venue was a fancy ballroom at the Waldorf Astoria. We shared the stage with Ed Bliss, author of a fine book, *Writing News for Broadcast*. Zinsser was promoting his own new book, the thirtieth-anniversary edition of which boasts "More Than One Million Copies Sold."

I, at the time, was bookless.

Since that meeting, I have accounted for a dozen or more of those million copies of *On Writing Well*, volumes which have been read, borrowed, marked up, loaned out, spindled, and mutilated.

At the age of ninety, the old man was still kicking my asymptote.

When I last checked an online bookseller's lists, Zinsser held the number-1 spot for all books on authorship. My *Writing Tools* came in at number 4 (and number 16 in a digital version). My book ranked number 2,115 among all sold on Amazon; his was number 360. There have been many days when my book has been number 2, but even then I continue to eat the Z-man's dust.

(As I write these words, I realize that this chapter will get him even more sales. On the track of writing books, I am still being lapped by the ghost of Zinsser.)

Because of our friendly rivalry, I am tempted to declare Zinsser's book overrated, the way that the uber-achiever in our category, *Strunk and White,* is slammed by certain types of teachers and scholars. I want to drop-kick Zinsser and then body-slam the puny writing god, the way the Hulk does Loki in *The Avengers.* But I just can't do it.

I can't do it because of two stinkin' pages. Two pages.

For the record, they are pages 10 and 11 in my edition. I've studied them until my eyes blur. I've shared them with countless aspiring writers, young and old. There have never—I say never!—been two pages in a writing text as practical, per-suasive, and revealing as pages 10 and 11. Echoing the jazz ethos articulated by the likes of Miles Davis and Tony Bennett, Zinsser demonstrates that in writing there are notes in a com-position (words, in his case) that the artist should leave out.

In context, pages 10 and 11 appear as a set piece between two chapters, one on simplicity, another on clutter. "Clutter is the disease of American writing," writes Zinsser on page 6. "We are a society strangling in unnecessary words, circular con-structions, pompous frills and meaningless jargon." On page 13, he begins the chapter on clutter with "Fighting clutter is like fighting weeds—the writer is always slightly behind. New vari-eties sprout overnight, and by noon they are part of American speech."

Zinsser is too tough on American writing, unable or un-willing to recognize the natural and necessary redundancies inherent in all language, and that jargon, while inflated, may suit the purposes of specialized groups of writers and thinkers.

What makes Zinsser's tough standards tolerable is the way he applies them to himself—on pages 10 and 11. On the bottom of page 11, he shows two pages of the final manuscript of chapter 2 of the first edition of *On Writing Well*. He says,

> Although they look like a first draft, they had already been rewritten and retyped—like almost every other page—four or five times. With each rewrite I try to make what I have written tighter, stronger and more precise, eliminating every element that's not doing useful work. Then I go over it once more, reading it aloud, and am always amazed at how much clutter can still be cut. (In later editions I eliminated the sexist pronoun "he" denoting "the writer" and "the reader.")

What you see on pages 10 and 11 is what looks like the typed version of manuscript pages decorated with dozens of proof-reading marks. It begins mid-sentence with this original text:

> [The reader]...is too dumb or too lazy to keep pace with the writer's train of thought. My sympathies are entirely with him. He's not so dumb. If the reader is lost, it is generally because the writer of the article has not been careful enough to keep him on the proper path.

Uncluttered enough for my taste, yet Zinsser goes to work: Crossing out "writer's" and "entirely" and "He's not so dumb" and "of the article" and even "proper" before "path." Here's what's left:

> [The reader]…is too dumb or too lazy to keep pace with the train of thought. My sympathies are with him. If the reader is lost, it is generally because the writer has not been careful enough to keep him on the path.

Zinsser cuts about 20 percent of the original version, a standard he applies throughout pages 10 and 11.

So why am I emoting over this passage? Because it shows the heart and head of a generous writer. Those pages with those editing marks reveal the mind of a disciplined writer at work. He will set no standard for us that he is unwilling to apply to himself.

Then there are the deletions themselves and the strategies behind them. Why do we insist on including phrases such as "in the article"? During a brief stint as a movie reviewer, I worked with an editor who repeatedly cut the phrase "in the movie" from my drafts. Where else would the damn scene be?

Why include "entirely"? Now if your sympathies are "partially" with him, we have another story.

And then there is "proper" before "path." I would never have cut it. I would have embraced the alliteration and the rhythm of a two-syllable word before a final monosyllable. But Zinsser is right! "Path" encompasses the meaning of "proper."

A year or so after I met Zinsser, I invited him to the Poynter Institute for one of my first writing seminars. He soon became animated in conversations about the craft. (The great writing teacher Donald Murray also attended.) I began the seminar with this exercise: I had retyped and made copies of pages 10 and 11—but without Zinsser's editing marks. Each writer had to edit the text with the goal of cutting unnecessary words. "Get rid of the clutter," I said.

What happened next was revealing and endeared Zinsser to me forever (damn him!). With a sincere but puzzled look, he admitted that he couldn't figure out what he had cut from his original text. There were problems he could not identify and solutions he could not remember and re-create. That, my friends, is the vulnerability that all apprentices feel—and some masters, as well.

In my last conversation with Bill Zinsser, he offered me words of encouragement: "Let's keep this mission going." I took him to mean the craft of writing, the humanity of writing, the power of storytelling in the interests of literacy, learning, community, and democracy. That is where I plant my flag, and so, I venture to say, do my brothers and sisters of the word.

LESSONS

1. Open this book to a random page. With a pencil, mark any word or phrase that you think does not contribute to the meaning of a passage or chapter.

2. Pick another page. As an exercise, imagine that you have been assigned to cut 10 percent. Mark the candidates for deletion.

3. Now apply this process to a sample of your own

published work. (A student paper will do.) Raise your standards. Cut 20 percent.

4. Finally, identify the clutter and weaker constructions in a draft you are working on now. Check your cuts with a writing helper to see if you agree.

3

Learn to live inside words. Recognize both their
literal meanings and their associations.

Writing Well
By Donald Hall

*Toolbox: You have language inside you. What a blessing. But
what if we flipped the switch? What if we imagined that we lived
inside the language, a fish breathing in the ocean? Writers swim
inside words. When you see words from the inside out, you learn
the absence of pure synonyms.* Sofa *is no longer interchangeable
with* couch. *Learn not just the literal meanings of words, but
their associations and connotations.*

In 1973, when Little, Brown published the first edition of *Writing Well* by Donald Hall, I was working on my doctoral dissertation, which was written quickly and not particularly well. It didn't matter. Over the objections of one reader, it was good enough to earn me a PhD at Stony Brook, a state university on Long Island. With degree in hand, I got my first teaching job at a branch campus of Auburn University at Montgomery,

Alabama. As a teaching assistant, I taught composition courses at Stony Brook and at least one writing course each quarter at AUM. *Writing Well* was my go-to text for this reason alone: It was well written.

It is always interesting to look at an old book you owned—and still own—to see what caught your attention back then, especially if you marked up the pages. On page 27, I marked up this passage, in which Hall discusses the work of Norman Mailer and John Updike:

> These writers are original, as if seeing a thing for the first time; yet they report their vision in a language that reaches the rest of us. For the first quality the writer needs imagination; for the second he needs skill. Without both qualities, he could not write the passage. Imagination without skill makes a lively chaos; skill without imagination, a deadly order.

The book went through at least nine editions. Hall went from being a writing teacher at the University of Michigan to a freelance writer to one of the most productive and versatile scribes in America, rising in 2006 to the status of Poet Laureate. A final book, *A Carnival of Losses,* was published in 2018 just weeks after his death at the age of eighty-nine.

By 1979 I was teaching journalists at a professional school called the Poynter Institute. I had learned that Hall had written two books about baseball, so I invited him to St. Petersburg, Florida, to visit spring training and to read his poems to a group of sportswriters. It was a joy to see a poet inspire these down-and-dirty scribes.

Many years passed without hearing from him. Somewhere—

I can't find it—I must have included in an essay praise for Donald Hall's *Writing Well*. Around Christmas of 2017, he mailed me a brief note:

Dear Roy,

It has been a while. I'm glad you quote the poet Donald Hall and his long-ago textbook Writing Well.

I enter my 90th year, with a new book coming in July: A Carnival of Losses, Notes Nearing Ninety.

Best to you,

Don

It was a great surprise to hear from him, and I wrote him back via land mail to Eagle Pond Farm in Wilmot, New Hampshire. Suddenly we were pen pals:

Dear Roy Peter Clark,

You are still there!...I'm glad to hear your praise for Writing Well. How many editions did I do? It drove me nuts, these obligatory editions driving out the used-book sales!...

You approach 70 as I approach 90....Yup, some of us continue to hang around. Who wants life without work? Lots of people, actually!

Best to you,

Don

Six months later he was gone, tributes being tossed like flowers on his grave, his final book arriving a month later. Who wants life without work? Good question, Don.

Another gift that Donald Hall left behind for me was the opportunity to revisit *Writing Well*. I rediscovered countless lessons and insights but will confine myself to passing along to you these three:

1. Words are inside you, but you can live inside words.
2. In writing and in life, you can have too much of a good thing.
3. You can learn the structure of something by making fun of it.

Writing Well is a composition textbook written by a poet. The advantage of that is a deeper appreciation for the individual word and families of words. It's as if a word has a door and you are invited to step inside.

To appreciate the word...the writer and the reader must first realize that no words can be synonyms. Some words are close to each other in meaning, close enough to reveal that they are not the same. The writer must know not just the surface definitions of words; he must go deeper and realize the families of contexts into which words have extended their associations—like "slice" with "knife" and even "cake." These families are the connotations of the word, and the associations we make with their denotation; "pepper" is not a connotation of "salt" but it is an association of it. Since the writer uses the whole family, it does not matter that he discriminates connotation from association. But he must know the insides of words; he must be a friend of the family.

Hall then brilliantly differentiates between these so-called synonyms: *to emulate, to imitate,* and *to ape.* All mean, in some sense, "to copy." Until the future poet laureate gets his eyes, ears, and hands on them:

> "To emulate" sounds fancy; also it usually implies that the imitation involves self-improvement. "To imitate" is neutral, except that everyone knows that an imitation is not the real thing; inferiority shadows the word. "To copy" is mostly to reproduce exactly, though like "to imitate" it states a lack of originality. "To ape" is to mimic, and to be comical or mocking about it. If you wanted to say that a young pianist imitated a famous virtuoso, but you carelessly use the word "ape" instead of "imitate," you would grant his style the grace of a gorilla. Context is all; the inside of a word must reinforce or continue the force of the context.

As I learned from Hall that I could swim inside words, I gained the ability to distinguish words that ring true from those that ring false. The first edition of *Writing Well* runs to 324 pages. Over almost four decades, two pages (46 and 47) are imprinted on my memory, example for example, almost word for word. The lesson, titled "False Color in Verbs," has inspired hundreds of revisions in my own work. I think of it as a kind of counter-lesson, that writers can learn a new trick, and then use it, and then abuse it until the effect becomes not satisfying but cloying or even offensive.

One of the first rhetorical distinctions many writers learn differentiates the active from the passive voice. In general, the lesson is "active good / passive bad." But an unhealthy preference for the active can lead, according to Hall, to a form of overwriting he calls "false color." To demonstrate this problem, Hall mocks two types of popular literature from the 1950s—the first written for men in crude adventure magazines:

> Hurtt scraped the scum from his lips and dug his finger into his nose. He scraped out a hunk of snot and snapped it at the Nazi bastard. Then he grimaced, swung his fist, and crunched the German's teeth into his gums.

Hall explains, "Tough writing is not the only kind of bad overwriting. Maybe pretty writing is worse…and it can rely on verbs for its nasty work, too."

> Songbirds trilled out my window, vines curled at the eaves, buds cocked their green noses through the ground, squirrels danced in dandelions, and Spring drenched the day with gladness.

It's possible that Hall copied these passages from men's magazines or romance novels, but I have a feeling they are parodies, written by Hall himself. This delightful move of his—to exaggerate a literary effect in order to understand how it works (or doesn't)—scattered throughout *Writing Well,* carries a lesson of its own: that one way to capture the essence of a particular genre or writing style is to make fun of it. If you make someone laugh in recognition, by Jove, you've got it.

LESSONS

1. One way to climb inside words is to explore the differences between so-called synonyms. Revisit how Hall does this with *emulate, imitate,* and *ape.*

2. With the help of a dictionary—I recommend *The American Heritage Dictionary*—explore the difference between these synonyms: *sofa* and *couch; naked* and *nude; charity* and *love.*

3. Keep in mind that words have literal meanings—their denotations—but also connotations. Explore this with colors. Holden Caulfield wears a red hunting cap. Captain Ahab seeks revenge on a white whale. *Blue* can have happy connotations (blue skies) or sad ones (got the blues). Play with *green, yellow, purple, brown, orange,* and *pink.*

4. A way to murder your darlings is to identify "false color" in your work, also known as overwriting, purple prose, and word drunkenness. Too many vivid words bump into one another, competing for attention. Apply this test: which of these words is most interesting or important? Murder the rest.

4

Shape a sentence for the desired effect.
To achieve clarity, put the main clause first,
with subject and verb together.

The Philosophy of Rhetoric
By George Campbell, D.D.

Toolbox: *Some sentences put the main thought at the beginning, others near the end. The difference matters. Sentences that make a point early seem more natural and conversational. Reading those sentences, the reader is more likely to focus on the content, and less on the writer. To create a special effect, a variation of the pattern with more of a flourish, save the trumpet blast till the end.*

In my search for the authors of good writing books, I always enjoy a pleasant surprise. One came in a reference from a college composition textbook published in 1904, *The Essentials of Composition and Rhetoric*. I found this in the introduction: "About the middle of the eighteenth century two notable books, Dr. Blair's *Lectures on Rhetoric* and Dr. Campbell's *Philosophy of Rhetoric*, widened the field of rhetorical theory by making it include all forms of literature."

Notice that the editor felt no need to include the first names of Dr. Blair and Dr. Campbell. It suggests that these authors and their works were well known in educational circles a century ago—the way we refer to Strunk and White today. I realized that I had copies of Dr. Blair's lectures in the deep mines of my book collection, but Dr. Campbell was a mystery. My bad, as they say. Three days later, a copy of *The Philosophy of Rhetoric* by George Campbell had been shipped to my doorstep.

In his time Dr. Campbell was a big deal, a Doctor of Divinity who believed strongly that God was best found not somewhere up in the sky but in the phenomena and experiences of everyday life. He is a key figure in the Scottish Enlightenment, a movement of Calvinist theologians, philosophers, and practical scholars who found an intellectual space in which reason and faith might be reconciled.

Dr. Campbell was born on Christmas Day, 1719. In the course of his life as a cleric and scholar, Campbell wrote on a variety of topics, but his intellectual passion focused on rhetoric. As a churchman he was pragmatic. The word of God was delivered from the pulpit, he reasoned, so the path to become a better preacher was the study of rhetoric. A founding member of the Aberdeen Philosophical Society, Dr. Campbell delivered parts of *The Philosophy of Rhetoric* as a series of talks to his brainy pals. The work was published in a significant year: 1776.

As a philosophical work of the eighteenth century, it offers a dense path for modern readers, especially those not comfortable with abstraction, technical example, and complex sentence structure. For students of rhetoric, it is a must-read. That said,

I found myself attracted to the most practical chapters, especially ones on the effect he calls "vivacity" and the strategy he describes as "the arrangement of words."

In the 1950s, a young woman—but never a man—with an outgoing personality might be described as "vivacious." My *American Heritage Dictionary* defines *vivacity* as "the quality or condition of being vivacious; liveliness," citing a phrase from Dickens: "the light and vivacity that laugh in the eyes of a child."

We might ask, "What makes for a vivacious, or lively, prose style?" Dr. Campbell might answer, "The arrangement of words." When I examined his examples, he seemed less interested than I am in "emphatic word order," the strategy that moves writers to highlight key words or phrases by placing them at the beginning, or even better, at the end ("Look at me!").

The "arrangement of words" refers to two significantly distinct kinds of complex sentences. Complex sentences contain one main or independent clause and any number of dependent or subordinate clauses. He uses traditional language to draw this distinction: When a sentence begins with the main clause and is followed by a sequence of dependent clauses, the sentence is called "loose." Perhaps that word applies to the way such a sentence trails off, rather than builds to a main clause.

When dependent clauses pile up at the start, when they prepare the reader for the main point, when they build until the meaning is almost inevitable, that sentence is called "periodic." (You can use as a mnemonic the idea that in periodic sentences the main action arrives near the period.) I avoid the terminology "loose" and "periodic," preferring the terms "right branching" and "left branching," borrowed from the ways modern linguists describe sentence structure. First, imagine that a sentence exists on a single horizontal line. When the subject and verb of the main clause begin a sentence, all the subordinate elements branch to the right. (Like the loose sentence.) When the main clause appears at the end, the subordinate elements branch to the left. (Like the periodic sentence.)

Follow this simple guide:

Right-branching, or loose sentence

Subject and verb of the main clause appear at the beginning.

Other elements branch to the right.

Example: "A tornado tore through Calusa City Thursday, where it bent palm trees to the ground, ripped shingles off roofs, shattered windows in skyscrapers, and sent children scurrying for cover."

Left-branching, or periodic sentence

Subject and verb of main clause appear near the end.

Other elements branch to the left.

Example: "After news of the tornado reached her, after a five-hour drive took her to the top of her street, after police checked her ID and gave her permission to walk down the block to where her house stood yesterday, Marissa prayed that she would find her cat."

Rhetoric invites us to consider the effect words will have on a reader or listener. Will the audience be informed, bemused, offended, encouraged, entertained, spent? It depends on not just the selection of words but their arrangement. Here is where reading Dr. Campbell pays dividends for both the enlightened reader and aspiring writer:

> On comparing the two kinds of complex sentences together, to wit, the period and the loose sentence, we find that each has its advantages and disadvantages. The former [the periodic sentence] savors more of artifice and design; the latter [the loose sentence] seems more the result of pure Nature. The period is nevertheless more susceptible of vivacity and force; the loose sentence is apt, as it were, to languish and grow tiresome. The first is more adapted to the style of the writer; the second to that of the speaker. [He argues that the most effective style has a mixture of both types of sentences. Some types of writing require more of one than the other.] In general, the use of periods best suits the dignity of the historian, the political writer, and the philosopher. The other manner more befits the facility which ought to predominate in essays, dialogs, familiar letters, and moral tales. These approach nearer the style of conversation, into which periods can very rarely find admittance.

Remember that when Dr. Campbell uses *period,* he is referring not specifically to that little dot (which he would have called a "full stop"), but to the structure in which the main clause comes near the end of the sentence.

His distinction is so important (to me as a reader and writer, and I hope to you) that I have summarized his thinking in more modern language:

- Some sentences put the main thought (subject and verb) at the beginning, others near the end.
- Sentences that get to the point early seem more "natural."
- They have a more conversational feel.
- They don't look like they are the product of artifice, of fancy writing.
- If you have too many of these straightforward sentences—especially of the same length—the effect can be tedious.
- Reading this kind of loose, easy sentence, you are less likely to notice the writer.
- This kind of sentence works best in speech—for instance, from the pulpit or lectern.
- The loose sentence works best for the kinds of public writing that are meant to be quickly understood: the essay, the news report, the letter, the popular story.
- The other kind of sentence, which puts the meat near the period, is harder to digest, but worth the chewing.
- With these you are more likely to notice the presence of the writer and the writer's craft.
- You are likely to find more of these in literary and intellectual genres: philosophy, history, political theory, especially if you are reading work from centuries past.
- Modern tastes prefer the loose to the periodic sentence, so you will find fewer of the latter; but that makes the occasional use of them more powerful.

LESSONS

Test the power of your own arrangement of words with these exercises:

1. For fun, take a paragraph with five or six sentences and reformat it so that each sentence exists on a single line. Examine each sentence to see which words and phrases appear in the beginning, middle, and end.

2. Try to identify the main clause, a group of words that could stand independently as a sentence. There may be more than one. If there is just one, where does it appear: closer to the beginning or the end?

3. For each clause, notice the position of the subject and verb. In general, the closer they are together, and the closer both are to the beginning, the easier the sentence will be to read.

4. Notice the language you save for the end of your sentences, especially the end of the paragraph. Even if the subject and verb come early, you can save something special for the end. Be alert for interesting language that gets lost in the middle of a sentence or paragraph. Can you move it to the beginning or end, where it will get more attention?

5

Work from a plan. Include a lead or an intro you can write without referring to notes.

Draft No. 4: On the Writing Process
By John McPhee

The John McPhee Reader
Edited by William L. Howarth

Toolbox: *The larger the writing project, the more you need a plan. You need it to organize your material, identify the parts, and reinforce a governing idea—a focus. If you lack a planning process, you can borrow one from another author, such as John McPhee. An important tool in his process is the "lead," a section of up to 2,000 words that helps the writer and the reader see what is ahead. Write this passage without referring to your notes. It will serve as a flashlight that shines down into the well of the story, illuminating the unknown.*

Two books sit on my desk. The first was published in 1976, the year before I migrated from university teaching to the newsroom. *The

John McPhee Reader is an anthology of a dozen excerpts of *New Yorker* pieces, most of which would become well-known nonfiction books. Forty-one years later, the second arrived on my doorstep, confirming an affinity four decades in the making. *Draft No. 4* is a collection of eight *New Yorker* pieces by McPhee on the craft of writing, reporting, and editing. The first book serves the courses of a banquet; the second reveals the secrets of how they were prepared.

By most accounts, John McPhee stands as one of the best American writers of nonfiction of the last half-century. By my count, McPhee, at the age of 88, has produced 39 books since 1965. (Shakespeare, remember, gave us 37 plays, and he didn't have to do much reporting.)

McPhee, a professor at Princeton, his alma mater and home base since childhood, has become something of a role model for me as I enter my seventies. Les Paul played guitar gigs at the Iridium Jazz Club in Manhattan into his nineties, and William Zinsser, though blind, was taking poetry lessons from a young tutor when he was ninety-two. McPhee still writes and teaches, and *Draft No. 4* extends his lessons to those beyond the tyros at Princeton fortunate enough to join his classes.

Here's the problem with choosing McPhee as a practical role model: He has lived a privileged writing life. He testifies that he writes what he wants, when he wants, at his own pace. He admits that on only two occasions has he acted upon an assignment suggested by an editor. On only two other occasions has he used a story idea suggested by a reader.

Some of McPhee's topics—geology, for example—might not have wide appeal, in spite of his skill as a vivid explainer and a nuanced profiler of characters. McPhee gravitates toward theme over straight chronology, creating too many impediments, some would argue, to building narrative energy. That said, at his best, he reigns supreme. McPhee, thank goodness, is a generous writer, never keeping his secrets to himself, but sharing strategies without imposing them on students or readers. Just remember his privilege, fellow writers. You and I may work on deadline. McPhee has license to extend his efforts "for as long as it takes." With that in mind, his tools and habits can work for writers across the board. Here is some choice advice from *Draft No. 4:*

- "You can build a structure in such a way that it causes people to want to keep turning pages."
- "Readers are not supposed to notice the structure. It is meant to be about as visible as someone's bones."
- "Often, after you have reviewed your notes many times and thought through your material, it is difficult to frame much of a structure until you write a lead. You wade around in your notes, getting nowhere. You don't see a pattern. You don't know what to do. So stop everything. Stop looking at the notes. Hunt through your mind for a good beginning. Then write it. Write a lead."
- "The lead—like the title—should be a flashlight that shines down into the story. A lead is a promise. It promises that the piece of writing is going to be like this."
- "I always know where I intend to end before I have much begun to write."
- "Writing is selection. When you are making notes you are forever selecting. I left out more than I put down."
- "Writing has to be fun at least once in a pale blue moon."

Over the years, I have developed a friendship with Bill Howarth, who taught in the English department at Princeton, and who edited and wrote an introduction for *The John McPhee Reader*. I was about thirty-two years old when I first read Howarth on McPhee. At thirty, I had written a newspaper column about the things I would like to accomplish by the age of forty. "Write one good book" was at the top. I even had a topic: teaching writing to children. For three years I had been visiting Bay Point Elementary, my three daughters' public school. Working with the language-arts teachers there, I began to experiment with how to teach writing to children, using some of the tools of journalism and nonfiction. Every child, for example, received a reporter's notebook. After every class, I sat and wrote for about fifteen minutes in a journal. Over three years, I had what I thought was wonderful material: writing lessons, case studies, profiles of students and teachers, examples of children's work, strategies, advice for parents, and, most of all, many fun and inspirational stories. Lots of stuff, but what now? How do you write a book?

The search party arrived in the nick of time in the form of John McPhee. I followed the Princetonian's methods—as described in depth by Bill Howarth—almost to the letter, working first by hand, then on a typewriter, and then on a computer— this was 1985, remember.

In imitation of McPhee:

1. Learn what you have. I transcribed my handwritten notebooks. As I typed, I added thoughts and phrases, captured from memory or called to mind by reading. I was already selecting, knowing early on that there were many elements I would not use. I made a photocopy of these elaborated notes and placed them in a binder.

2. Identify the parts. I read the notes—and took more notes on my notes—looking for themes, categories, patterns that might become building blocks of structure.

3. Draft a lead. I sat down and attempted to write—without referring to my notes—the first draft of a lead. It was not a one-paragraph lead for a feature story, but a 1,500-word commentary on why the teaching of writing to children is so important.

4. Find a focus. I shared my lead with a few trusted friends to let them know where I was headed and also to gain confidence in what would become the focus—the governing idea—of the work.

5. Hunt for chapters. Using the lead as a flashlight, I coded the raw material with structural notes—key words, phrases, and acronyms that would become narrative or thematic elements, perhaps even chapter titles.

6. Move things around. I copied these key structural elements—such as Writing as Punishment or Publishing Student Writing—on a set of index cards.

7. Play with sequence. I played with these cards for a long time, shuffling them, setting them down on the rug (where my dog, Lance, trying to help, nosed them). I set them down in a variety of sequences until I found an order that offered the most promise.

8. Create a storyboard. I taped these cards to the wall of my home office. (For later projects, I used a bulletin board.)

9. Set the table. I took duplicate sets of notes and coded them according to my structural categories. I scissored them into parts and organized the parts into file folders identical to the titles on my "chapter" cards.

10. Off you go! I took out file #1 and began to draft.

In 1987 Heinemann Educational Books published *Free to Write: A Journalist Teaches Young Writers* by Roy Peter Clark. I cannot describe the pride and joy of holding the first copy of my first book in my hand. I have worked on more than a dozen book-length projects since then, and each one was produced through some form of the process I learned from McPhee and Howarth four decades ago. I pass it along to you. Go ahead, write your book. Welcome to the club.

LESSONS

1. When working on any writing project, collect much more than you think you need.

2. After collection comes selection. To select well, you need a governing idea—call it a focus.

3. One way to find your focus is to write a lead, an opening passage. McPhee uses a lead as a flashlight. It can be short, even on a long work ("Call me Ishmael"!). It can be as long as a full chapter if necessary.

4. If you are stuck, drowning in material, try putting everything aside. Take a breath. Write a lead section without referring to your notes. Let your memory guide you to the most interesting and important elements.

II

Voice and Style

Every writer I have coached has desired to develop a personal style and achieve an authentic voice. Style and voice. Voice and style. Ben Yagoda, one of America's most versatile writers, uses those words interchangeably to signify expressions of a writer's craft. My mentor Don Fry describes voice as an illusion: an effect of sound created by all the moves a writer makes. The word *style* has two discrete meanings, as exemplified by *The Elements of Style*, in which Will Strunk Jr. gets all conventional and his student E. B. White all rhetorical. Strunk emphasizes the patterns all good writers should follow; White shares tools that will make your writing sound distinctive, not like everyone else's.

Gary Provost offers an elegant example of how a single choice—the length of a sentence—can influence how a work sounds and how it is experienced by the reader. That wisdom is endorsed by Ursula K. Le Guin, who argues that "every sentence has a rhythm of its own," which then contributes to the rhythm of the entire work.

Robert Taylor and Herman Liebert's *Authors at Work,* a collection of old manuscripts, makes visible the patterns of revision that tune a writer's voice or spruce up a work's style. It is so encouraging to discover the rough work of famous writers and the ways they tune their voices during revision.

While revision often comes near the end of a process, Vera John-Steiner reveals what happens when creative people have a vision at an early stage and begin to describe that vision through "notebooks of the mind." Before there are words on paper, there can be illuminating sketches, charts, diagrams, shapes, scratches of inspiration.

When it comes to reading, writing, and storytelling, technology influences meaning, from the printing press to television to computers and the internet. In *Wired Style,* Constance Hale points to the convergence of literary and digital styles and the experiments in voice that require a writer to be "multilingual."

Each book invites us to listen to how we "sound" on the page or the screen. As we read our work aloud, we listen for the voice that represents the best versions of our writing selves.

6

Recognize two contradictory meanings of *style*.
Be prepared to abandon the agreed-upon style of
a group to express your individual style.

The Elements of Style
By William Strunk Jr. and E. B. White

Toolbox: *The meaning of the word* style, *as in the book* The
Elements of Style, *is mercurial. Just when you think you've contained it, it squirts away, assuming a new shape and significance.
Some words with the same spelling have opposite meanings. If
you "sand" wood, you make it smooth. If you "sand" ice, you
make it gritty. The word* style *is almost like that. With some style
books, the goal is consistency: we agree—or not—to use the serial
comma. But style is also an approach to writing that makes an
author's work distinctive. We recognize a particular author by his
or her style. These two definitions are not mutually exclusive, but
they can rub, causing a creative friction. You may have to violate
a group's style in order to express your individual style.*

The Elements of Style is the great-granddaddy *and* the great-
grandmommy of all books on writing. I say granddaddy and

grandmommy not just to avoid the universal masculine, but because it is the work of two authors, not one: William Strunk Jr. and E. B. White. A century ago, Strunk was an English professor at Cornell, and White became his most famous student, one of the most versatile writers of the twentieth century. A veteran of *The New Yorker*, White wrote as a reporter, editorialist, correspondent, essayist, poet, and novelist. To generations of children and their parents, he was best known as the author of *Stuart Little* and *Charlotte's Web*. Strunk the Professor and White the Author. Quite a pair. Their names became shorthand for the title of what Strunk and his students knew as the "little book." That little book became big enough in its influence to have sold more than ten million copies. *Strunk and White*.

Almost anything you need to know about *The Elements of Style* can be found in the 2009 book *Stylized* by Mark Garvey, who describes his work as a "slightly obsessive history." Any fan of *Strunk and White* will be fascinated by Garvey's detailed chronicle of the writing guide, informed by correspondence between White and the publishers. Longtime admirers of the little book, along with its harshest critics, can learn from commentators gathered by Garvey, including Dave Barry (humorist), Sharon Olds (poet), and Adam Gopnik (critic). In oral-history style, these well-known authors testify as to how they found the advice in *Strunk and White* formative and, at certain moments in their lives, deformative.

My original title for this chapter was "Why Strunk and White still matters (or matter) (or both)." If you take *Strunk and White* as the name of a book, yes, the book still matters. If you take it as the names of two people, then, yes, the original author and his reviser both still matter. It all matters, and here are some reasons why.

It is short. The original edition, written and privately published in 1918 by William Strunk Jr. for his Cornell students, was only 43 pages. The 1920 version published by Harcourt, Brace and Howe was a mere 52 pages. It has seven sections: the rules of usage, principles of composition, matters of form, commonly misused words and expressions, spelling, and a final section of exercises.

It is inexpensive. In 1970, the year I graduated from Providence College, I purchased a Macmillan paperback edition of *The Elements of Style* for 95 cents. Books, especially college texts, were a lot cheaper back then. If you could buy something for less than a buck, you were golden. But I have learned a little trick from investigative journalists who never fall for the fallacy of the nominal dollar. I calculate what the 1970 book would cost today. The answer from one inflation calculator is $6.17.

Publishers have learned that you can make more money on a popular book by creating new editions with new features. I currently own eight editions of *The Elements of Style:* a Dover reprint of the 1918 version; a 1934 edition, published by Harcourt, Brace and Co., and edited by a colleague of Strunk's named Edward A. Tenney; and six editions of *Strunk and White*.

It is popular. Would I eat a McDonald's burger just because I read a sign that said billions and billions have been served? Yeah, I might. And I own a half-dozen pairs of Converse All-Stars sneakers—better known as Chuck Taylors or Chucks—knowing that 800,000,000 pairs have been sold in the last century. When it comes to writing books, popularity matters. Because of its slim size and low cost, *The Elements of Style* could be assigned as a text by generations of teachers. Those two benefits made it easy to pass along, from student to student, from editor to writer. James Jones, an author who worked with the famous Scribner's editor Max Perkins, once said of him that Perkins prescribed books to his authors like a doctor passing out pill samples. *Strunk and White* was used that way, as the writer's little helper. If a writer needed to be more concise, more organized, a little plainer? Here, just take two of these, a Strunk AND a White, and write something in the morning.

It comes from an academic perspective, and then a professional one. One of the traditional distinctions in the literary world is the one between academic writing and professional writing. As a grad student, I sat in a meeting in which some English professors were making fun of the prose of a journalist of high reputation. Whether they were motivated by jealousy or simply belonged to a different "discourse community," a different club of readers and writers, I didn't see their point.

So what might have been discordant became harmonic when the popular author, White, agreed to participate in the creation of a new version of his professor's old book. Two aspects of the origin story are illustrative. It was 1958 when a college friend sent White a copy of Strunk's "little book." Not only did White not have his own copy, but he had forgotten all about the book, though his memories of his professor were vivid.

In other words, his professor's self-published guide was not formative, at least not in a direct way. White was by disposition uncomfortable with technical grammar and conventional approaches to usage. "Writing is an act of faith," he wrote, "not a trick of grammar." In a life of White written by Melissa Sweet for young readers, she notes "Even though Andy [White's nickname] had agreed to work on the revised edition of *The Elements of Style* (under the condition that it stayed true to Strunk's original text) he did not consider himself a grammarian. 'When I finally can't take any more grammar,' he wrote, 'I hop on my bicycle and go scorching up and down the highway to remove the cobwebs.'"

Some of the harshest criticism of *The Elements of Style* is that it favors a style of writing—lean and undecorated—no longer in fashion. To the extent that Strunk focuses on conventional usage, he is a target of descriptive linguists who can bring to the table countless examples of canonical writers who are assertively un-Strunky in their usage.

Let's take punctuation as an example. It's possible that I developed my preferences from Professor Strunk. These include a devotion to the serial comma and the use of an apostrophe and *s* to form the possessive singular, even when the noun (with a few exceptions) ends in the letter *s*. So it is *Charles's gun*, not *Charles'* as the stylebook of the Associated Press would have you observe. Somehow "faith, hope, and love" feels more like St. Paul with that comma before *and*—again, not to AP, though. When I read a British newspaper and see a helpless little comma floating outside quotation marks, I do want to toss it a lifeline and pull it into harbor. So we scroll on, writing against the tide, borne back to a past we did not invent, when other writers and editors from other writing clubs made these decisions for us.

Professor Strunk admired Sir Arthur Quiller-Couch and his books on reading and writing, which tended to focus more on rhetoric and literature than grammar and usage. So it's important to recognize those places where Strunk crosses the line from Standard English to spotlight a specific rhetorical strategy. It comes as Strunk's #18: "Place emphatic words of a sentence at the end." My version of that is Writing Tool #2: "Order words for emphasis." As a favorite example—high-school teachers refer to it as a "mentor text"—I note that Shakespeare, being a far better writer than I, announces in *Macbeth,* "The Queen, my lord, is dead." I would have rendered it, "The Queen is dead, my lord," in an effort to keep subject and verb together. The Bard prefers placing an important word (*Queen*) at the beginning and the most important word—the news, if you will—at the end, right next to what Yanks call the period but Brits call the full stop.

On my rereading of Strunk, I discovered that the professor took the strategy a step further, to my delight, and onto my workbench: "The principle that the proper place for what is to be made most prominent is the end applies equally to the words of a sentence, to the sentences of a paragraph, and to the paragraphs of a composition." That had not occurred to me until I read it a week ago, and I now recognize its value in my writing and look forward to testing it out.

E. B. White turned *The Elements of Style* into a blockbuster. He made three distinctive contributions:

1. He attached his celebrity to the work. By 1959 White was among America's most popular writers, and his reputation gave

the work an aura of literary hipness that its academic origins lacked.

2. He lionized the author. His *New Yorker* essay, which became an introduction, was a compelling profile of a character—direct, persistent, plainspoken, devoted to a cultivated use of the English language in the public interest. This passage by White—though a little wordy—stands out as memorable:

> "Omit needless words!" cries the author on page 21, and into that imperative Will Strunk really put his heart and soul. In the days when I was sitting in his class, he omitted so many needless words, and omitted them so forcibly and with such eagerness and obvious relish, that he often seemed in the position of having shortchanged himself—a man left with nothing more to say yet with time to fill, a radio prophet who had outdistanced the clock. Will Strunk got out of this predicament by a simple trick: he uttered every sentence three times. When he delivered his oration on brevity to the class, he leaned forward over his desk, grasped his coat lapels in his hands, and in a husky, conspiratorial voice, said, "Rule Seventeen. Omit needless words! Omit needless words! Omit needless words!"

In an earlier work, I mischievously rewrote that passage to omit needless words. Why do we need "coat" to modify "lapels," for example? Where else would his lapels be? This was not the first time the student silently defied the master to create sharp and interesting prose.

3. White earns the right to coauthorship (and equal royalties)

with a section titled "An Approach to Style," a brief discussion with a list of twenty-one "suggestions and cautionary hints." As I reread them, I realize that a few are stuck in my mind, and they speak to me, like Jiminy Cricket, when I am tempted toward either laziness or exhibitionism. So I try to "Work from a suitable design," although that design might come after much exploratory writing. I avoid qualifiers, except when I need them. And, because my ear is not that good, I can count on my fingers the times I've tried to use dialect.

White's advice is rhetorical. Applied, it creates what passes for "style." When you think of the word *style,* realize—under Strunk and White—that the word is a contranym (like *cleave* and *cleave*) that can mean two opposite things, depending on context.

In the Strunkian sense, "style" denotes an agreed-upon usage—writing *Charles's* rather than *Charles'*—because we have agreed that doing so is better. We turn it from a choice into a convention, a social contract within a group or a culture. For consistency and clarity—to avoid confusion or distraction—we decide to do things the same way. We gather the provisions in something called a stylebook.

In the Whitean sense, "style" is achieved when a writer expresses herself with an identifiable distinctiveness. E. B. White did not want to sound like anyone else in his writing. He wanted to sound like himself. He was greatly rewarded for the accomplishment. Both these meanings of style can coexist. If you need reminders how, I know a little book you can own. Reread it. Learn why it still matters. Why they still matter. *Strunk and White* has persuaded millions of reluctant writers that the writing craft is not an act of magic, but the applied use of both rules and tools.

LESSONS

1. Remember, *style* has two meanings: the conventions that writers adhere to and the distinctive elements of language that set writers apart.

2. When you enter a new discourse community or writing club, see if it has a stylebook. By all means, learn it. Agree to the social contract designed to govern certain standards of usage.

3. Conventions are agreements, not rules. *Style* also refers to the eccentric, sometimes rebellious decisions you make as a writer.

4. If you find your writing preference to be at odds with a stylebook's—and you will—give the distinctive usage a try. You will be tempted to sneak it by alert copyeditors. You'll have better luck if you give them a heads-up.

7

Vary sentence length to create a pleasing rhythm.
Think of each period as a stop sign.

*100 Ways to Improve Your Writing: Proven Professional
Techniques for Writing with Style and Power*
By Gary Provost

Steering the Craft: A 21st-Century Guide to Sailing the Sea of Story
By Ursula K. Le Guin

Toolbox: *Short sentences sound truthful. Writers use them to
grab your attention. Longer sentences take you on a journey,
showing you the snowy, rusty cityscape along the edge of the
tracks as the train rumbles by. By length alone—short, medium,
long—sentences send secret messages to the reader. With variation, sentences can take on a musical rhythm, from legato to
staccato. As in music, pleasure comes from the combined experience of repetition and variation.*

Imagine we are standing in a bookstore on Central Avenue in
St. Petersburg, Florida. It is named after the family that owns

it—Haslam's—and has evolved over eighty years into one of the oldest and biggest in the Southeast. It is said to be haunted by Jack Kerouac, who met the end of his road in St. Pete in 1969. It is occupied by not one but two cats, Teacup and Beowulf, who may or may not let you pet them. Your chances are better if you are holding tribute in the form of something smelly to eat.

You are an aspiring writer but want to step on the gas in your craft. You need the verbal equivalent of nitrous oxide in your street-racing muscle car, something to blast you to another level of learning and performance. You want to write more. You want to get published. You want to make money.

I escort you through the bookstore into the section on writing, which contains both new and used works. I point out a number of good choices (including more than a dozen books described in *Murder Your Darlings*). You want a new book, not a used one, but you don't have much money, only eight dollars. "That's all I got," you fret. "I guess I can't afford to buy a good writing book."

"Not to worry, my young bard," I reply. I reach down for a thin tan-and-blue volume by Gary Provost, *100 Ways to Improve Your Writing*, published in 1985 by Mentor Books and in print ever since. Price: $6.99. Page for page, penny for penny, this may be the most useful writing book ever written. Its author, Gary Provost, was a productive and versatile writer, a champion of the freelance tribe, a scribe who burned out like a Kerouac Roman candle at the age of fifty.

Among its virtues, *100 Ways* may have the most charming and offbeat dedication of any writing book in history:

As a freelance writer I live and die by the mailbox. During the past twenty years, I have sent and received more than forty thousand pieces of mail that had some part of my heart attached to them. And during that time there haven't been more than one or two mishaps concerning the handling of my mail. Though I have laughed at post office jokes and have made a few myself, the fact is that the United States Postal Service has the highest success record of any business I have ever dealt with. For that reason this book is dedicated to the men and women of the post office at South Lancaster, Massachusetts 01561, and to postal workers everywhere.

It's hard for me to imagine a writer generating 2,000 pieces of mail a year. That said, nothing that I have written has pleased my son-in-law Dan, a veteran postal worker, more than Provost's dedication.

Provost had a long and productive relationship with *Writer's Digest*, which published parts of *100 Ways* before the chapters were assembled into a book. The table of contents reveals a structure predicated on numbered lists:

I. Nine Ways to Improve Your Writing When You're Not Writing
II. Nine Ways to Overcome Writer's Block

He offers *five* ways to do this, and *eleven* ways to do that, until the numbers add up to the magic 100. As there are only 156 pages to the book, it gave the author a good target for each piece of writing advice: about a page and a half, no time for theories or elaborate discourse, but more than enough space for tips with a sharp point.

Chapter 10 is titled "Twelve Ways to Avoid Making Your Reader Hate You." It includes such common advice as Avoid Jargon, Avoid Clichés, Avoid Parentheses, Avoid Footnotes. (Advice from me would include "Avoid the word *avoid* because there will come a moment when, say, a footnote provides a perfect solution.) I do like "Don't Play the Tom Wolfe Game":

> If you have read any of Tom Wolfe's early books, you know that Wolfe employed a lot of visual GIMMICKS like ZOWeeee!!!!, lively little passages full of CAPITAL LETTERS, and unUSual Punk Chew A Shun....!!!?
>
> I call that the Tom Wolfe game, and it was fine for Wolfe. It was fun. It worked. It became part of his writing personality. It's his.
>
> But ninety-nine percent of the time this sort of thing fails. It draws attention to the gimmick and away from the content. It reminds readers that they are reading, and it occasionally brands the writer a moron.
>
> Certainly the appearance of your story is not irrelevant. Clean paper, bold print, white space—all of these things affect the success of the story. But writing is not primarily a visual art. It is more like music than oil painting, and the extent to which it must depend on the shape, size, and color of those squiggly little lines is the extent to which it is not writing, but is something else.
>
> If you cannot state a good reason for doing SOMEthing LYKE Thhhhiiiissss!!!, don't do it.

Elmore Leonard expressed a similar antipathy to exclamation points, suggesting that writers were allowed perhaps one exclaimer for every two books. Like Provost, he gave Tom Wolfe a get-out-of-jail-free card. I would love to eavesdrop on a heavenly conversation between Provost and Leonard now in 2020, the age of emoticons and emoji. Why bother with a bland exclamation point when you can decorate your messages with a pair of googly eyes or a smiling pile of dung?

When my editor, Tracy Behar, was advising me on the potential content of this book, she warned against unnecessary repetition of advice or examples from my previous five books with Little, Brown. I am not as scrupulous on this matter as she—one reason we make a good team—only because I think "Remember, writing is not magic; it's a process" is such a formative idea that something like it belongs at the beginning of any writing book.

In that spirit, I would like to include a brief passage from Provost's book that also appears in *Writing Tools*. The passage has been quoted countless times from writers discovering it in my work and, on occasion, misattributed to me. Writers favor it as a kind of "mentor text," a piece of writing that reveals its architecture and composition to the reader. It coaches us on why and how we should vary the length of our sentences:

This sentence has five words. Here are five more words. Five-word sentences are fine. But several together become monotonous. Listen to what is happening. The writing is getting boring. The sound of it drones. It's like a stuck record. The ear demands some variety. Now listen. I vary the sentence length, and I create music. Music. The writing sings. It has a pleasant rhythm, a lilt, a harmony. I use short sentences. And I use sentences of medium length. And sometimes when I am certain the reader is rested, I will engage him with a sentence of considerable length, a sentence that burns with energy and builds with all the impetus of a crescendo, the roll of the drums, the crash of the cymbals—sounds that say listen to this, it is important.

So write with a combination of short, medium, and long sentences. Create a sound that pleases the reader's ear. Don't just write words. Write music.

Ursula K. Le Guin may be the most famous American writer that I had never heard of. She died in January 2018, just as I was beginning to build steam for this book. Her passing and the tributes that followed caught my attention. In one tribute, *Tampa Bay Times* book editor Colette Bancroft wrote,

> Le Guin was indeed a force. Best known as a writer of science fiction and fantasy, she wrote in many other genres as well, publishing over her half-century career 20 novels…, 13 children's books, several translations and numerous collections of short stories, poetry and essays. Her books were translated into 40 languages and sold millions of copies worldwide.

Among her many awards was the National Book Foundation's Medal for Distinguished Contribution to American Letters.

It happens sometimes. You think of yourself as a well-read person until an author dies and you realize that, in spite of all her publications and awards, she was invisible to you. Not long after the news of her passing, a stylish book cover caught my eye: *Steering the Craft: A 21st-Century Guide to Sailing the Sea of Story*. Hmm. Nice title, I thought. Two meanings of the word *craft*; a parallel between steering the craft and sailing the sea. Seven words in the title, four of them, including the last three, beginning with the letter *S*.

Its author? Ursula K. Le Guin.

Originally published in 1998 as *Steering the Craft: Exercises and Discussions on Story Writing for the Lone Navigator or the Mutinous Crew*, it found a new life in a 2015 edition by Mariner Books. When an artist dies, there is often new attention to her work, and for Le Guin that includes attention to her writing book. *Steering the Craft* comprises a sequence of loosely connected pieces of advice, enhanced by famous literary examples and practical exercises, but it lacks the architecture that would make it a classic. When I find such a structural weakness in a writing book, I ignore it, turning my attention to the ground, looking for gold coins. Within its modest 141 pages, there are rewards aplenty. These include a lexicon of common, but important, literary terms. There is a nifty guide on how to create a support group for local writers, how to organize it, how to keep it going, along with rules of the road for both the author and those who critique him or her.

Le Guin is at her most passionate and practical when, like Gary Provost, she gets down to the sentence level. She offers remedies for common writing illnesses, including the eye-catching "conjunctivitis": "Stringing short sentences together with conjunctions is a legitimate stylistic mannerism, but used naively, it sets up a kind of infantile droning that makes the story hard to follow."

Her parody rings true: "They were happy and they felt like dancing and then they felt like they had been reading too much Hemingway and it was night." If that feels too self-consciously rhythmical, then where does the better music in a sentence come from? She writes,

> Every sentence has a rhythm of its own, which is also part of the rhythm of the whole piece. Rhythm is what keeps the song going, the horse galloping, the story moving.
>
> And the rhythm of prose depends very much—very prosaically—on the length of the sentences.

She rebels against a contemporary fetish that "the only good sentence is a short sentence." More punning: "A convicted criminal might agree. I don't."

Her take is that

> very short sentences, isolated or in a series, are highly effective in the right place. Prose consisting entirely of short, syntactically simple sentences is monotonous, choppy, irritating. If short-sentence prose goes on very long, whatever its content, the *thump-thump* beat gives it a false simplicity that soon just sounds stupid. See Spot. See Jane. See Spot bite Jane.

A good test of the value of advice in a writing book is whether its author practices what the work preaches. Here's a paragraph from a chapter titled—lowercase—"the sound of your writing":

> Most children enjoy the sound of language for its own sake. They wallow in repetitions and luscious word-sounds and the crunch and slither of onomatopoeia; they fall in love with musical or impressive words and use them in all the wrong places. Some writers keep this primal interest in and love for the sounds of language. Others "outgrow" their oral/aural sense of what they're reading or writing. That's a dead loss. An awareness of what your own writing sounds like is an essential skill for a writer. Fortunately it's quite easy to cultivate, to learn or reawaken.

With Provost's clever demonstration of sentence variety in mind, I decided to count the words in the seven sentences in Le Guin's passage: 11, 32, 14, 12, 4, 16, 10. Notice that her sentences not only vary in length but in structure, from the initial short simple sentence, to the compounding of clauses, filled with evidence, in the second. I look forward to the experience of reading Le Guin's honored prose. For now, she has the last word: "A good writer, like a good reader, has a mind's ear."

LESSONS

1. Read drafts of your work aloud. Listen for those passages that have a monotonous rhythm.

2. Revise the boring parts by varying the length of your sentences. If necessary, vary just about everything. Remember that the number and placement of periods in a passage will govern the rhythm. Each period is a stop sign.

3. Purposeful repetition works if you are trying for a special emphasis. But you can establish a pattern based on repetition, then give it an interesting twist at the end.

4. Find a passage of your writing you think works for the reader. Now count the number of words in each sentence. While there is no "correct" algorithm, consider revising if you see too many sentences of the same length.

8

Use visual markings to spark your creative
process. Also use them to signify your revisions.

Authors at Work
Edited by Robert H. Taylor and Herman W. Liebert

Notebooks of the Mind: Explorations of Thinking
By Vera John-Steiner

Toolbox: *Draw pictures of your writing ideas. Create maps of
your process. Visualize your revisions. Think charts, diagrams,
lists, story shapes. Use circles, spirals, triangles, pyramids, stick
figures, and arrows—lots of arrows. These blueprints can guide
your thinking from conception (those scribbles on napkins)
through the final changes in the margins of your text. Even in the
digital age, edit one draft on hard copy to better envision both
your path and destination.*

It is no secret that I am a disciple of Donald Murray, the influential writing teacher at the University of New Hampshire
whose work extended from composition classrooms to news-

rooms such as the *Boston Globe*. The word *disciple* has messianic implications—and I embrace them, not in any spiritual sense, but in the sense that ever since Murray rode his steed into Writing Town, nothing has been the same.

One of his many gifts to me was a special book titled *Authors at Work*. It is a collection of facsimiles of literary manuscript pages, from John Locke (1704) to Dylan Thomas (1953)—just a year short of a quarter millennium of creativity. Murray was so excited by this 1955 museum exhibition of manuscripts that he purchased a number of copies of this limited-edition catalogue and dispensed them like decongestants to blocked and breathless writers.

Let's travel back in time from our digital age to the Romantic Era via manuscript exhibit 13 in *Authors at Work*. The author, Percy Bysshe Shelley, decides to revise the title of what will become one of his most famous poems. In clear penmanship he has written at the top of the page "To the Sky-Lark." Dissatisfied, he deletes *the* and replaces it with *a:* "To a Sky-Lark." In this case, the word *delete* is a euphemism. He takes his pen and scratches out the definite article—like really scratches (/\/\/\/)— and writes *a* above the line. It doesn't matter for the moment *why* he makes this change. (I make my case in *The Glamour of Grammar.*) What matters is that he makes the change at all. At the end of an author's road, the little changes—even *the* to *a*—often mean the most.

As I examine these manuscripts over the years, they continue to thrill me. They are windows into the craft, character, purpose, audience, and quirks of the authors who created them.

The main lesson from this book is not just to revise—

everyone knows that. Beyond the obvious, know that there are predictable patterns of revision, visual representations of three recurring imperatives:

- Take this out.
- Put this in.
- Move this around.

Here are some of them (I am copying and paraphrasing language from the catalogue; direct quotes are from Herman W. Liebert):

- Joseph Addison "revises as he writes," rejecting certain phrases and making a new start on the same line of writing.
- Alexander Pope's poetic lines read smoothly, but only after "laborious re-drafting." A few early verses survive the revision, and he is polishing to the end.
- Samuel Johnson, one of the most famous literary figures of the eighteenth century, testified that he would compose lines of poetry in his head, as many as fifty at a time, while he paced back and forth in his room. On lazy days he wrote down only half-lines, knowing he could fill them in from memory later. The manuscript shows his claims to be true.
- Voltaire shows a distinctive style of composition as two different handwritings appear on the manuscript page. Voltaire writes a draft, then adds corrections. Another hand—probably that of a secretary or an amanuensis—recopies the draft and incorporates the author's changes.
- Richard Sheridan, author of the play *The School for Scandal,* writes quickly but makes extensive use of marginalia.

On the left, we can see where the names of the speakers are listed to keep things straight.

- Frances Burney changes the order of key words two or three times. "A long insertion is pinned to the page displayed."

- James Boswell drafts his *Life of Samuel Johnson* on the right pages of his folio, leaving room for long additions on the left side. Having collected many letters and other written material, he marks places for insertion with the phrase "Take it in." In the twenty-first century, the digital phrase "cut and paste" is familiar, but consider the analog version. "Sometimes he sent copy to his long-suffering printer in pieces several feet long, made by pasting together sheets of his journal."

- Charles Lamb "scrapes out rejected words with a sharp instrument" and writes the preferred phrase over them.

- Honoré de Balzac includes almost as much new language in his revisions of a corrected proof as appeared in the original.

- Charles Dickens "marks at least one correction in almost every sentence."

- Thomas Carlyle brings exhaustive attention to detail in his notes and working papers, manuscript, corrected galley proofs, and corrected page proofs. He uses all sorts of paper: envelopes, tiny slips, collections of scraps pasted together, folded dossiers.

- Henry James retains, after revision, only 76 words of dialogue from a whole page of typescript. More than 200 words have been blotted out.

- Dylan Thomas writes at least 70 drafts of his poem "Prologue."

If you want to emulate these authors and advance in your craft, you must revise, revise, and then revise some more. Even if most of your word processing is done on the computer, you can learn much about the strengths and weaknesses of a draft by working on paper. As these manuscripts show, you can do that in various ways:

- Neatly run a pencil through a single word or line.
- Scratch out a word or phrase and replace it.
- Blot or cross out long passages.
- Insert words, phrases, passages anywhere they will fit: over a line, in the margins.
- Cut and paste with scissors and tape.
- Draft on the right, leaving room for revision on the left.
- Use the margins to add, correct, amplify, stack, rethink, or communicate with others.

Keep in mind the big steps: take this out, put this in, move this around.

Thomas French, who won a Pulitzer Prize in 1998 for feature writing, testified that an important stage in his writing came when he saw pages of *Authors at Work* for the first time. They confirmed for him that the finished copy of published authors was often the product of careful, almost endless, sometimes eccentric revision. In an introduction to the catalogue of manuscripts, Herman W. Liebert describes the aim of the exhibition "to move backward by this means as near as possible to the creative moment and to follow the subsequent evolution of writers' work."

So far in this chapter we have examined the signs and signals writers make to mark their revisions, mostly near the end of the process. A similar set of markers helps writers, and other creative people, envision the work, often before a single sentence appears on the page or the screen.

As you think of your own writing process, consider that moment, perhaps a tipping point, when you prepare a text and are ready to share it with someone else. That can come early in the process: you can scribble a line on a paper napkin and share it with the person sitting across from you. More often, it comes later, sometimes much later, and sometimes—yes, never. You may write ten drafts of an entire novel and lock the final version in a drawer.

When is your writing ready to be shared? Before the digital age, the answer to that question depended upon the quality of paper you were using. If you were writing on scrap paper or in a reporter's notebook or in something you might call a journal or daybook; if you were writing on colored paper—yellow or blue, or on anything with a spiral binding; these would all be indicators that the prose was, for now, for your eyes only.

By the time you got to a better stock of paper—as in the manuscript pages described above—you were signaling a desire not just to learn or discover, but to communicate. It might be for your spouse, friend, teacher, or editor, but the page was now ready to be handed over to someone else. Until you reach that point of sharing, you will benefit from jotting "telegrams to yourself," a clever and useful phrase from Vera John-Steiner, the author of the brilliant 1985 book *Notebooks of the Mind*.

This was another of Donald Murray's favorite books, and he shared it widely. You can tell that I liked it—through several rereadings—via the countless pencil markings I left inside: circles, underlines, check marks, observations in the margins. I am not just reading the text; I am having a conversation with the author.

John-Steiner, a Holocaust survivor and a professor of linguistics and educational psychology at the University of New Mexico for more than 40 years, interviewed more than 100 subjects widely considered thoughtful and creative, chosen from a rich variety of disciplines. Among them were journalists, poets, psychologists, composers, biologists, philosophers, photographers, physicists, choreographers, painters, and anthropologists. Her goal, like Liebert's, was to identify early expressions of creativity, the points at which thoughts are expressed through gestures, words, and images.

In addition to testimony from living subjects, John-Steiner unearthed evidence from the actual notebooks, journals, diaries, and blueprints of the famously gifted. The one weakness of the book is that these are described, but, with two exceptions, never pictured. On a left-hand page we see a sketch labeled "Darwin's Tree," taken from one of his notebooks. Under the words "I think," we see evolving what may have been a preliminary notion of the origin of human beings.

To the right of that evolutionary tree, we see a page from the working papers of Merce Cunningham, a choreographer. On it we see initial visions of a dance, signified by a pattern of stick figures, names of steps, and the letters *L R L* (left, right, left). Whether you are creating a pictorial representation of natural selection or a dance for the New York City Ballet, you have to begin somewhere.

What is called in social science a "protocol analysis" allows the researcher to learn the preliminary steps and organizing habits of the reflective practitioner. Whatever contraption is being created—scientific theory, a sonata, poetry—it often begins with markings not meant for others to see. Postcards to yourself.

John-Steiner's chapter "Verbal Thinking" includes a case study from the author Virginia Woolf. On a late September day in 1938, Woolf notes in a diary that she is too tired to write the next chapter of a biography in the usual way. Instead, she creates a list of the elements she might include, jotting them down "in a staccato, thinking-aloud manner":

> Suppose I make a break after H's death (madness).
> A separate paragraph quoting what R. himself said.
> Then a break.
> Then begin definitely with the first meeting.
> That is the first impression: a man of the world, not a
>   professor or Bohemian. Then give facts in his letters to
>   his mother.
> Then back to the second meeting.
> Pictures: talk about art. I look out of window.
> [...]

Give the pre-war atmosphere. Ott. Duncan. France.
Letter to Bridges about beauty and sensuality.

Here is what John-Steiner sees:

> These notes are jottings to the self; they assist the writer re-
> membering an organization of important details and concepts
> that emerge in the sequence of her work. Use of a telegraphic
> style makes it possible to gallop ahead, exploring new connec-
> tions, a task that is much harder when the writer's intention
> is to shape connected and readable prose. Often when there is
> some transcribed record of the way in which writers plan their
> work, it takes the form of these very condensed thoughts.

I have this simple move I use when I coach struggling writers. Perhaps the writer is blocked, confused, or overwhelmed.
We may be drinking coffee. I grab a paper napkin. "Just tell me
what you are thinking about. What kinds of things *might* be in
your story?" (The word *might* turns out to be liberating.) Suddenly I am taking dictation:

> Almost 50 years since Jack Kerouac bled to death in St. Pete,
>   Florida
> He died at 47 a bitter drunk old man
> End of the road
> Still signs of him around city
> Flamingo bar
> Haunts Haslam's bookstore

These are notebooks of the mind. They don't even have to be notebooks. Napkins of the mind can be good enough.

LESSONS

1. Visual thinking and planning are crucial tools for word people, especially at the beginning of a project. For your next piece of writing, try drawing a picture or diagram of what you'd like to achieve. You need not be an artist: stick figures, geometric shapes, arrows, and spirals will do.

2. Keep a stack of index cards nearby. Different colors will help. Use a card to send yourself a note on your writing plans for the day. A postcard to yourself: "Dear Roy. Wish you were here. I am trying to rewrite the Lessons for the book. Could use your help!"

3. Use index cards to signify the parts of your project. Each card can represent a scene, segment, or chapter. Move the cards around to find a meaningful sequence.

4. Remember the three methods of revision: put this in, take this out, move this around. If you are stuck, move from the computer screen to a printout. This will give you a wider view of the architecture of the work to see how the parts might better fit together.

9

—✦—

Tune your voice for the digital age. Experiment
with language and forms of delivery.

Wired Style: Principles of English Usage in the Digital Age
By Constance Hale and Jessie Scanlon

Toolbox: *I studied classical piano as a boy, using muscle memory
to master works by Mozart and Beethoven. But I was enjoying
rock 'n' roll. To play like Little Richard required me to change the
way I listened to music. I had to learn chord progressions and
improvisations. In the same way, writers in the digital age must
expand their range. Readers now expect not just a conventional
voice, but a distinctive one, a writer willing to experiment with
language. This means not getting trapped in the jargon of technology, writing on a richer variety of cultural experiences (the Bible
and Twitter), using colloquial language to achieve sophisticated
effects, and, at least on occasion, finding a way to combine high
seriousness with deep irreverence.*

When I first read her name, Constance Hale, I thought it
sounded like a weather report. I love names so much that I

can't help playing with them, digging down into them, speaking them aloud as if they were part of a song lyric. Known to her friends and admirers as Connie, let's just say that in her career as a teacher and author, she has demonstrated constancy as a champion of good writing and effective use of language. She has run influential writing conferences at Harvard and Berkeley. She is the author of *Sin and Syntax: How to Craft Wickedly Effective Prose*; and *Vex, Hex, Smash, Smooch: Let Verbs Power Your Writing*, one of the few books to give due credit to strategic use of the passive voice. She has earned the moniker "E. B. White on acid," a great blurb applied to a book that opened my eyes at a sleepy moment: *Wired Style: Principles of English Usage in the Digital Age*.

Hale and her coauthor Jessie Scanlon were assigned the task of establishing the house writing and usage style for *Wired* magazine at a time when the traditional literati and the newly coined digerati were competing for attention. Technology has always brought new words into the language and bent old ones to new tasks and concepts. Published in 1996, *Wired Style* is a special book. No other style guide took on writing for the digital age with such ambition and verve. There is a bilingual, bidialectal, code-switching quality to the work, with a deep appreciation for traditional literary values alongside enthusiastic encouragement to write in exciting new voices in new formats for new audiences, a recognition that the alphabet, the printing press, and the internet stand as the most important information technologies in human history.

About 150 pages of my edition constitute an A-to-Z dictionary of terms essential to the development of digital technology for the purposes of communication. If you are seventy years old, for example, and too embarrassed to ask your grandkids what a meme is, you can find out here:

> Contagious idea. Thought virus. Unit of cultural inheritance. Rhymes with scheme.
> Evolutionary biologist Richard Dawkins introduced the word (though not the idea) in *The Selfish Gene*. His meaning: an idea that functions in the mind the same way a gene functions in the body. An especially infectious idea is a **viral meme.**

Hale and Scanlon created an excellent 1996 glossary, defining a rich variety of words, concepts, and institutions that span the digital world, from popular acronyms such as *IMHO* ("in my humble opinion") to popular culture, such as the influence of *Star Trek* and other science fiction imaginings. As I browse through these from the vantage point of someone who is not a digital native, I recognize many terms that still have currency in 2020. The problem, of course, is that digital culture changes so quickly that the rate of obsolescence is rapid. As a result, once-practical terms—such as *floppy disk*—have the same status as *typewriter* or *transistor radio,* words for objects that have become nostalgic curiosities. There are no mentions of Facebook or Twitter. A book, by definition, is not the best vehicle for managing the rapid transformations of digital culture. To which I say, "So what?" *Wired Style* created the foundation upon which all subsequent digital glossaries might be built.

More intriguing are the twenty-four pages of introduction,

in which the authors put forward the ten principles of wired style. Here they are, summarized:

- The medium matters.
- Play with voice.
- Flaunt your subcultural literacy.
- Transcend the technical.
- Capture the colloquial.
- Anticipate the future.
- Be irreverent.
- Brave the new world of new media.
- Go global.
- Play with dots and dashes and slashes (not to mention !@#<<$*).

Each of these imperatives is explained and well illustrated, although, as with the glossary, some examples now feel a bit out of date.

Of all of these, I found most significant the encouragement "play with voice." That clause is built on two words that need some definition when it comes to the craft of writing:

Play: This verb denotes and connotes forms of action we associate with youthful exuberance, laughter, fun, and entertainment. I would argue that most forms of writing—even obituaries—are forms of play. Even Shakespeare's most gruesome tragedies (anyone read *Titus Andronicus* lately?) are called plays. In the context of writing for the digital age, think of experimentation: mash up elements that might not belong together; make contraptions of meaning using an increasingly rich variety of genres and platforms.

For about three years, early in the history of the Poynter Institute's website, I wrote about 400 columns under the pseudonym "Dr. Ink." There was a Pygmalion effect to my creation of this pompous pointy-head, a self-appointed expert who never used the word *I* as he explained journalism, politics, or popular culture but enjoyed referring to himself in the third person: "Dr. Ink looks down his perfectly shaped nose at anyone who follows AP Style and fails to use that final comma before *and* in a series."

Voice: Although *voice* usually refers to speech that can be heard, in writing it can refer to the effect of words on the page or screen that are not spoken aloud. We read a text and think "he *sounds* angry" or "she *sounds* funny." Someone asked me recently about a writer on Twitter: "Why does he always sound so whiny?" I read several tweets and decided—yes, whiny, though I had never heard a recording of this author's actual voice.

Newspapers and magazines have that special ability to project a multiplicity of voices, even in a single issue. In Tuesday's newspaper we might read numerous reports written in a fairly plain and mostly neutral style; but on the editorial page we find opinions written in an institutional voice. Signed columns carry the most distinctive voices, the kind we might recognize even without a byline. Letters to the editor range in tone from measured to screeching. We haven't even mentioned the voices of the sports columnist, the food critic, the advice columnist, or the authors of classified ads. These voices are not all pleasant or effective, but they all sound like something.

To develop your voice in the digital age, pay close attention to the writers who "speak" to you on websites, blogs, and social networks. One of my favorite writers on Twitter, for example, is Mary Karr, an author we will discuss later in this book. Consider this example on her struggles as a writer:

Mary Karr: "After 2+ years bent over a wanna-be book—after throwing out first 82 then 178 pages—have wrangled & calf roped about 8 pages to the ground. Fall down, get up, dust off. Singing like a boss lady."

That text could only have been written in the digital age. Notice the use of numbers, shorthand language, dashes and ampersand, sentence fragments, but with an extended metaphor! She is playing with voice.

Wired Style projects the metaphor of voice into the digital age. Catch this from Hale and Scanlon:

In this era of "client/server databases," "vertical portals," and "high-bandwidth networks," we are awash in data. But good writing is not data. We turn to literary journalism not just for information but for context, culture, spirit, and color. We respond to voice. Not the clear-but-oh-so-conventional voice of Standard Written English. Not the data-drowned voice of computer trade journals. And not the puréed voice of the mainstream press. The voice of the quirky, individualist writer.

Voice captures the way people talk. Voice adds attitude and authenticity. Voice is the quality of writing that lets the reader know that a story is coming from *someone* who has been *somewhere*.

In her online profile, Hale explains:

> I am a writer based in San Francisco. I grew up on the North Shore of O'ahu, where I spoke "proper" English at home and Hawaiian creole (or "Pidgin English") at school. I'm sure that this "bilingual upbringing" gave me my obsession with language. I travel to Hawai'i often, and to stay connected to that culture I study the hula in California. Although my six books may not seem connected, they do if you understand my origins.

I have a sudden vision. Connie and I are performing at a writing conference in which I am playing Hawaiian songs on my ukulele and she is performing the hula. (*Ukulele*, by the way, derives from two words meaning "jumping flea," most likely a metaphor for the fingers moving quickly from string to string.) But it is her "bilingual upbringing" I find most intriguing. Let's agree that all of us are capable of communicating in a variety of ways to a variety of audiences. Think of the difference between your love note and your complaint to the bank. What I now realize about *Wired Style* is its tolerance for the richest variety of voices, from the most literary to the most technical. All the voices, in the end, must sound like you. But you do not suffer from multiple personality disorder. No, you are a student of the word in a world hungry for meaning.

LESSONS

1. A great virtue for writers in the digital age is versatility. You must practice writing short and long, fast and slow, in reports and stories, in multimedia forms, across media platforms.

2. Wired writing is not an abandonment of older forms. Headlines matter more than ever. Stories are everywhere. But these can now be expressed on websites, blogs, social media, even via #hashtags. You can write as a friend, follower, commenter, quick-take artist, clickbaiter, or snarky troll. Study the best writers in these genres and see how they work.

3. For fun, try creating an alternative online identity. Please do this for fun and learning, not for vicious mischief. Give your digital doppelgänger a name and a writing voice that is different from yours. Play around. See what you learn.

4. It turns out that the internet is not an information superhighway. It is, instead, a polluted ocean with buried treasure sitting here and there on the bottom. Neutralize the poison of the propagandists, hackers, conspiracy theorists, trolls, and bullies by devoting your online efforts to the public good.

10

———✦

Turn the dials that adjust the way you sound as a
writer. Read the work aloud to make sure it
sounds like you—or a little better.

*The Sound on the Page: Great Writers Talk about Style and Voice
in Writing*
By Ben Yagoda

Toolbox: *Think of your writing voice as a version of your am-
plified singing voice. If you were on stage, you would be singing
into a microphone and through a sound system, where your voice
would be influenced by certain controls: volume, bass, treble,
echo. Your writing voice has those kinds of levers, too: whether
you use I or we; whether you write stories or reports; whether
you quote Aristotle or your local street philosopher. Learn how to
manipulate these levers to discover and deliver your best writing
voice.*

I am ready to say it now with more force: Of all the effects created by writers, none is more important or elusive than that
quality called voice. Good writers, it is said, want to "find" their
voice, and they want that voice to have "authority," a word from

the same root as *author*. They want to be "authentic." If the writer went on a quest to find a sacred object or special power, it might very well be called voice.

To echo Connie Hale, in the digital age voice is more important than ever. Writers need to develop their own "brand," an identity that suggests reliability and quality. With so many sources of information to choose from, readers scan their computers and mobile devices for writers who deliver. Those writers, I would argue, have recognizable voices, not in the way they speak, but in the way they write.

(When I thought about the writer's voice in the digital age, it led me to this brainstorming list of subgenres and modes for 2020: blog posts, status updates, tweets, text messages, clickbait, snark, shaming, trolling, mansplaining, linking, tech jargon, and branding, to name a few.)

Style, by one definition, feels like an external quality, something that you wear, a fashion; voice, though it can be modulated, expresses a more durable integrated quality, something that comes from within. Elton John can wear outrageous glasses as a stylish trademark, or not. His voice, whether he sings "Crocodile Rock" at Wembley Stadium or the ballad "Candle in the Wind" at Westminster Abbey during the funeral of Princess Diana, is distinctively, authentically his. To think of a writer as a singer is not much of a stretch. To "make it sing" has always been newsroom slang for good writing. The language we apply to music—*rhythm, theme, sound, crescendo, reprise, composition,* and, yes, *voice*—explains effects in writing as well.

Adapting the classic definition of pornography, we know voice when we see it—or hear it. William Safire and George

Will were both older, white, male conservative columnists, yet their readers could easily distinguish between them even without benefit of a byline. Few readers would confuse Anna Quindlen with Maureen Dowd, even though both write from a liberal, feminist perspective. The voices of these writers are so distinctive that they shout their identities to the reader from the screen or the page.

The fact that voice is to some extent integral rather than added on can be illustrated in an anecdote from the poet David McCord. He remembers how he once picked up an old copy of *St. Nicholas* magazine, which printed stories written by children. One story caught his attention, and he was "suddenly struck by a prose passage more earthy and natural in voice than what I had been glancing through. This sounds like E. B. White, I said to myself. Then I looked at the signature: Elwyn Brooks White, age 11." McCord recognized the elements of style—the voice—of the young author who would one day grow up to write *Charlotte's Web* and so much more.

What I have looked for but never found is what we musicians call a fake book—but for writers: a simple, straightforward text on the music of writing that includes practical strategies for setting, tuning, or modulating your writing voice. If Don Fry is correct that voice is the "sum" of an individual's writing strategies, which of those strategies are essential to creating the illusion of speech? To answer that question, think of a piece of sound equipment called a graphic equalizer. This is the device that mixes the range of sounds in a sound system by providing about thirty dials or levers or stops, controlling such things as bass and treble. Push up the bass, pull down the treble, add a little reverb to configure the desired sound.

If we all had a handy-dandy writing-voice modulator, what ranges would the levers control?

I've identified and isolated these choices:

1. Level of language: What is the level of language? Is it concrete or abstract—a 1956 Mickey Mantle baseball card or a phrase like *hero worship*—or somewhere in between? Does the writer use street slang or the logical argument of a professor of philosophy?

2. Choice of person: What "person" does the writer work in? Does the writer use *I* to create a familiar voice? Or *we* to express the collective, as in a labor union? Or *you* to sound conversational? Or the most common, *they*, to seem more detached? Or all of these?

3. Source and range of allusion: What are the sources and the range of allusions? Do these come from high or low culture, or both? Does the writer cite a medieval theologian or a professional wrestler? T. S. Eliot or Wild Bill Hickok?

4. Density of metaphor: How often does the writer use metaphors and other figures of speech? Does the writer want to sound more like a poet, whose work is thick with figurative images, or a journalist, who uses them only for special effect?

5. Sentence length and structure: What is the length and structure of the typical sentence? Is it short and simple? Long and complex? Or varied?

6. Distance from neutrality: Does the language sound

neutral, objective, dispassionate? Partisan? Or on fire and engaged?

7. Inclusive to exclusive: Does the prose exhibit a plain style, a common voice, one that invites in many readers from many discourse communities? Or does it speak to an exclusive club of readers, either through slang or jargon?

8. Conventional to experimental frames: Is the voice what we might expect to hear from a particular genre or platform, be it a sonnet, headline, or blog post? Or does it seek to cross conventional boundaries to create something surprising or even shocking?

9. Original to derivative: Is the voice clearly borrowed from another writer or text, the way musicians sample musical phrases from the familiar work of others? Or does it seek to be radically original, a voice that readers regard as distinctive?

Consider this simple example. In Toronto, a man pleads guilty to the rape, murder, and dismemberment of a ten-year-old girl. No one can be entirely neutral in the face of such horror, but it is instructive to see the different approaches to this story by the fiercely competitive Toronto newspapers.

The Sun, a tabloid in the British style, offers this headline: "ROT IN HELL."

The Globe and Mail gives us "HEART OF DARKNESS."

The Star weighs in with "HIS 'DARK SECRET.'"

The voice of the headline writer differs in each of these approaches, and the difference can be marked by the distance from neutrality. The least neutral is, of course, "Rot in Hell," a phrase the headline writer picks up from the local columnist inside the paper. His lead, for the record, is "Rot in hell, you son of a bitch...."

Less evocative but still opinionated is the *Globe and Mail's* "Heart of Darkness," which a small percentage of readers will recognize as an allusion to the title of a Joseph Conrad novella. This choice is inspired by Christie Blatchford's lead: "The darkness of a man's heart is a story as old as the hills, but rarely has there been offered such a stark and intimate viewing of it as yesterday at the main Toronto courthouse."

Closest to neutral is the approach of the *Toronto Star*. The quotation marks in "His 'Dark Secret'" indicate to the reader that the words come from a source and are not necessarily the opinion of the writer or the newspaper. Not surprisingly, the lead to the story is the most straightforward: "[Name of killer] described it as his 'dark secret,' an overwhelming desire that consumed his life, a fantasy, he told detectives, to have sex with a young child."

Here's a larger point: That the writer's voice may be more audible when it is shrieking or shouting or cursing. But the voice of the strategically neutral writer is still a voice, one that we need when we try to get at the truth without fear or favor.

As a writer, I am drawn to other writers, especially the versatile ones. Their versatility—in length, genre, tone, topic—creates spaces where I can reach out and connect. Ben Yagoda is near the top of my list of contemporary American writers. He and Kevin Kerrane coedited *The Art of Fact,* an anthology of literary journalism. He has written books about *The New Yorker,* Will Rogers, the American Songbook, and my personal favorite, Dr. Ruth Westheimer, the diminutive diva of sex advice, whose accent and candor burned up cable television programming in the days when MTV was actually interested in music.

Ben (I can call him that; we have been on programs together) also writes on writing. In his book on voice, *The Sound on the Page,* he gives his own insights and advice along with those of dozens of successful authors. His book includes chapters and sections such as "Music and Style"; "Style and Personality"; and "Finding a Voice, Finding a Style."

I am struck by the way in which Ben uses the words *voice* and *style* in parallel, that is, as equal elements, as in his subtitle: "Great Writers Talk about Style and Voice in Writing." Style and voice; voice and style. But this is misleading. I wish I had a computer program handy that would count—in Ben's work and mine—the exact number of times the two words are used. For Ben, *style* would outnumber *voice;* for me the numbers might be reversed.

Let's contrast Ben's treatment of the two words. Here, he specifically takes on *voice:*

> Writers often talk about finding their voice. It's an odd use of the common metaphor—a speaking voice is there for us all along and doesn't require a search party—but it's undoubtedly accurate. And so while it's true that some writers seem to be blessed with a style-by-birthright, needing only to refine or develop it, many others have a moment on their road to Damascus when, all of a sudden, the words tumbling out sound *right* for the first time.

So when we think of the distinctive nature of a writer's expression, is *voice* a synonym for *style*? Or are there important differences? Just for fun, I headed for the *OED* to search for original meanings. Huzzah. I found seven full columns of definitions and historical citations under *style* as a noun. The name derives from a pointed object—a stile, a stick used for writing on tablets of clay. Among the twenty-six discrete definitions, many are associated directly with forms of writing, eventually expanded to other creative forms of expression, from art, to music, to fashion. In our common usage, we all tend to distinguish the style of a work from its content. The idea is that even if we might be bored by the content of a writer's work, we may be attracted to the way it is written.

Let's go back to Ben for an example from his introduction:

For the first of many times, I present as an example Ernest Hemingway. What is Hemingway's content? He has some fishing and war stories that are pretty good, if a little short in the action department, and some ideas about honorable and dishonorable behavior that would puzzle many contemporary readers. His characters, especially in the novels and most especially in the later novels, tend to be tiresome. But his style! Take a look at the first paragraph of one of his first stories, "The Three-Day Blow."

Here Ben quotes Hemingway:

The rain stopped as Nick turned into the road that went up through the orchard. The fruit had been picked and the fall wind blew through the bare trees. Nick stopped and picked up a Wagner apple from beside the road, shiny in the brown grass from the rain. He put the apple in the pocket of his Mackinaw coat.

Back to Yagoda:

The first striking thing about this passage is the action it describes appears to be in no way dramatic, significant, or interesting. The second is that it could only have been written by Hemingway....Even if by some chance you have not read his work, you will, if you are at all an attentive reader, be struck by the unified, consistent, and ultimately hypnotic sound and *feel* of it. We note the plain words and short sentences, of course— so pronounced that the comma in the third sentence feels like a consoling arm around our shoulder and the three-syllable *Mackinaw* at the end a gift outright—but also the way these technical features create a mood. The reluctance to commit to a complex sentence, a Latinate word, an adverb, or even a pronoun (repeated *Nick* and *the apple* instead of substituting *he* or *it*), the urge to describe the world precisely even at the risk of using eight ungainly prepositional phrases in one paragraph: the more familiar one is with this writer, the more one understands that his stylistic choices express a state of mind, a philosophy of perception, and a morality that we now communicate with one word—*Hemingway.*

What Ben describes as the composing elements of style, I experience as voice, that is, something I think I am *hearing* rather than seeing. Let me offer an example from Ben's own use of language and expression of craft. This is from his introduction: "This book began with a single and simple observation: it is frequently the case that writers entertain, move and inspire us less by what they say than by how they say it. *What* they say is information and ideas and (in the case of fiction) story and characters. *How* they say it is style." Notice how he uses italics to emphasize certain words, such as *What* and *How*. Please read those sentences aloud. Notice now how the italics influence the way you pronounce those words. Ben's rare use of an exclamation mark in the Hemingway passage has a similar influence. It means you read the verbless sentence "But his style!" in a different tone of voice than if it were merely "But his style."

With *The Sound on the Page,* Ben Yagoda has done us (me) a great favor. He has written something for us (for me) that I want to honor by writing back. Writers can speak to other writers from the page or screen, a conversation that does not require us to read the words aloud.

LESSONS

1. Read a piece of your own writing aloud to a friend or an editor. Ask your colleague, "Does this sound like me?" Discuss the response.

2. Read a piece of your own writing aloud. Make a list of adjectives that you think define your voice, such as *heavy* or *aggressive* or *tentative.* Now try to identify the effects in your writing that led you to these conclusions. Finally, what strategies in your writing cause these effects? Can you *hear* problems in the story that you cannot *see*?

3. Read any daily newspaper. Read as many of the leads as possible. Mark them according to their distance from neutrality. Which sound neutral or objective? Which sound opinionated or partisan? Which ones are hot? Cold?

4. Name a writer whose voice appeals to you. Why does it? Read a passage from that writer aloud. Pick adjectives that describe that voice: *confident, consoling, savvy*. Find the elements in the passage that inspire those descriptions.

III

Confidence and Identity

Donald Murray coached writers in classrooms and newsrooms, two places where aspiring writers might become discouraged. Some students never feel they belong in the writers' club. Even in newsrooms, folks who write often prefer being called reporters. Many obstacles must be overcome: from bouts of apprehension, to writer's block, to procrastination, to impostor's syndrome, the fear that, in spite of your accomplishments, your weaknesses will one day be exposed, and you will be forced to walk the plank.

Anne Lamott admits to many anxious moments as a writer. Her encouragement to her students anticipates the inevitability of "shitty first drafts." Peter Elbow turned writing instruction into a kind of group therapy, where students, bogged down with inertia, learned to bust loose with intense episodes of "freewriting," a form of fast drafting in which the work seems to be accomplished by the hands rather than the head or heart. You could find meaning, wrote Elbow, in a small community of writers, its members armed with a protocol of smart thinking and critical support.

Two women, writing about writing in the 1930s, sought to lift writers from their depression during the Depression. Dorothea Brande preaches a discipline that could encourage the frustrated writer, urging writers to create rituals of drafting and revision, down to what beverages work best while doing so. Brande wants to help writers, but she is a tough taskmaster. Brenda Ueland, on the other hand, is a dynamo of inspiration. Speaking especially to women who might feel undermined by their social and domestic roles, Ueland offers page after page of "You can do it, sisters and brothers of the word."

It's hard to imagine an author who writes with more confidence than Stephen King. For sheer productivity, few writers can match him. He admits his identity as a writer was shaped by reading bad stuff and learning what *not* to do. He also preaches the requirements of craft, developing a rigorous writing habit, choosing a time and place where you can do good work, with a target number of words per day. Yes, on the seventh day, King rested.

11

———+•

Learn the steps of the writing process. Good
writing is not magic, but it's full of surprises.

*The Essential Don Murray: Lessons from America's Greatest
Writing Teacher*
Edited by Thomas Newkirk and Lisa C. Miller

Toolbox: *Before you master the requirements of your particular
genre, understand the steps of the process all writers must climb:
finding story ideas, gathering the material you need, discovering
a focus, selecting your best stuff, envisioning a structure, building
a draft, revising all parts of the process over time. For each step,
you can find strategies that will help you solve problems and
make meaning.*

Five huge boxes sat at the loading dock of the Poynter Institute
not long ago, waiting for the FedEx truck to pick them up. They
were filled with more than 125 file boxes containing the literary effects of Donald M. Murray, in my opinion the most
influential writing teacher America has ever known. The pre-
cious content of those boxes—including 100 of Murray's experimental daybooks—was headed home where it belongs: to

the University of New Hampshire. Our hope was that students, teachers, scholars, and journalists would now be able to get their eyes and hands on those documents. When they did, they would see a writer and a teacher hard at work, trying to make sense of the English language and the writing process, and trying to help all of us get better as writers.

Murray had a profound influence on those of us who taught writing at Poynter. If I was Arthur, he was Merlin. If I was Frodo, he was Gandalf. If I was Luke Skywalker, he was Yoda— only a big Yoda with a round face, a Santa beard, and a wardrobe, with suspenders, purchased at Walmart.

Don and I arrived at common ground from opposite directions, like two trains in an algebra equation. He flunked out of high school twice, experienced World War II as a paratrooper, got an English degree from UNH in 1948, and headed for the newsroom of the *Boston Herald*. In 1954, at the age of 29, he won the Pulitzer Prize for editorial writing for a long series of opinions on military preparedness. He was the youngest writer ever to win this prize.

A decade later, he returned to UNH as a writing teacher and became a founding parent of an approach to composition teaching that emphasized process as well as product. His practical theories about writing helped changed the way it was taught at every educational level. At professional conferences, he held, but did not desire, a kind of papal status, and his disciples, including me, maintained a zealous appreciation of him as a tribal leader of the word.

I came to journalism from the opposite direction, as a teacher of literature and composition, hired to coach writers at the *St. Petersburg Times* in 1977. The following year Don was hired to coach at the *Boston Globe,* developed a popular column there, and continued to write almost every day until his death in 2006 at the age of eighty-two.

Any expression of Don Murray's published work is worth a writer's attention. Most of these books, but not all, were written for an academic audience, teachers and students who were wading, at least knee-deep, into the craft. The key works, in chronological order, are as follows:

A Writer Teaches Writing (1968)

Writing for Your Readers (1983)

Write to Learn (1984)

Read to Write (1986)

The Craft of Revision (1991)

Happily, in 2009, admirers from both the academy and journalism edited *The Essential Don Murray: Lessons from America's Greatest Writing Teacher.* The problem with collections that have the word *essential* in the title is the implication that work not contained therein might be considered inessential. No threat of that here. The editors, Thomas Newkirk and Lisa C. Miller, have chosen wisely, capturing in chapters that feel more like little doorways the range and influence of Murray's work. Chapter titles and subtitles reveal that range:

Teach Writing as a Process Not Product

How Writing Finds Its Own Meaning

Write before Writing
The Daybook
Voice of the Text
Writing Badly to Write Well
One Writer's Secrets
Notes on Narrative Time
All Writing Is Autobiography

In an afterword, one of Don's most fervent students and closest friends, Chip Scanlan, speaks for many of us when he testifies: "Don's process approach transformed the way I thought and wrote; it represents the single most important element of my education as a writer and subsequently as a teacher, an influence so powerful it transformed me into a disciple dedicated to spreading his word as often and far as possible."

In 1995, Poynter published an essay by Murray, titled "Writer in the Newsroom." We still distribute it, in monograph form, on special occasions. You do not need to work in a newsroom to appreciate the ideas and experiences of a versatile writer and true mentor of the craft.

Writer in the newsroom: A lifetime apprenticeship
By Don Murray

Sixty-one years ago Miss Chapman looked down at me and said, "Donald, you are the class editor." So much for career planning.

Forty-seven years ago, after having survived infantry

combat, college, and a first marriage, I found myself in the city room of the old *Boston Herald*, determined to learn the newspaper craft and get back to writing great poems.

Now, at seventy, I return each morning to my writing desk apprenticed to the writer's craft.

Monday morning I write my column for the *Boston Globe*; Tuesday through Sunday I draft yet another book on writing, a novel, a poem. Unemployed, I am blessed by not having to take weekends and holidays off, do not suffer any vacations. *Nulla dies sine linea*—Never a day without a line: Horace, Pliny, Trollope, Updike.

Chaucer said, "The lyf so short, the craft so long to lerne." I now know he did not speak with complaint but with gratitude.

The Japanese artist Hokusai testified: "I have drawn things since I was six. All that I made before the age of sixty-five is not worth counting. At seventy-three I began to understand the true construction of animals, plants, trees, birds, fishes, and insects. At ninety I will enter into the secret of things. At a hundred and ten everything— every dot, every dash—will live."

My bones may creak, I may live on a diet of pills, I may forget names, but when I shuffle down to my computer I see Miss Chapman standing in the corner of the room, nodding encouragement.

A lapsed Baptist, I bear witness to the salvation of a writing life. I do not testify for all writers, just this apprentice to a craft I can never learn. The sculptor Henry Moore said:

"The secret of life is to have a task, something you devote your entire life to, something you bring everything to, every

minute of the day for your whole life. And the most important thing is—it must be something you cannot possibly do."
I evangelize. I wish you failure. I hope you have not yet learned to write but are still learning. If you are confident of your craft and are writing without terror and failure, I hope you will learn how to escape your craft and write so badly you will surprise yourself with what you say and how you are saying it....

I do not consciously seek; I wait, accepting the lines and images that float through my mind, sometimes making mental notes, sometimes scribbled ones.

I live in a curious and delightful state of intense awareness and casual reflection that is difficult to describe. Perhaps it is like those moments in combat when the shooting and the shelling stop and you can hunker down behind a rock wall and rest. In a poem I wrote a few weeks ago, I found myself saying that I was "Among the dead, the dying, / more alive than I have ever been."

At that moment in combat I celebrated life, noticing the way a blade of grass recovers from a boot, studying how the sky is reflected in a puddle in the mud, even enjoying the perfume of the horse manure the farmer will use to nurture the spring planting—if there is a spring....

Readers create their own drafts as they read mine, they read the family history of their own blood. Reporters and writers—indeed all artists—set up shop where there is birth and death, success and defeat, love and loneliness, joy and despair.

After I leave my writing desk, I lead a double life. I am a mole, living an ordinary life of errands, chores, conversations with friends, reading, watching TV, eating and—at the same time—I am a spy to my life, maintaining an alertness to the commonplace, the ordinary, the routine where the really important stories appear.

I am never bored. I overhear what is said and not said, delight in irony and contradiction, relish answers without questions and questions without answers, take note of what is and what should be, what was and what may be. I imagine, speculate, make believe, remember, reflect. I am always traitor to the predictable, always welcoming to the unexpected....

I write easily, and that is no accident. I remind myself that John Jerome said, "Perfect is the enemy of good" and follow William Stafford's advice that "one should lower his standards." I write fast to outrace the censor and cause the instructive failures that are essential to effective writing.

I write to say I do not know. That is my terror and my joy. I start a column with a line or an image, an island at the edge of the horizon that has not been mapped. And I do not finish the column unless I write what I do not expect to write 40 or 60 percent of the way through. My drafts tell me what I have to say. That is true of my nonfiction books, my fiction, my poetry. I follow the evolving draft....

I look back at that thin—no longer skinny—young man in the *Boston Herald* city room so long ago and realize that I did with dumb instinct what I do by design today.

After walking on my first byline when the cleaning women put the first edition down to protect a scrubbed floor, I developed a healthy disinterest in what I had published. I felt no loyalty to what I had said and how I had said it.

When I learned how to write a story the way the editor

wanted it, I experienced a playful desire to unlearn it, to see if I could do it differently. I kept saying I wonder what would happen if.... And today each draft is an experiment. I try short leads and long leads, telling the story all in dialogue or with no dialogue, starting at the end and moving backward, using a voice that I have not tried before, making up words when the dictionary fails.

I sought mentors, asking people at other desks how they were able to write a story I admired. I asked the best reporters if I could go along on my own as they reported a story. They were surprised and said yes; but when the union got wind of it, I was told to knock it off.

I looked at the assignment book and freelanced stories that were not scheduled to be covered. I tried features on my own and surprised editors with stories they did not expect— and often did not want.

I wrote weddings and fashions for a suburban weekly, volunteered to review books, freelanced on Saturday for the sports department, took graduate writing courses at Boston University and wrote stories so experimental I could not even figure out what they meant.

I drove Eddie Devin, the best editor on the city desk, home at 1 a.m., put a fifth of whiskey on the kitchen table, handed him a week's carbons of my stories, and was taught how I could improve....

I read compulsively to see what other writers can do and I still do today; I hunted down craft interviews such as the *Paris Review's Writers at Work* series and copied down the lessons I learned about my craft, and I still do that today....

I wish you a craft you can never learn—but can keep learning as long as you live.

LESSONS

Donald Murray argues that all writers must solve the same problems in every piece of writing. The solutions may differ, but the challenges are the same. For your next writing project, use this checklist to help you identify where you are in the process:

1. **Discover a good idea:** The long-term goal is to see the world as a storehouse of story ideas.

2. **Collect stuff:** Fill your notebooks with information, quotes, scenes, details, data, and much more. Even novelists and poets gather raw material for their art.

3. **Find a focus:** This is the central act of writing, the discovery of what the work is about, an idea or a feeling expressed in a lead, a theme, a thesis, a piece of dialogue, a title or headline.

4. **Select the best:** A strong focus helps you choose the best material from all you have gathered.

5. **Build a structure:** You need a shape, a blueprint, and architecture, either original or traditional. Even a haiku has a beginning, a middle, and an end.

6. **Write a draft:** Rehearse the work in your head. Start writing at any time. Lower your standards at the beginning.

7. **Revise:** The word means to "see again." This applies to more than the words you choose. You can revise all parts of the process.

12

Keep writing; things will get better. Never be discouraged by the inadequacies of early drafts.

Bird by Bird: Some Instructions on Writing and Life
By Anne Lamott

Toolbox: *No writer writes the perfect story, one perfect word at a time. In writing, perfect is the enemy of good. Since imperfection is necessary, it also becomes desirable. Never be discouraged by early problems in a text. It is a cognitive distortion to think that "shitty first drafts"—to use Anne Lamott's earthy term—make you a shitty writer. With experience, you will learn that such early writing is not sculpture, but clay, the stuff in which you will find the better work.*

When, over the course of a quarter century, a writing book retains its sales and popularity, when it commonly ranks high in surveys as among the best, when it is quoted in other books, essays, and workshops on the craft—that means something. Popularity matters. I don't mean the kind that drives sales of lurid novels. I mean the kind that signifies utility, as when the parents of baby boomers like me raised their kids with the help of *Baby and Child Care* by Dr. Benjamin Spock. For writing guides, it is the kind of popularity that drove *On Writing Well* by William Zinsser to sales of more than a million, the kind that *The Elements of Style* acquired when E. B. White added his thoughts to a work created by his college teacher William Strunk Jr.

That reflection brings us to another writing book: *Bird by Bird: Some Instructions on Writing and Life* by novelist, memoirist, activist, and author Anne Lamott, a work first published in 1994 and a top-selling writing book ever since.

When we evaluate writing books, it helps to distinguish between two kinds. One is primarily about craft: how to write. The other is about identity: how to live the life of a writer. My books, for example, fall into category A, with dollops of category B as a sweetener. When I analyze a poem by T. S. Eliot, for example, I might mention that Eliot died when I was a junior in high school and that I played the electric piano in a Long Island garage band named T. S. and the Eliots. *Bird by Bird* has the virtue of sharing Lamott's wisdom on how to write with how to live the life of a writer.

Anne Lamott is primarily a memoirist whose books, such as *Traveling Mercies* and *Plan B*, recount her journeys of faith, prayer, and church as she coped with the struggles of life, including depression and addiction. There are few writers on these topics who write with as appealing and forgiving a voice as Lamott's. She writes the kind of books that you pass along to a friend who might need a booster shot of care and encouragement.

Here is a passage I marked up from *Traveling Mercies* in which she describes trying to decide whether to let her seven-year-old son go paragliding:

Later that afternoon I went to sit alone by the river. Cottonwood fluffs flocked upward through the sunbeams as if hearing a call, and children ran along the edge of the river like little bankers, gathering stones and pebbles, grasses and twigs. I prayed to know what to do, and I kept thinking I was hearing an answer, but it was like a one-woman Ping-Pong game: I decided he could go, I decided he couldn't, I decided he could. I realized that I was getting crazier with every passing moment, and that since you can't heal your own sick mind *with* your own sick mind, I needed to consult somebody else's sick mind. So I called all of my smartest friends.

Half said I should let Sam go, half acted as if I were considering buying Sam a chain saw for his birthday. But all the ones who believe in God told me to pray, so I did. Here are the two best prayers I know: "Help me, help me, help me," and "Thank you, thank you, thank you." A woman I know says, for her morning prayer, "Whatever," and then for the evening, "Oh, well," but has conceded that these prayers are more palatable for people without children.

Needless to say, I still didn't know what to do.

That personal, self-deprecating, confessional voice makes its way—some would say too often—into *Bird by Bird,* mostly to good and practical effect. One of the best and most personal lessons is embedded in the title.

In most of my favorite books—with the possible exception of *The Postman Always Rings Twice*—the title of a book, sometimes the phrase itself, appears somewhere in the text. So it is in *Bird by Bird*. Lamott describes an incident in which her brother, at the age of ten, cannot build any momentum on a school report on birds. His sister describes little brother as "immobilized by the hugeness of the task ahead." But this story has a deus-ex-machina resolution: "My father sat down beside him, put his arm around my brother's shoulder, and said, 'Bird by bird, buddy. Just take it bird by bird.'" Perhaps I should have titled the work you are reading *Book by Book*.

No diamond is without a flaw, and no writing book I know lacks a false note. The most amusing but perhaps least useful strategy in *Bird by Bird* comes near the end, when Lamott advises fiction writers how to develop characters out of their own life experience. This alchemy, she argues, is most effective when that mean old man described in your most recent bestseller does not recognize himself and sue you.

> I know that if you write a novel about your marriage, and your spouse is a public figure—a politician, say, or a therapist—and you say really awful inflammatory things about this person, all of which may be true, including the part about his wearing the little French maid's outfit when you made love and that awful business with the Brylcreem, you will get a visit from your publisher's lawyer, who will be very anxious and unamused. The problem is that the publishing house will be liable for millions of dollars in damages if this spouse of yours can convince a jury that he or she has

been libeled. The best solution is not only to disguise and change as many characteristics as you can but also to make the fictional person a composite. Then throw in the teenie little penis and anti-Semitic leanings, and I think you'll be Okay.

Most fictional characters turn out to be composites, of course, drawn from real life, but flavored by invention. Better, I think, to remember that dead men and women can't sue. And in litigious times, that "teenie little penis" might become measurable evidence of actual malice.

This leads me to Lamott's most practical advice for writers: Develop the capacity to tolerate "shitty first drafts" as a necessary stage upon which to build something acceptable, even beautiful. As for shitty first drafts (I prefer to call them "zero drafts"): "All good writers write them. This is how they end up with good second drafts and terrific third drafts." There are very few writers, she argues (and she hates them), who are "typing fully formed passages as fast as a court reporter." She calls that illusion the "fantasy of the uninitiated."

She ups the ante with intensifiers: "For me and most of the other writers I know, writing is not rapturous. In fact, the only way I can get anything written at all is to write really, really shitty first drafts." For her, this draft is a "child's draft, where you let it all pour out and then let it romp all over the place, knowing that no one is going to see it and that you can shape it later." There is a kind of shame in this—almost like being in the middle of potty training. The key protection is that "no one is going to see it."

To which I am tempted to respond: "Why not? I'd love to see it. I would consider a bad draft from a great writer a blessing, a treasure trove I might learn from." But these are her nasty drafts, not mine. Her descriptions of her own work are filled with angst. She feels in a "panic." She suffers from impostor's syndrome: "It's over.... I'm ruined. I'm through. I'm toast."

She looks for antidotes to the poison. She learns to tell those negative voices in her head to shut up. She will need those critical voices, but later in the process. She teaches herself to look for the gold nugget in that awful, offal first work. She turns writing into the mechanical act of typing, thinking with her fingers until an idea or image appears. She applies "bird by bird" to her own serial progress. All of this is in service to trusting that process, remembering that you have driven through this tunnel before, and that you have always made your way into the light of day.

This is useful:

Almost all good writing begins with terrible first efforts. You need to start somewhere. Start by getting something—anything—down on paper. A friend of mine says that the first draft is the down draft—you just get it *down*. The second draft is the up draft—you fix it *up*. You try to say what you have to say more accurately. And the third draft is the dental draft, where you check every tooth, to see if it's loose or cramped or decayed, or even, God help us, healthy.

As I reread *Bird by Bird*, given that Lamott's spiritual memoirs are so consoling, I was surprised at the violence of the language she uses to describe her methods and her feelings toward them. (I concede that this comes from someone who has written the book *Murder Your Darlings*.) This violent diction can be taken as vintage hyperbole from writers, like Red Smith, who describe the struggle of writing as opening a vein. She writes about "keeping those crazy ravenous dogs [of doubt] contained." She even talks about an exercise in which she closes her eyes, listens to the cacophony of hostile voices, and makes believe that each one is a mouse, which she then picks up by the tail and deposits in a mason jar: "Then put the lid on, and watch all these mouse people clawing at the glass."

Kids, I assure you, it doesn't have to get that bad. Just send those mice back into the field, or feed them a little cheese and get on with your work. Do not believe that suffering and self-doubt are the *necessary* collateral damage of producing good writing. The goal for productivity—and, dare I say, satisfaction—is not to hate your shitty drafts, but to learn to love them, and yourself.

Years ago, I met a fifth grader named Mark who had been taught by a great teacher named Mary Osborne that "sloppy copy" early in the process is a good thing. Revision would lead to better drafts. When Mark met me, he was proud of his finished story, which would be published in a school booklet, but even prouder of the eleven drafts—all attached to his final copy—that helped him cross the goal line.

LESSONS

1. Tolerate the inadequacy of your early efforts. Frame these not as impediments to excellence, but as necessary stages to a solid draft. "Bad" drafts do not make you a bad writer.

2. Trust your process. Believe that the work will get better if you just keep at it. Embrace the motto of the great Texas bowler Billy Welu, who in his television commentary said that you may have to roll that ball on the edge of the alley so it can hook into the pocket for a strike. "Trust is a must," said old Billy, "or your game is a bust."

3. Try writing "zero drafts," early exploratory work that does not require complete sentences. Early writing teaches you what you know and what you still need to learn.

4. You will reach a point where you cannot judge the quality of your draft. This is when you call for help. But be judicious. Have helpers who are encouraging or critical or knowledgeable. Pick the helper you need when you need him or her.

13

Write freely to discover what you want to say.
Use a "zero draft" to move you toward
a first draft.

*Writing Without Teachers: Techniques for Mastering the Writing
Process*
   and
Writing with Power
By Peter Elbow

Toolbox: *Writers help themselves by writing sooner than they
think they can. Before a first draft, try a "zero draft," early scrib-
blings that may not even reach sentence form. Freewriting—
fast drafting without self-censorship—is another path toward
liberation. In these early forms of writing, the goal is not communication. You write here to compile, remember, and gain
knowledge. "What do I already know?" you ask yourself. "And
what do I still need to learn?"*

I would like to introduce you to two good writers: Christopher
Scanlan and David Finkel. I consider both to be friends and
have worked with them as journalists, authors, and teachers. To

observe them—and interview them—reveals two different approaches to the craft. I would argue that they solve the same writing problems in different ways, but you would not know that by examining their working materials.

Scanlan, known as Chip, is a freewriter: he writes as fast as he can, sometimes for ten or twenty minutes, sometimes longer. He begins with an idea, of course, but not an outline. The freewriting creates a discovery draft. It often, but not always, digs up something special, a small gold coin that had been buried in sand. That coin inspires another episode of fast writing, but this one a little more focused. On and on Chip writes, until the shape of something more permanent emerges, a more traditional first draft materializes, and revision can begin.

I once heard David Finkel, who knows Chip, express skepticism on how such a freewriting process is possible. While Chip is speeding, David appears to be thinking, working out in his head steps that Chip undertakes with his hands. When David begins to draft, he works on a sentence until he feels it is just right, and then the next, and the next, building a version that will be in pretty good shape by the time he reaches an ending. This process does not require David to be stuck in his chair for hours on end. In a congenial newsroom, he was often seen circumnavigating it, solving problems as he strolled from watercooler to restroom and back to his computer.

This tale of two writers is meant to be cautionary. It is possible for two writers to employ different methods and yet finish the work at equal quality in the assigned time. Please do not draw from these examples that writers can be so different in their methods that they must be engaged in a different process.

I adhere to Donald Murray's scripture that all, or almost all, writers are trying to solve the same problems, sometimes with different tools. Both Chip and David need to find something to write about; both gather tons of material; both find a focus; both seek to select their best content; both create (or fill) an architecture; and—whether they draft fast or slow—both must revise.

Whether it works for you or not, you should grow familiar with the elements of freewriting, and you will find them described in two important books in the history of writing pedagogy. The first is *Writing Without Teachers,* the second *Writing with Power,* both by Peter Elbow. I have had the pleasure of working with Peter at two conferences, and there are few authors or teachers who have had a more liberating effect on student writing than he has. His theories and techniques, which he developed in his years teaching and directing the writing programs at colleges and universities, have a group therapy quality to them—students are asked to write fast, rewrite fast, and share their work with other writers in a humane way. His approach is more democratic than that of his respectful adversary, David Bartholomae. Bartholomae believes that college students must earn the status of writer, while Elbow declares students of writing to be writers from the beginning.

In *Writing with Power,* Elbow divides the writing process into two steps: "creativity" and "critical thinking." He argues that during acts of creating—such as brainstorming story ideas—it is essential to silence critical voices. Those voices need to be heard and inspire revision, but not so early that they become blood clots in the flow of invention. He then returns to what always seems to be his favorite method, first articulated in *Writing Without Teachers:*

> Freewriting is the easiest way to get words on paper and the best all-around practice in writing that I know. To do a freewriting exercise, simply force yourself to write without stopping for ten minutes. Sometimes you will produce good writing, but that's not the goal. Sometimes you will produce garbage, but that's not the goal either. You may stay on one topic, you may flip repeatedly from one to another: it doesn't matter. Sometimes you will produce a good record of your stream of consciousness, but often you can't keep up. Speed is not the goal, though sometimes the process revs you up. If you can't think of anything to write, write about how that feels or repeat over and over "I have nothing to write" or "Nonsense" or "No." If you get stuck in the middle of a sentence or thought, just repeat the last word or phrase till something comes along. The only point is to keep writing.

According to Elbow, the goal is not to produce good or bad writing, but to kickstart the process: "The goal of freewriting is in the process, not the product."

Freewriting is one of those methods I use strategically rather than habitually. It works best for me on airplanes. Rather than read a mystery novel or play a video game, I favor the spiral notebook and use it to turn thinking and dreaming into language. On a round trip to Denmark I scribbled the raw material for what would become the book *Help! For Writers*. On another long journey, I scribbled fifteen chapters of a novel (currently unpublished) called *Trash Baby,* about a boy who finds an abandoned baby next to a dumpster.

On certain days, even freewriting feels too rigorous for me. Maybe I don't want to spend ten minutes scribbling as fast as I can. I prefer a process called zero-drafting, which has, for me, greater flexibility and more pointed utility than some of the steps professed by Elbow. That said, the good professor deserves your attention. He transformed his own young writing problems into practical theories about creating, critiquing, and sharing. Even if you choose not to use Elbow's strategies, it's good to know you have them at your...ahem...elbow if you need them.

WRITING THE ZERO DRAFT

Years after being introduced to Elbow's theories on freewriting, I came across a concept called writing the zero draft. I did not invent that term, but I am about to take credit for a riff on that strategy called "subzero drafting." If you do a Google search on "zero draft," you will find many interesting and useful links from authors and writing teachers. Joan Bolker writes that she learned the term from Lois Bouchard, but no one stakes a claim to it. In contrast to Calvin Trillin's "vomit out" draft, the zero draft seems almost warm and fuzzy. Drawn from teaching strategies of composition theorists such as Peter Elbow, the idea is to write quickly and early without the inhibitions that petrify into paralyzing procrastination or writer's block. (My editor asks me to distinguish between zero drafting and freewriting.

Some writers may experience no difference at all. For me, zero drafting is more liberating because the standards are even lower than those for freewriting. I freewrite with sentences. I can zero draft with fragments. I freewrite on the computer. I can zero draft on the back of an envelope.)

The zero draft, then, is the writing—maybe the scribbling—that happens before you are ready to call something your first draft. As I was drafting this sentence, for example, I had about twenty-five zero drafts for chapters of *Murder Your Darlings,* and I would write a few more before I turned back to read them cold to see which ones deserved to be turned into first drafts. With each draft, my standards get higher until each word will have to prove its worth.

Perhaps there is language that comes even before the zero draft. Can there be a subzero draft? The idea comes in part from Geoff Dyer, writing about the postmodernist scholar Roland Barthes in a foreword to *Camera Lucida:*

> Barthes liked "to write beginnings" and multiplied this pleasure by writing books of fragments, of repeated beginnings; he also liked *pre*beginnings: "introductions, sketches," ideas for projected books, books he planned one day to write.

Think of a subzero draft as a *pre*beginning. It's not a story, but story dust. It occurs at the first moment that random thoughts, ideas, images turn into language. For me, the blank canvas most likely to catch them before they evaporate is the simple paper napkin.

At the Banyan coffee shop, I might jot on a napkin a creative list, a comparison/contrast diagram, the names of books I want to read or give away. In this context, the content is not important. What matters is the quick creation of a set of possible elements for an essay, key questions to be answered, with some evidence to be checked, weighed, and organized.

The napkin—and other spaces for quick writing—has a good history. On the Blueline blog, Raine Mercer lists authors who began famous works on scrappy paper:

- Richard Berry scribbled the lyrics for "Louie, Louie" on a piece of toilet paper.
- Stephen King wrote the idea for the book *Misery* midflight on a cocktail napkin.
- Paul Lauterbur, while munching a burger at a diner, sketched out a blueprint for Magnetic Resonance Imaging, better known as MRI, on a napkin. Thanks, Paul!

Music, fiction, science—and the lowly napkin has a history of aiding journalists in their investigative pursuits as well. A review by Nandini Balial of the famous journalism movie *All the President's Men* praises a scene in which Dustin Hoffman, playing Carl Bernstein, interviews a reluctant bookkeeper, played by Jane Alexander: "He takes his time, asking questions slowly, scribbling on matchbooks, napkins, tissue paper. The lengthy scene, one of the film's best, feels like slowly guiding a deer in the headlights off the road."

Ginni Chen, in "10 Surprising Surfaces Famous Writers Have Written On," offers a list of surprising spaces for early scribbles. In addition to the sacred napkin, she lists index cards, cardboard (a favorite of Gay Talese), scrap paper, scrolls, book margins, butcher paper, walls, the backs of receipts or grocery lists, even air-sickness bags.

To all these, I must add the palm of the human hand. Maybe I'm partial to those movies where an attractive woman meets a man and writes her number on his palm. If it happened to me, of course, the number would last only until my visit to the men's room, where the antibacterial soap would eradicate that moment forever.

Let's end with journalism. When the great Don Murray was coaching writers at the *Boston Globe,* he watched reporters with great care. One had the assignment of writing about the tall ships coming into Boston Harbor. Murray heard the reporter ask his editor "How much time do I have?" The editor said, "about thirty minutes." The reporter said, "Great. I've got time for dinner."

Murray stalked the cocky writer to the cafeteria and watched as the scribe, with a bagel and a cup of coffee, scribbled a few notes on a napkin. It turned out to be a brief plan, four or five items, that, back at his desk, propelled the writer to meet his deadline just in the nick of time.

LESSONS

1. If you like to write one sentence at a time until each meets your high standards, continue to do so—as long as you meet your deadlines and the expectations of your teachers and editors.

2. If you miss deadlines or underperform, consider freewriting as an alternative. Lower your standards at the beginning of the process, discover your best material in preliminary drafts, and then raise your standards through revision.

3. At some point thoughts become words. You have choices:

a. Prebeginnings or subzero drafts: lists or points or phrases you scribble on Post-it Notes

b. Zero draft: writing dashed out just for yourself, to capture your ideas

c. Freewriting: fast, fast writing with a time limit to try to discover your focus

d. First draft: writing in traditional sentences, your butt in the chair, your mind and hands searching for the right words

4. You need a writing routine—with an escape hatch. If you are having trouble writing on a computer, pick up a legal pad and pencil. If you can't write at your desk, take your laptop to the cafeteria. The ambient noise may help.

14

—————+—

Say it loud: "I am a writer." Assume the identity of a writer, especially at moments of self-doubt.

Becoming a Writer
By Dorothea Brande

If You Want to Write: A Book about Art, Independence and Spirit
By Brenda Ueland

Toolbox: *A goal of mastery of any craft is self-identification. Consider the difference between task and role; becoming and being; craft and a sense of mission and purpose; the how and the why. Many play golf and music but do not think of themselves as golfers or musicians because, after all, they are not Tiger Woods or Jimi Hendrix. If you write, a day may come when you identify yourself as a writer. You are not the Scarecrow. You don't need a credential to prove you have a brain. Your credential is your writing. Learn to take encouragement anywhere you can find it.*

Both of my parents came of age in the 1930s during the Great Depression. My father, Ted Clark, was an honor student in his eighth-grade New Jersey school but could not afford to go to high school. He and his father dug ditches and did electrical work wherever they could find it. My mother, Shirley Marino, was the first member of a large Italian family (thirty-five first cousins!) on the Lower East Side of New York City to graduate from high school. Before she married my dad in 1942 at Fort Benning, Georgia, she took jobs as a bookkeeper and turned over most of her pay to her parents.

Any complaints by modern Americans about how we are living through tough times should be tempered by a look back at history. The period between the two great wars saw social disruption that threatened the fabric of American culture and democracy—and the world. The civic and business institutions that had created America—including thousands of banks—failed miserably. In the aftermath of the Russian Revolution and the seeming collapse of American capitalism, people worried that communism would spread across the land, and with it, violent upheaval.

Writing in *The Nation*, NYU scholar Joanna Scutts describes how these social, political, and economic factors created reactionary movements, some of them harmless, some of them dangerous. One dangerous movement—we still see its ugly manifestations—is called fascism. The title of Scutts's article is "Fascist Sympathies: On Dorothea Brande," an author who, it turns out, wrote an influential book about writing. What are we to make of this?

Before Hitler came to power, there were forces in American culture—including eugenics and a radical form of individualism—that would find fertile ground in the Third

Reich. Fascism opposed communism. Fascism also opposed an economic system supposedly controlled by Jews. Violent anti-Semitism goose-stepped its way to what we now call the Holocaust.

According to Scutts, one fascinating side effect of this culture in the 1930s was what we now think of as the self-help movement. If you could not depend on the government or even your bank, you could depend upon yourself. If you could not do anything to reform society, you could reform yourself. In a way, your problems and inhibitions were self-imposed, as if there were a little voice in your head telling you—in modern parlance—how much you suck. The solution was "mind over matter." This attitude was expressed in popular culture as well. The music of the Depression era invited you to walk "On the Sunny Side of the Street," to expect on a rainy day "Pennies from Heaven," and to remember that "The Best Things in Life Are Free."

One of the most popular self-help books of that time was written by Dorothea Brande. The 1936 guide titled *Wake Up and Live!* sold in the millions and inspired a Broadway musical by the same name. Scutts describes it as "a slim, simple work of pop psychology that advocated a radically individualistic form of self-improvement. It urged readers to place their own success above all other commitments and to train their mind to overcome the fear of failure." The book's most heartfelt advice: "Act as if it were impossible to fail." Success, in other words, was a triumph of the will.

In spite of its popularity, *Wake Up and Live!* is not Brande's most enduring work. That status goes to one of the best writing books of the twentieth century, *Becoming a Writer,* first published in 1934. It might have been titled *Wake Up and Write!* I own three editions of *Becoming a Writer* and count it as an inspiring favorite. Only recently did I notice that there is no author's biography in recent editions. "Who is this woman?" I wondered aloud, who could write so forcefully about the craft. Perhaps she was an unappreciated feminist hero. Scutts praises *Becoming a Writer* as a "briskly pragmatic guide to literary success."

Here's the difficult truth: In addition to her personal literary success, Dorothea Brande was also known as the spouse of another literary light named Seward Collins, described by Scutts as "one of the leading proponents of American fascism." You could make a movie about Collins, an affluent Princeton graduate who collected erotica, had a bad affair with Dorothy Parker, created the conservative political journal *The American Review,* and hung out with the leading literary figures of his day. With the recent resurgence of extreme right-wing movements, it is important to remember that American fascists—I'm tempted to include the great American hero of the day, aviator Charles Lindbergh—were not operating on the fringes of the political culture, but through it. A Catholic priest from Michigan, Father Charles Coughlin, built a radio show that attracted millions of listeners with a style of nativist ranting that sounded a bit like Hitler's.

If we were to expel from the canon of literature authors who had, early in the twentieth century, expressed some form of anti-Semitism, there would be quite a long line—in England and America—headed for the exit. But Brande and her husband,

Collins, who expressed admiration for Hitler and Mussolini, took it to dangerous levels. In reviews, Brande attacked Jewish authors as a group for their "stupidities," which, she said, "cannot be denied." In a 1936 interview with a pro-communist periodical, Collins is quoted as saying: "I am a fascist. I admire Hitler and Mussolini very much. They have done great things for their countries." In response to a question about Hitler's persecution of the Jews, Collins replied: "It is not persecution. The Jews make trouble. It is necessary to segregate them."

One more tidbit about the Brande-Collins couple. Their theories of "mind over matter" led to a fascination with the spiritual and the occult. As for that collection of erotica? Perhaps if they didn't mind, it didn't matter.

This leaves me in a quandary. Can I find in *Becoming a Writer* any of the dangerous associations Scutts identifies in *Wake Up and Live!*? It makes a bit of sense to see Brande's writing guide as a kind of self-help book for aspiring writers. Freud's theories were circulating in the 1930s, and there is plenty of evidence in Brande's writing book that she was taken by his ideas about the conscious and unconscious mind. She suggests exercises using a kind of self-hypnosis with a strong "mentalist" aroma.

Here's the question you should ask me: Knowing what you now know about Brande, can you see any hint of fascism or religious intolerance in her writing guide? My answer: No. Will you ever recommend *Becoming a Writer* to aspiring authors, young and old, ever again? My answer: Yes. Can we watch and enjoy movies, music, books created by morally defective artists? Can a bad person write a good book? Let's see.

ENTER BRENDA UELAND

To understand the strengths and weaknesses of *Becoming a Writer*, we can hold it up against a contemporary volume, *If You Want to Write* by Brenda Ueland. It turns out that not one but *two* of my favorite writing books were written in the 1930s by *two* American women: Dorothea Brande, who was from Illinois, and Brenda Ueland, who was from Minnesota. In striking ways, these books serve as counterweights to books such as *The Elements of Style* by William Strunk Jr., which was very much about the imposition of certain standards of writing and grammar and patterns of composition that you should follow.

In an earlier chapter, I drew a distinction between types of writing books. One might be called "how to write," the other "how to be a writer." In 1934 Dorothea Brande's focus is right there in the title: *Becoming a Writer*. It's an old philosophical distinction, the difference between Being and Becoming. I would argue, following the lead of one of my best students, Jackie Johnson, that the blurry line between being and becoming is crossed when a person identifies as a writer.

This certainly defines my path. By 1977 I would have described myself as a young scholar, a passionate reader of literature, a composition teacher. By the time I was approaching thirty, I had written thousands of reports and stories, including a 300-page doctoral dissertation. Yet I would never have dared call myself a writer or an author. Then in 1979 I had my byline on more than 250 stories, reports, essays, and reviews in the

St. Petersburg Times. "Hmm," I remember wondering one day, "maybe I could be a writer."

I now see these distinctions as somewhere between senseless and self-destructive. If you talk, you are a talker. If you golf, you are a golfer. If you write, you are a writer. The self-identification will help you link a chain to becoming a better writer; before you know it, you will see Being and Becoming begin to merge. You *are* a writer, and because you are, you will never give up becoming better and better at your craft.

There are countless ways to grow in your craft, but the two most common are

1. Take a course on writing.
2. Read a writing guide.

Both Brande and Ueland express skepticism on the utility of these methods, arguing that in writing courses you will be exposed to obvious advice and a small army of nitpickers critiquing your work. They suggest that authors of writing books are too often not good writers themselves, and that the approaches such authors recommend will lead you toward conventionality rather than originality.

Though they share that opinion, it is their differences that matter. Whereas editions of *Becoming a Writer* seem determined to veil some of the darker aspects of Brande's biography and professed values (fascism never looks good on the résumé!), Ueland's life story is up front where everyone can see it. Inside my copy, there are two photos of the author, one from

1938, the year she wrote her book, and one from 1983, when she was 91, two years before her death. In the latter, she looks the camera in the eye, with wild hair, a man's black tie, and a sporty striped jacket.

She writes that she was "born on Lake Calhoun in a happier time (before automobiles). A large white house (a thousand rooms and one bath). A large wooden windmill that creaked on a summer day, a horse, pony, cow, and happy chickens wandering freely in the plushy sward."

Her father, we learn, was a lawyer and a judge, and her mother a leader in the suffrage movement. As for her professional life:

> Brenda Ueland spent many years living in New York, where she was part of the Greenwich Village bohemian crowd that included John Reed, Louise Bryant, and Eugene O'Neill. After her return to Minnesota, she earned her living as a writer, editor, and teacher of writing, and lived an active and vital life until her death, at the age of 93, in 1985.

She was pals with Carl Sandburg, who, she says, declared *If You Want to Write* to be "the best book ever written about how to write." It is certainly a contender, especially if you are looking for encouragement.

Here's more from the back cover: "Brenda Ueland was the author of two books, many articles and short stories, and a long-time teacher of writing. In her 93 years, she published six million words, was knighted by the king of Norway, and set an international swimming record (for over-eighty-year-olds). She said she had two rules she followed absolutely: to tell the truth, and not to do anything she didn't want to do."

Inside *If You Want to Write*, aspiring writers—especially women—find nothing but encouragement. "So remember these two things," writes Ueland, "you are talented and you are original. Be sure of that."

But Ms. Ueland, I might ask, if I am so talented, why am I procrastinating?

No wonder you don't write and put it off month after month, decade after decade. For when you write, if it is to be any good at all, you must feel free,—free and not anxious. The only good teachers for you are those friends who love you, who think you are interesting, or very important, or wonderfully funny.

But Ms. Ueland, I don't have any friends who love me that much. "Well then you must imagine one."

I might give Ueland gold stars for a rich variety of compelling chapter titles (a skill she would have applied magnificently in the digital age):

- Everybody is talented, original and has something important to say
- Be careless, reckless! Be a lion, be a pirate, when you write
- Why you are not to be discouraged, annihilated, by rejection slips
- Why Women who do too much housework should neglect it for their writing

While there is no reference to Brande, I begin to see Ueland's book, written four years after Brande's, as a response to *Becoming a Writer*.

Brande's work, influenced by Nietzsche, was all about the triumph of the will, a word that appears prominently in her work with a capital letter: *Will*. While her book contains practical advice—why you need two typewriters and how to decide what beverage to drink during your writing—it turns useful habits into rigorous disciplines. For example, Brande offers exercises to help you write whenever the opportunity arises, "on the dot of the moment," with no excuses permitted.

She transforms from coach to taskmaster. Succeed, she demands, or stop writing:

> Right here I should like to sound the solemnest word of warning that you will find in this book: If you fail repeatedly at this exercise [writing at a moment's notice], give up writing. Your resistance is actually greater than your desire to write, and you may as well find some other outlet for your energy early as late.

This comes across not as encouragement, but as a military order: "These two strange and arbitrary performances—early morning writing, and writing by prearrangement—should be kept up till you write fluently at will." (There's that word "will" again.)

Compare that to Ueland's rejoinder:

That is why I hope I have not said in this book anywhere "You must let it out…You *must* write." There is too much pressure of duty and fear on you already, on everybody,—too many "musts" for the talent in you to begin to shine in a free and jolly way.

I don't warn you against action. I just want to cheer you up by saying that nervous, empty, continually *willing* action is sterile and the faster you run and accomplish a lot of useless things, the more you are dead.

She italicizes the word *willing* and adds a footnote that includes this sentence: "People by 'will' do remarkable things. But this is for soldiers and money-grubbers who are committed to all sorts of evil that their imagination and love tells them is horrible and senseless."

Let me bring Brande back into the game. The anti-Semitism of the age did not prevent her from incorporating the work of a certain Austrian Jewish doctor named Freud. The very best advice in her book, and perhaps the most useful psychological advice for any author, is not to judge the work too harshly too early in the process. You can't will every sentence to be perfect. To make progress you must silence that critical voice in your head—Freud's "watcher at the gate"—whose negativity causes self-doubt and discouragement. If you think of that internal voice as coming to you externally through your speakers, the volume at the beginning should be turned way down—even muted—and then gradually turned up as you move through drafts. For the last draft, that voice may be a dictator (sorry, Dorothea), forcing you to decide between *a* and *the*.

Ueland's final chapter begins with a quote from Blake: *He Whose Face Gives No Light Shall Never Become a Star:*

> But if (as I wish) everybody writes and respects and loves writing, then we would have a nation of intelligent, eager, impassioned readers; and generous and grateful ones, not mere critical, logy, sedentary passengers, observers of writing, whose attitude is: "All right: entertain me now." Then we would all talk to each other in our writing with excitement and passionate interest, like free men and brothers, and like the people in paradise, whom Dostoyevsky described in a story: "not only in their songs but in all their lives they seemed to do nothing but admire each other." The result: some great, great national literature.

She then adds a numbered list "to sum up." I am tempted to convert Ueland's words into a happy writing pledge. Her list includes the following pieces of advice:

- Know that you have talent, are original and have something important to say.
- Write freely, recklessly, in first drafts.
- Don't fret or be ashamed of what you have written in the past.... We are too ready (women especially) not to stand by what we have said or done.
- If you are never satisfied with what you write, that is a good sign. It means your vision can see so far that it is hard to come up to it.
- Don't always be appraising yourself, wondering if you are better or worse than other writers.

One final note on Dorothea Brande. I sent a message to my old friend Arthur Caplan, one of America's most influential experts on biomedical ethics. I remember his involvement in a debate concerning medical research by the Germans during the Third Reich. Is it possible that even a small piece of medical research conducted by Nazi doctors might have created some knowledge that would prove to be for the benefit of mankind?

He replied:

Evil, bad, pernicious, bigoted, criminal and disgusting people create things of wonder, beauty, and even inspiration all the time. The moral question is how important, unique, and encouraging of awful behavior is the work. I think we can and surely do "use" morally suspect work in science, medicine, the arts, humanities, and media all the time. But, we should acknowledge the flaws and misdeeds explicitly of the "authors," explain the use, and note that we won't whitewash the evil in pursuit of utilizing the good. So I don't pull down every statue of Columbus, Lee, Stalin, etc., but I would insist on descriptions of who they were and what they did and why the statue is still important.

So I would not tear down a statue of Dorothea Brande—if there were one. I'd rather put my energy into erecting one of Brenda Ueland.

LESSONS

1. Writers are notoriously filled with self-doubt, even self-loathing, when the rejection letters pile up. You need antidotes for this poison. Begin as you write by controlling the critical voice in your head, the watcher at the gate who stifles your imagination and creativity. That voice tells you that you suck and have no right to call yourself a writer. Confronting such negativity with creativity *proves* you are a writer.

2. Embrace Ueland's encouraging vision. Identify as a writer. You need no credential other than words on the page or the screen. Become a writer by writing.

3. Encouragement for writers comes from other people: readers who offer their appreciation; teachers and editors who voice their approval; friends and loved ones whose affection feels unconditional. These responses need not be random. Immerse yourself in supportive communities of readers and writers: classes, workshops, book clubs, online support groups that welcome creative people.

4. It would be a good exercise in critical thinking for you to read the books by Brande and Ueland, then compare and contrast them. I stand with Art Caplan's notion that bad people can create works that help and inspire others. I give myself permission to extract those moments of light, as long as I am honest and transparent about the darkness. If you are a bad person, I hope your good writing will turn you into a good person.

15

———✦—

Develop the writing habit. Find a reliable work
space, free of distractions, where you can aim for
a daily level of production.

On Writing: A Memoir of the Craft
By Stephen King

Toolbox: *Stephen King offers an odd bit of advice: that you
should read bad writing so you can learn what not to write. More
practical is the way in which King serves as a role model of productivity, a prodigious one to be sure. He claims he can write a
novel in a season. That's four books per year. This pace comes
from the elements of a writing habit: a reliable and comfortable
place to write, the equipment and materials you need, protection
from the distractions of television or digital media, a self-imposed
daily target—up to 2,000 words a day. I promise you will not
reach his standard, and neither can I. But we don't have to. We
can scale it down as fits our personalities and responsibilities.
Regular writing is a habit you should not kick.*

Many famous writers write about writing, if not in books, then
in essays. George Orwell, as always, springs to mind. A famous

or popular writer can lend credibility (perhaps author-ity) to the text. And $ales. *The Elements of Style* by William Strunk Jr. was a cultish academic curiosity until his famous student E. B. White got his hands on it. Next thing you know—ten million sold!

In 1979, I interviewed a young author of scary stories, named Stephen King. I had read King's first three novels: *Carrie, 'Salem's Lot,* and *The Shining,* all of which had been turned into movies. King was promoting a book called *The Dead Zone.* To show you how early this was in King's career, my final question was "Are you a millionaire yet?" To which he answered something like "Not yet, but check with me next year." King was well on his way to becoming America's King of Horror, selling more than 300 million copies worldwide of his sixty creepy, crafty novels, and showing no signs of letting up.

You can tell from *The Shining* that King was interested in the writing process and the writer's struggles. In probably the most memorable sequence of any of King's films, Jack Torrance, played by Jack Nicholson, turns from struggling novelist into ax-wielding maniac. Snowbound, cabin-fevered, trapped in an old haunted hotel, the author seems to be making progress on his book until his wife discovers that he is capable of writing only a single sentence repeated page after page: "All work and no play makes Jack a dull boy." A dull boy with a sharp ax.

Is King the most popular living author to have written a writing book? I think the answer may be yes. Is the book any good? The answer is certainly yes. Was it easy for King to write about writing? By his own account, no. For a man who likes to draft a novel in ninety days, King struggled with *On Writing,* letting it hibernate in a desk drawer for months and months. Maybe the book was unlucky, or cursed, or whatever King trope works for bad fortune. In 1999 during a simple walk along a Maine roadway, King was struck by a van driver who was distracted, not by technology, but by a dog, loose in the back. The multiple injuries were devastating, requiring a helicopter transport and emergency medical attention. The recovery was long and painful. Somehow, it allowed him to return to his writing book, his survival giving us the opportunity to enjoy many more novels, as well as the television and movie versions of King's imaginative work.

King's recovery, popularity, and productivity have made *On Writing* one of the bestselling writing books of the twenty-first century. I believe it is the most successful book he has published outside the genre for which he is considered a master. Lots of popular authors prefer to keep their writing secrets to themselves. (I can't tolerate them.) Some also prefer to keep their personal lives to themselves. By writing against those grains—by exposing his life and his craft—King shows himself to be another generous writer. Although they are the works of very different authors, you can place *On Writing* on a shelf beside Anne Lamott's *Bird by Bird,* which also mixes writing advice with memoir.

King's personal stories always wind up attached to a practical writing lesson. Here begins a short chapter on the relationship between reading and writing:

If you want to be a writer, you must do two things above all others: read a lot and write a lot. There's no way around these two things that I'm aware of, no shortcut.

Although he claims to be a slow reader, he says he reads sixty to seventy books a year, most of them fiction. I wondered where he finds the time, since he adheres to a rigorous writing schedule, with a self-imposed daily output of 2,000 words.

In a cool anecdote, King describes his youthful affection for a sci-fi pulp fiction author named Murray Leinster. King claims affection for Leinster's magazine stories even though they were filled with thin characters, ridiculous plots, and an annoying overuse of the adjective *zestful,* a word King claims to have avoided.

Funny, even interesting, but so what? For King, every act of reading is a workshop for the developing writer. Reading great fiction, *The Grapes of Wrath,* may inspire, but also intimidate. Reading bad fiction may be more practical: It can show you what *not* to do. He writes,

Asteroid Miners... was an important book in my life as a reader. Almost everyone can remember losing his or her virginity, and most writers can remember the first book he/she put down thinking: *I can do better than this. Hell, I am doing better than this!* What could be more encouraging to the struggling writer than to realize his/her work is unquestionably better than that of someone who actually got paid for his/her stuff?

When King moves from personal stories to a more systematic view of craft, he offers writers—especially storytellers—tips that cover not just writing strategies but also useful habits. To summarize some of my favorites:

On productivity: A fast draft of a novel should take a "season," about three months. For King that means ten pages a day, about 2,000 words. For new writers, he suggests a total of 1,000 words per day, with the prospect of one day off a week. Have a regular comfortable place to write, limiting the distractions of technology—no televisions, no phones.

On the strategic parts of the novel: You need a narrative that propels the story in sequence, description that immerses the reader in another time and place, and dialogue that brings the characters to life and reveals what makes them tick.

On story, theme, plot: Story is more important than plot. Story can lead you to theme, but not the other way around. A *"what-if"* question can propel the action: *"What if* vampires invaded a small New England village, as in *'Salem's Lot?"*

On description: "It begins in the writer's imagination, but should finish in the reader's." For King, character details need not be exhaustive. Just a few "well-chosen details" are enough for readers, who can fill out the rest.

On pacing: "Mostly when I think of pacing, I go back to Elmore Leonard, who explained it so perfectly by saying he just left out the boring parts. This suggests cutting to speed the pace, and that's what most of us end up having to do (kill your darlings, kill your darlings, even when it breaks your egocentric little scribbler's heart, kill your darlings)." You'd think that someone with King's literary habits would prefer the original *murder* or even shoot for something more gruesome. Slaughter your darlings?

* * *

Some of the most vulnerable authors on the planet are those who write about grammar, or writing, or even writing books. I am fortunate enough to have Little, Brown as my publisher. This is my sixth book for the company that once gave literary life to Emily Dickinson and J. D. Salinger. As I walk the tightrope, an army of helpers hold the net, including text editors, copyeditors such as the eagle-eyed Kathryn Rogers, proofreaders, fact-checkers, and designers. I would like to report that not a single grammatical mistake, spelling, or factual error has ever found its way into print. No can do.

I invite readers, as I am doing now (rclark@poynter.org) to call to my attention any errors you discover in this book. I will work hard to minimize them. But, in every book, I come to learn three or four have wiggled through the net: writing "correlative" conjunction when I meant "coordinating"; misspelling a German word; saying Williams College when I meant Wellesley. Seeking forgiveness for myself, I am inclined to grant it to my fellow authors.

So Stephen King has written a popular and influential writing book in which he advises writers to "avoid the passive tense." Since King uses so many active verbs in his eerie novels about rabid dogs and demonic clowns, he obviously meant to write "avoid the passive voice," not "avoid the passive tense." Tense and voice are two different characteristics of verbs, so it's important not to confuse them. It's a small mistake in a friendly and useful book.

LESSONS

1. Nothing contributes more to becoming a productive writer than a daily habit. Remember that a page a day equals a book a year. King shoots for 2,000 words per day. But even 200 words (with 65 days off) gives you 60,000 words per annum.

2. You do not have to exercise every day to gain the maximum health benefit. In the same spirit, do not be discouraged by violating your self-imposed writing schedule. Don't strive for a self-defeating impossible pace of productivity. To riff on Pete Seeger: Start small. Keep going.

3. A good writing habit is enhanced by a comfortable writing space, which can be private (a back bedroom) or public (a window seat at the coffee shop). Minimize distractions and temptations, especially those that pour from media—old and new. Music—off. Television—off. Video games—off, off, off. iPhone—off. Social media—off. All these provide important expressions of culture and information. Use them for research. But none of them will help you sleep—or write.

4. Read a lot and write a lot. Don't just read good stuff, which can be intimidating. Enjoy some bad stuff, knowing you can write better.

IV

Storytelling and Character

What do stories mean, and *how* do they mean? I have spent most of my life trying to figure out a good and practical answer. I got help from New Zealand scholar Brian Boyd, who asks a question that might be borrowed from Darwin: How do stories help us survive? The answers are cosmic as a galaxy, but practical as a shoelace.

Boyd is amazed that we have evolved to tell not only true stories but fictional ones. Critic James Wood grabs the baton to explain *How Fiction Works*. He rejects the traditional limitations of reliable and unreliable narration, endorsing an approach he calls the "free indirect style." The effect of this strategy is to make the experience of literature feel more like real life.

The Canadian scholar Northrop Frye elucidates our experience of narrative, explaining that when we read a story for the first time, we experience it in sequence: scene follows scene. Recalled in memory, certain scenes may stand out but not in a linear way. Instead, moments and movements endure, best described by words such as *theme* and *myth*.

I would love to listen in on a conversation between Frye and playwright and teacher Lajos Egri. Egri turns a theme—in the form of a brief and pointed premise—into an engine that summarizes and generates the action of a play.

The British author E. M. Forster wrote a bunch of novels and then stopped. He also wrote many other works worth reading, especially *Aspects of the Novel*, a text that transformed the way creative writing was taught in schools throughout Great Britain. Most handy were his distinction between flat and round characters and his explanation of why both have their place in storytelling.

Journalists write stories, of course, but not as often as you think. More often they write reports. Reports point you there. Stories put you there. A literary movement was created in the 1960s by journalists such as Gay Talese and Tom Wolfe, who make the case that nonfiction writers can, indeed, borrow the strategies of novelists, but only if they are willing to do more reporting, not less.

16

Understand the value of storytelling.
Guide readers in identifying dangers to avoid
and people who will help.

On the Origin of Stories: Evolution, Cognition, and Fiction
By Brian Boyd

Toolbox: *Reports convey information. Stories expand our experience. We have brains big enough to give us language, and that gift allows us to tell stories—nonfiction and fiction. The purposeful writer can draw energy from the two essential benefits of storytelling:*

- *We can identify dangers to our survival: a disease, an outlaw, that storm brewing in the Gulf.*
- *We can teach ourselves how to work together to achieve goals and solve problems.*

Keeping those ends in mind will help you connect your craft to a higher purpose.

As I begin this chapter (on a Monday), eight boys from Thailand have been rescued from a flooded cave, with efforts still ongoing to save four more and their soccer coach, who accompanied them into the caves on an adventure. By now people across the globe know that the Wild Boars, the soccer team of twelve youths—one just eleven years old—were trapped by heavy rainstorms. They had gone on this trek before without incident. An international team of engineers, workers, and divers gathered for the rescue, an exit so tricky that it took the life of one experienced diver involved in the rescue. With high hopes that all the remaining players come out alive—and be restored to health—it feels like the right time to ask some big questions about the nature of *this* story and the power of *all* stories.

What makes an event worthy of news coverage? It turns out that news judgment is a strict taskmaster. It prevents us from telling the story of every child who is in mortal danger. We must pick and choose. Stop for a moment and ask yourself how many children in America and around the world are at this very moment in jeopardy, in danger of the loss of their health and lives. They may be victims of gun violence in Chicago or civil war in Syria, or they may have been torn from their parents at a border or lost their parents to opioid addiction, or they suffer from lead poisoning, or they live on islands or in territories in danger because of extreme weather or other catastrophes. I have no data to share with you, but the perils in this paragraph must afflict children by the millions.

So why did these twelve boys and their soccer coach in a cave, in a country halfway around the world, capture and keep our attention? Why has their story received hour-by-hour coverage in every form of news delivery yet invented? I am going to try to answer that question using two books and three separate rubrics of story analysis and news judgment:

- a famous list of news qualifiers by an influential journalism professor
- an attempt to match this story against familiar narrative archetypes
- a literary scholar's explanation of why such stories—all stories—are necessary for human survival

MENCHER'S FACTORS FOR NEWSWORTHINESS

Melvin Mencher was arguably the most influential teacher at the Columbia Graduate School of Journalism, a demanding mentor famous for his aphorisms about the process of reporting ("Don't report from the office chair"). He was also author of the most important college journalism textbook of the twentieth century, *News Reporting and Writing*. In the tenth edition of that book, he lists seven factors that create newsworthiness. Here they are, with my notes on how they fit the story of the Thai boys in a cave.

Timeliness: Timely news alerts came one after the other. News that boys were lost, that they were discovered alive, that plans were under way to rescue them, that the first boys were brought out safely....

Impact: There was life-and-death impact on these children and their loved ones, of course, with an emotional impact on the Thai people. But in terms of young lives in danger, there were far fewer than produced by the immigration crisis in the U.S. or refugee families fleeing from Syria.

Prominence: The Wild Boars and their coach were not famous people or part of a prominent institution. Although entrepreneur Elon Musk got involved and created some headlines related to the rescue, by and large, this category doesn't fit.

Proximity: The news came from far away. This category does not apply.

Conflict: This story did not contain the usual forms of news conflict: hot wars, political or policy debates, cops and criminals, but there is a struggle involving humans fighting against the forces of time and nature.

The Unusual: In earlier editions of his book, Mencher referred to this as "the bizarre," but "the unusual" is better, with less of a negative connotation. Perhaps, more than any other traditional category, this one best fits the news out of Thailand.

Currency: A story may have timeliness and then build up steam over time, like the Watergate hearings or the trial of O. J. Simpson. This story will remain in the news until, we hope, all are rescued and, in the days to come, they are nursed back to health, returned home, and get to enjoy the celebration of their rescue.

Applying Mencher's rubric, I come up with four relevant categories of newsworthiness: timeliness, the unusual, conflict, and currency, which is to say that his rubric, while helpful, does not fully explain the magnetism of these events and these stories. Beyond the journalistic, I would argue that the story of twelve boys trapped in a cave derives its power from literary precedents, a kind of primal, archetypal narrative energy that makes us both afraid and hopeful.

CLARK'S ARCHETYPES

1. With the exception of the coach and rescuers, the story was about boys, not men. We wanted the miners in Chile to be rescued. We want these children back even more. We want them returned to their mothers and fathers and brothers and sisters.

2. Twelve is a number we recognize as having meaning. Jesus led his twelve disciples. There are twelve days of Christmas, twelve inches in a foot, and twelve eggs in a carton. Bakers sell goods by the dozen. (English has a specific word for a group of twelve!) A million children form a macrocosm. Twelve children form a microcosm, a little world, in which everything is contained.

3. My colleague Wendy Wallace notes that this story evokes so many of our primal fears: claustrophobia, darkness, drowning, suffocation, starvation, ripping children from their parents. It's Hansel and Gretel, but in a cave in the dark.

4. Author Tom French argues that the best narratives have engines, that is, questions that only the story can answer for the reader or viewer: *guilty or not guilty, dead or alive, who shot J.R.?* We have multiple engines here: Will the boys be rescued? How will that come to pass? What condition will they be in when they get out? Will this happen before the monsoons set in?

5. Because those questions are not answered all at once—there is delay, the passage of time, enforced waiting—this creates suspense. We have mini-cliffhangers (cave-hangers?)

along the way: a rescuer is killed, it's starting to rain, they are bringing out the stronger children first, they are running out of air in the cave.

6. Descent into the underworld. Near my desk I have a copy of Dante's *Inferno*. His *Divine Comedy* begins, of course, with his getting lost in a dark wood and finding a guide, the poet Virgil, to lead him down into the circles of Hell, a necessary journey that will end with an ascent through Purgatory into Paradise. That story derives from both Classical and Christian models. The musician Orpheus descends into the underworld trying to rescue his wife. Jesus, after his Crucifixion, descends into the underworld to grant salvation to lost souls. For the Thai boys, the descent into the cave is neither metaphorical nor allegorical, but oh so real.

7. Rebirth. The descent works best as a narrative element if there is a return to the surface, through the dark tunnel into the light. Here is where I over-interpret the events in Thailand. (It's how we roll.) Earth is the mother. The cave is her womb. In it are her children huddled in the wet darkness. To be reborn, they must pass through narrow passages that require struggle, dangers, and even death. Looking at the diagrammatic representations of the rescue, it is almost impossible not to see a long, complicated birth canal that requires, in addition to the rescue team, an umbilical rope leading back to light, breath, and new life.

BOYD'S THEORY OF STORIES AND HUMAN SURVIVAL

If Mencher offers factors of newsworthiness, and ancient arche-types kick things up a notch, both are mere prologues here to the literary theories of a New Zealand scholar named Brian Boyd. I bumped into his book at a reading festival. The title grabbed me, even though I did not at first recognize in it an allusion to Darwin: *On the Origins of Stories: Evolution, Cognition, and Fiction.*

Boyd is a practical, insightful, and versatile critic, a Nabokov expert who immersed himself in the science of evolutionary bi-ology, a reader who takes us "from Zeus to Seuss." This is not just a clever phrase. One big section of his book applies his the-ories to a reading of Homer's *Odyssey,* another to *Horton Hears a Who!* by Dr. Seuss.

For as long as I have been studying literature in a serious way (more than fifty years), we English majors (actually our teachers) have been vigilant against reductive scientific inter-pretations of complicated works of art. When it comes to "his genes made him write that," we don't want to hear it. Boyd is no reductionist. He ventured into Darwinian science and came out not only unharmed but armed with powerful frames to help us understand both language and literature.

From his theoretical vantage point, God or Darwin (from my bias, maybe both) gave human beings a brain. More accu-rately, humans evolved over millions of years to have a brain of a certain size. That brain gave us language. And that capacity for language gave us the ability to tell stories. That power comes with lots of benefits.

If a wolf tried to attack me at the edge of the forest, or if a cop car was hiding on the other side of Thrill Hill waiting to give me a speeding ticket, I could tell you what happened to me. As a result, your experience would expand. Without having to walk near the forest or drive over the hill, you would know that danger lurked there. You might choose to avoid it.

But, wait, there's more! In real life I have never seen a wolf anywhere, and I'm not sure I have ever even stood at the edge of a forest. (I have to get out more!) But I have driven too fast over Thrill Hill and gotten a ticket from the police officer waiting on the other side. I can tell you true stories based on events that actually happened. Or I can make things up, telling you the kinds of stories we categorize as fiction: No, it wasn't a wolf at the edge of the forest, sir, it was a unicorn, a centaur, and a dragon from Saturn.

Stories not only enrich human experience, they are a form of virtual reality. When Romeo and Juliet die tragically, the audience weeps—even though the dead are only acting. This great capacity to tell and learn stories, from an evolutionary perspective, increases the potential of our survival as a species. Another way of putting it: If stories did not help us survive, we would not have the ability to tell them.

But *how* is this magic set in motion? Boyd leads us along two paths. On one path, stories teach us how to live together. We can't survive alone. There are dangers out there, and we need to work together—to collaborate—to protect ourselves and procreate. On the other path, stories identify the sources of danger, from murderers and tyrants to typhoons and plagues, the many ways in which violence, disorder, natural disaster, greed, and intolerance threaten a safe and peaceful order.

An efficient manifestation of this pattern can be found in stories told over the years in the television series *Law & Order*. Each episode begins with a typical New Yorker finding a corpse, signifying a horrible disruption of the social order. For one half-hour the police will investigate the murder and make an arrest; for the second half-hour prosecutors will bring the accused to trial, and a jury will issue a verdict. Order mostly restored.

In the story of the twelve boys in a cave there is no villain to speak of—no Judas, Iago, or Cruella de Vil. The coach has, since the rescue, apologized and been forgiven. But other kinds of dangers have been exposed. To name them in the kindest way, we can call them inexperience, folly, naïveté, unpreparedness, an underappreciation of the unpredictable power of nature. From this story, I will learn to be more cautious about entering caves, and not just the literal ones. On the other hand, maybe my grandson—who is thirteen—will experience the story and nurture a desire to become trained as an expert diver, someone willing to travel to other countries and risk personal safety to help others. He can learn to collaborate.

That is the ultimate value of this amazing story, one worth remembering for many years. Once upon a time twelve boys and their coach got trapped in a deep, dark, dank cave, and over days and days people from all over the world thought of them and prayed for them and sent their best and bravest to rescue them so that they could be well, and grow up, and have children, and be able to tell their children, and their children's children, a truly amazing story, one that sounds like fiction but comes from real life.

In the end, all the boys and their coach were rescued and all the rescuers—save one—emerged from the cave alive and well. In story terms, that is a wonderful payoff, one that confirms the validity of Boyd's greater vision:

> For the great bulk of the 600-million-year evolution of mind on Earth, this ability to think in sustained fashion beyond the here and now has not been available to *any* species. But humans not only have this ability; we also have a compulsion to tell and listen to stories with no relation to the here and now or even to any real past. And by developing our ability to think beyond the here and now, storytelling helps us not to *override* the given, but to be less restricted by it, to cope with it more flexibly and on something more like our own terms.

Whatever you write, and for whatever audience, you can find inspiration and strategic energy from tapping into Boyd's two great benefits of storytelling.

> In both factual and fictional forms, stories can consolidate and communicate norms, providing us with memorable and shared models of cooperation that stir our social emotions, our desire to associate with altruists (like Dr. Seuss's Horton), and our desire to dissociate ourselves from cheats and freeloaders (like the suitors whom *The Odyssey* repudiates and Odysseus routs).

In spite of his scholarly command of both literary and Darwinian theory, Boyd expresses amazement at the capacity of human beings to tell stories. I am inspired by his sense of wonder, and it thrills me to think that those of us who tell and receive stories participate in an act of survival that carries with it the experience of joy.

LESSONS

1. Think of stories as microcosms, little worlds that contain much larger truths. In your research, keep your eyes open for the small example that represents or dramatizes your theme or central idea.

2. Most stories reveal recognizable patterns, some deeply embedded in human history and myth, such as the descent into the underworld. This cultural truth does not require the writer to call too much attention to these archetypes. Not every cave is a womb or tomb.

3. Recall now and then the dual purposes of storytelling, from the perspective of human survival: to identify with those who are helpers and altruists and to reject those who pose a threat of social disorder.

4. Somewhere in the process, ask yourself the writer's most purposeful question: Why am I writing this?

17

Prefer the complex human narrator.
Try alternatives to the all-knowing or completely
unreliable storyteller.

How Fiction Works
By James Wood

Toolbox: *When you write a story, figure out who is the teller. Who is my narrator? What does that person know? What are his or her motives and backstory? What is the limit of that person's knowledge? We used to have two choices, narrators who were reliable or unreliable. A third choice is called the "free indirect style." It is not easy to master, but worth the effort. It lends credibility to the narration by replacing omniscience with a degree of uncertainty, an unsteadiness that reflects the way humans actually know the world.*

I grew up learning that there were two kinds of narrators in fiction—and maybe nonfiction as well. The first was the omniscient third-person narrator, the voice that knew everything about everything and everybody, a voice that was solid, authentic, and most of all, reliable.

I don't write much fiction, but in 1999, I was invited to write a serial novel for the New York Times Newspaper Group. In the month leading up to the year 2000, *Ain't Done Yet* appeared in twenty-four newspapers across the South. This adventure with a doomsday theme for the coming millennium was set in my hometown of St. Petersburg, Florida. It began:

Crossing the Sunshine Skyway Bridge never failed to depress Max Timlin, even on this perfect morning when squadrons of brown pelicans flew across a sky so blue it looked digitally enhanced.

"I hate Nature!" he screamed at the windshield and smacked the palm of his hand against the steering wheel so hard it stung. Max sat in his dream car, a 1965 Mustang convertible, black with a cream-colored interior, purchased as a consolation prize after his second divorce. The top was down, and as he gunned the car's famous oversized 289 engine, a balmy breeze became a windstorm that whipped through the ravaged wasteland that once was his hair. "I hate Nature, I really do," he said calmly now, and clicked on the radio.

Max was the hero of this story, a veteran reporter hired to investigate a cult with end-of-the-world fantasies. As an inexperienced fiction writer, I chose what seemed like the simplest, least subtle narrative structure: a single, linear plot (no subplots); a protagonist who appears in every scene; a mini-cliffhanger at the end of each of twenty-nine daily chapters; and a third-person, know-it-all narrator. Notice everything he knows: the location of the action, the color of the sky, the name of the bridge, the name of the protagonist and what he is driving, what he is saying, his marriage history, what the wind does to his hair.

The second kind of narrator possible, of course, was one who would tell the story from the first-person point of view. Because of this narrator's inside perspective, he or she could not be objective. This kind of storyteller is, almost by definition, a stakeholder, an insider who is constantly learning. This narrator lacks God's eye. Nick Carraway in *The Great Gatsby* is such a narrator—someone trying to figure things out, which means that unreliability creeps in and he cannot be trusted completely, not because he is lying, but because he is human.

"It was a queer, sultry summer," writes Sylvia Plath in her semi-autobiographical novel *The Bell Jar*, "the summer they electrocuted the Rosenbergs, and I didn't know what I was doing in New York." Exactly. What was she doing there—besides beginning to go mad?

And who felt more unreliable than Holden Caulfield when he whined,

> If you really want to hear about it, the first thing you'll probably want to know is where I was born, and what my lousy childhood was like, and how my parents were occupied and all before they had me, and all that David Copperfield kind of crap, but I don't feel like going into it, if you want to know the truth.

So I went through life—and graduate school!—checking off one of two boxes, the Reliable Narrator (check), or the Unreliable Narrator (check). Then one day I cracked open a book titled *How Fiction Works* by author and critic James Wood. I got to Wood the long way around. I have had a tendency to glom on to particular critics, readers of literature whose insights improved my vision. It probably started with T. S. Eliot, who died when I was in high school. Then there was Leslie Fiedler with his eye-popping, myth-mapping, homoerotic interpretations of American literature. Harold Bloom joined me for a long marriage, until I divorced him for an affair with Camille Paglia. Then James Wood, who teaches at Harvard and writes for *The New Yorker*, grabbed me with *How Fiction Works,* leading me back to his earlier collection of critical literary essays titled *The Broken Estate.*

When I consider that list of critics who have come my way over the last half-century, I think I see something they have in common (in spite of their obvious differences). They are, to my mind, *practical* critics. They help me, not just by the transfer of content or knowledge. They make me better at the *practice* of reading and writing.

This from Wood is encouraging:

In this book I try to ask some of the essential questions about the art of fiction. Is realism real? How do we define a successful metaphor? What is character? When do we recognize a brilliant use of detail in fiction? What is point of view, and how does it work? What is imaginative sympathy? Why does fiction move us? These are old questions, some of which have been resuscitated by recent work in academic criticism and literary theory; but I am not sure that academic criticism and literary theory have answered them very well. I hope, then, that this book might be one which asks theoretical questions but answers them practically—or to say it differently, asks a critic's questions and offers a writer's answers.

A critic's questions and a writer's answers. Yes.

When I popped open *How Fiction Works,* I had to confront the degree to which my bipolar attraction to reliable/ unreliable narrators was blinding me to much more complex, much richer experiences of literature—and of life. I had to learn another way, a form of complex narration known as the free indirect style. Even when I began to wriggle out of the old handcuffs of defining the role of the narrator, it took me several rereadings to get the technique of free indirect style— and to embrace its advantages. This hard work was my way of honoring Wood, not a complaint about a lack of clarity on his part. Some things that are hard to get are worth the work it takes to get them. Free indirect style turns out to be one of them.

Wood debunks the traditional definitions: "Actually, first-person narration is generally more reliable than unreliable," he writes, "and third-person 'omniscient' narration is generally more partial than omniscient." Using a simple example, Wood shows us what would be generally regarded as traditional third-person narration:

He looked over at his wife. "She looks so unhappy," he thought, "almost sick." He wondered what to say.

Wood compares that narration to this:

He looked at his wife. Yes, she was tiresomely unhappy again, almost sick. What the hell should he say?

What makes this free indirect style? "The husband's internal speech or thought has been freed of its authorial flagging; no 'he said to himself' or 'he thought.'" Wood appreciates the gain in flexibility. "The narrative seems to float away from the novelist and take on the properties of the character, who now seems to 'own' the words."

This distinction offered me an invitation. It drove me back to the fragment of my own fiction, shared near the beginning of this chapter. What I had thought of as straight third-person narration contained seeds of the free indirect style. Remember: "Crossing the Sunshine Skyway Bridge never failed to depress Max Timlin, even on this perfect morning when squadrons of brown pelicans flew across a sky so blue it looked digitally enhanced."

As I read it now, it feels as if the thoughts and words belong less to me and more to Max. It flips the pathetic fallacy, where nature identifies with the mood of human beings. I am sad and crying, and so, naturally, it's dreary and rainy outside. But not in this passage. Max understands that he is more depressed than usual *because* the beautiful weather and scenic panorama make most humans happy. I think I am catching on, and as you read Wood's book, I predict you will, too.

Wood calls as an expert witness to the power of the complex narrator the German novelist W. G. Sebald, an author who favors the free indirect style, rather than the all-seeing, all-knowing one. According to Sebald:

> I think that fiction writing which does not acknowledge the uncertainty of the narrator himself is a form of imposture which I find very, very difficult to take. Any form of authorial writing where the narrator sets himself up as stagehand and director and judge and executor in a text, I find somehow unacceptable. I cannot bear to read books of this kind....I think these certainties have been taken from us by the course of history, and that we do have to acknowledge our own sense of ignorance and of insufficiency in these matters and therefore to try and write accordingly.

I have read two of Sebald's novels, *The Rings of Saturn* and *The Emigrants,* and found them compelling but challenging because they did not strike me as fictional enough. They have a travelogue feel, with fictional characters bumping into real people in real places. Photos without captions exaggerate this effect. Should I be concerned that I can't read Sebald and decide what is reported and what is made up?

In the chapter "W. G. Sebald's Uncertainty" in *The Broken Estate,* Wood explores Sebald's technique. I pay close attention, not because I want to write like Sebald, but because I am always trying to solve the larger question of how to make stories more true, more real. Most of my attention has been on what I perceive as the unethical embedding of fictional elements in what purports to be nonfiction, such as made-up scenes or composite characters. But what if a novel—a form in which events are supposedly fictional—turns out to be 98 percent true? What am I to make of that? If I can solve this problem, maybe I will have a new writing strategy on my workbench.

I need Wood's critical eye to help me see straight as a writer:

The Emigrants reads like fiction—and *is* fiction—because of the care and patterning of Sebald's narration, because of its anguished interiority, and because Sebald so mixes established fact with unstable invention that the two categories copulate and produce a kind of truth which lies just beyond verification: that is, fictional truth.

I want to know more about fictional truth.

For Sebald...facts are indecipherable, and therefore tragic.... Though his deeply elegiac books are made out of the cinders of the real world, he makes facts fictive by binding them so deeply into the forms of their narratives that these facts seem never to have belonged to the actual world, and seem only to have found their proper life within Sebald's prose. This, of course, is the movement of any powerful fiction, however realistic: the real world gains a harsher, stronger life within a fiction because it receives a concentrated patterning which actual life does not exert. It is not that facts merely *seem* fictive in Sebald's work; it is that they actually *become* fictive even though they remain true and real.... They become fictive not in the sense that they become untrue or are distorted, but in the sense that they become newly real, in a way parasitical of, yet rivalrous to, the real world.

It is easier for me to see the ways in which facts became poetic when they are found in verse, as when Sandburg describes Chicago as the "Hog Butcher for the World." Now it's my job to continue to learn how a novelist uses facts in such a concentrated pattern that they transform their shape, or maybe take on an aura, an intensified feeling. This is how I learn from the best literary critics, such as Wood: The author writes the text; the aspiring writer (me) reads the text; the critic appreciates the text; the aspiring writer reads the critic, learns a new move, then tries to apply it in his or her writing.

LESSONS

1. Whether you desire to become a novelist or not, read fiction like a writer, with special attention to the language of the narrator, which is all we have to go on, after all. Develop a built-in reliability meter. In short, do you believe what the narrator is telling you? Why or why not?

2. Traditional criticism gives us reliable or unreliable narrators, but Wood prefers storytellers who deliver in the "free indirect style." Think of this style as ironic, in that the reader sees beyond what the narrator reports.

3. Wood describes an expression of this style that can be felt "when the gap between an author's voice and a character's voice seems to collapse altogether; when a character's voice does indeed seem rebelliously to have taken over the narration altogether." He cites this opening from Chekhov: "The town was small, worse than a village, and in it lived nothing but old people, who died so rarely it was even annoying." Wood points out the absence of traditional neutrality in this narration, which spices it up and signals the free indirect style.

4. Try writing a bit of fiction, a vignette, or just a scene. Write it three times, with three different forms of narration: third person (reliable, omniscient); first person (unreliable because of limits to knowledge); free and indirect (third person but with the feel of a character's viewpoint).

18

———→

Write for sequence, then for theme.
Readers want to know what happens next and
also what it all means.

Fables of Identity: Studies in Poetic Mythology
By Northrop Frye

Toolbox: *For as long as there have been stories, authors have played with time, and so can you. We say that life is experienced in chronological order, but that does not take into account dreams or memories. Stories have the power to distract us from daily life and plunge us into narrative time. Our experience of story time differs with each reading. Our first reading is usually sequential, a compulsive drive to discover what happens next. At some point our memory takes control. "What happens next?" is replaced by "What does it all mean?" Those questions give writers a dual responsibility: We attend to both what happens and what it means. We move from scenic action to matters of theme, myth, and archetype.*

What a journey this book by Canadian scholar Northrop Frye has made since 1963 to arrive in my hands and now, by allusion, into my work. It delivered to me exactly the set of critical ideas I needed, just when I most needed them. As a graduate student I became familiar with Frye's scholarly work, especially the 1957 *Anatomy of Criticism*, maybe one of the last great works of ambitious, systematic literary criticism until the postmodernists began to tear the cathedral down.

As must be clear by now, I will take good reading and writing advice wherever I can find it. That eclecticism led me back to a St. Pete bookstore, 321 Books, where I paid three bucks for Frye's *Fables of Identity*. My volume was acquired and then kicked out of not one but two college libraries. With the Library of Congress number PR503.F7, it was stamped as having been accessioned by the Yankton College Library in South Dakota on April 20, 1973. It must have been too cold up in Yankton because at some point it heads south to join the collection at Clearwater Christian College in Florida. The stamp on the copyright page says, in block letters: CLEARWATER CHRISTIAN COLLEGE DOES NOT NECESSARILY APPROVE OF THE VIEWS EXPRESSED IN THIS PUBLICATION. That notice makes me happy. I live about twenty miles from Clearwater, a city populated by many Scientologists, and I was cheered that a small Christian school would be willing to make available to students sophisticated literary theory that had not been tested for orthodoxy. Books have a way of finding you when you need them.

Most of *Fables of Identity* consists of literary essays on the work of canonical writers as diverse as Milton, Twain, Shakespeare, Blake, Byron, Dickinson, Yeats, Stevens, and Joyce— writers who can be identified by their last names alone. What stand out for me are the introductory chapters on myth, fiction, and archetypes.

An excerpt:

> Some arts move in time, like music; others are presented in space, like painting. In both cases the organizing principle is recurrence, which is called rhythm when it is temporal and pattern when it is spatial. Thus we speak of the rhythm of music and the pattern of painting; but later, to show off our sophistication, we may begin to speak of the rhythm of painting and the pattern of music. In other words, all arts may be conceived both temporally and spatially. The score of a musical composition may be studied all at once; a picture may be seen as the track of an intricate dance of the eye. Literature seems to be intermediate between music and painting: its words form rhythms which approach a musical sequence of sounds at one of its boundaries, and form patterns which approach the hieroglyphic or pictorial image at the other. The attempts to get as near to these boundaries as possible form the main body of what is called experimental writing. We may call the rhythm of literature the narrative, and the pattern, the simultaneous mental grasp of the verbal structure, the meaning or significance. We hear or listen to a narrative, but when we grasp a writer's total pattern we "see" what he means.

I have read few paragraphs in literary criticism over a half century that have excited me as much as that one does. My enthusiasm comes from a highly formal idea positioning literature somewhere between the work of musicians and painters. That insight would be interesting enough, but it leads me to another that has endless potential for both reader and writer.

At this point, Frye is saying

1. We experience music one way.
2. We experience painting another way.
3. We experience literature both ways.

When it comes to narrative (use *story* or *plot* if you prefer), we experience it sequentially, that is, scene after scene after scene. In popular fiction, something unusual happens at the beginning (a death, a disappearance, an arrest); that action raises questions that only the story can answer. (Who killed that person? Will they find the missing child? Is the person in custody innocent or guilty?) According to Frye, if the work is done well (or even if it isn't) we follow along, turning the page until that moment of "recognition," usually near or at the end, of the outcome. ("Elizabeth and Darcy must wed—of course!") That is literature as music.

But when we reflect on the work later, in tranquility or in an argument, we may well remember high points ("gold coins" in Don Fry's good term), but not sequentially. Instead, we remember the work more as a whole, using words to describe its theme, meaning, tone, significance, relevance. Here's an inventory of what I remember about the film version of Ian Fleming's *Goldfinger:* Bond catches Goldfinger cheating at golf; Goldfinger captures Bond, puts him on a metal slab, and aims a laser beam between his legs; Bond makes out with a beautiful woman and then discovers her body covered in gold paint; Oddjob, the Korean bodyguard, throws his derby like a Frisbee, cutting off the head of a statue; Bond seduces Pussy Galore for a literal roll in the hay. I remember well a moment near the end when Bond is rescued by a technician who turns off the nuclear bomb in the bowels of Fort Knox just in time, so that the read-out stops at 007. So yes, I have a general sense of a story arc, and a general sense of what came earlier and what came later, but to a large measure it doesn't matter. What matters is my fifteen-year-old response to the movie: that was so freaking cool!

I belong to a school of thought that distrusts too much emphasis on "the theme" of a work. I prefer the plural *themes* because a work is often about many things. I could argue that the more ambitious the work, the more varied the themes. That said, the themes usually fit together, not in the sense of the classical unities, but for the sake of an aesthetic coherence; we like that *click, click, click* sound when the pieces of a puzzle snap into something whole.

"In the direct experience of a new work of fiction," writes Frye, "we have a sense of its unity which we derive from its persuasive continuity." Even a bad plot—fiction or nonfiction—ties discrete scenes into a coherent whole. He argues that when the story becomes more familiar to us, we pay less attention to its sequence of episodes and more to a different form of unity, which he describes as theme.

Frye labels the "total design" of a story as a myth or an archetype, a broad, deep pattern that comes down to us from millennia of stories about gods and their encounters with one another and with human beings. For instance, when the late Margot Adler, granddaughter of psychoanalyst Alfred Adler, wrote stories for NPR, she became aware of the connection between contemporary narratives and ancient myths. When she descended with police officers into the caverns of New York City's subways and found a kind of sub-tropolis for the otherwise homeless and dispossessed, she saw it as a descent into the underworld, common in the old stories of Orpheus, Jesus, and Dante.

Here is more from Frye:

> In myth criticism, when we examine the theme or total design of a fiction, we must isolate that aspect of the fiction which is conventional, and held in common with all other works of the same category. When we begin, say, *Pride and Prejudice,* we can see at once that a story which sustains that particular mood or tone is most unlikely to end in tragedy or melodrama or mordant irony or romance. It clearly belongs to the category represented by the word "comedy," and we are not surprised to find in it the conventional features of comedy, including a foolish lover, with some economic advantages, encouraged by one of the parents, a hypocrite unmasked, misunderstandings between the chief characters eventually cleared up and happy marriages for those who deserve them.

In summary, Frye argues that when we read a new novel "we are aware of its continuity or moving power in time." When critics study the work of storytellers, they judge the artist's ability to create "a sharply focused reproduction of life." That occurs in the sequence of narrative. But there is a form of unity in such a work beyond narrative sequence. Frye calls it "the formal cause that holds the work together," a real "unity in the design."

What would happen, I wonder, if we used the word *focus* to represent all other words about the higher meaning of a work of writing: the thesis, the theme, the logos, the nut, the peg, the point, or slant? I feel comfortable with the idea that a poem, for example, has a focus. Yeats's "The Second Coming" is centered on the idea that in a chaotic world of war and rebellion "the center cannot hold." Shirley Jackson's short horror story "The Lottery" has a focus: that blind adherence to traditional rules leads inevitably to the scapegoating of the marginalized and vulnerable. In a focused work all the key moments in the narrative can be used as evidence of something pointed.

If a story has focus, it means that:

- At the highest level, it's about one thing.
- All the evidence supports that thing.
- There is nothing that sticks out—unless the author wants it to.
- There are several ways to express the main idea: *title, subtitle, photo and caption, thesis, theme, nut, lead, premise, pitch.*
- All members of a team producing that story know what it's about, and can act on it.
- The writer knows what to put in and what to leave out.

You may use terms like *theme, archetype,* and *central idea.* If you are looking for a better one, try *focus.*

LESSONS

1. Learn the difference between the way a narrative is experienced sequentially and how it is experienced from memory.

2. While you are building a story in sequence, think about how the reader will reflect upon the story after the fact, in tranquility.

3. Ask yourself throughout your writing process: Is my focus sharp? Have I given readers enough evidence to discern and retain the focus I intend?

4. Consider all the words used to express focus: *premise, theme, thesis, lead,* etc. Which ones do you find most helpful, and why?

19

Distill your story into five words—maybe three.
Use the "premise" or other tools to articulate
what your work is really about.

*The Art of Dramatic Writing: Its Basis in the Creative Interpretation
of Human Motives*
By Lajos Egri

Toolbox: *There's a quality in prose I call "altitude." It describes
that moment when the story "takes off" from what happens to
what it means. In the last chapter, the Canadian scholar Northrop
Frye describes this movement in an academic way. Playwright
Lajos Egri taught a more practical way. He believed in writing
a "premise," a short sentence that summarizes what the work is
all about. "Great love defies even death" describes the premise of
Romeo and Juliet. You may not have the premise in your bag of
writing tricks, but you need something like it. The capacity to encapsulate has different names in different writing disciplines: the
theme, the nut, the point, the angle, the take, the thesis statement,
even the hoo-ha (an old Yiddish exclamation of surprise, in this
context slang for the moment a reader figures out what a piece of
writing is about). Say it in five words.*

Lajos Egri, a veteran playwright, conducted writing classes, first in New York and then in Los Angeles. Many successful playwrights and screenwriters took his course and studied from his book *The Art of Dramatic Writing*. It's a tribute to both teacher and text that they inspired practical writers to create movies and plays that audiences continue to enjoy.

Egri was one of the millions of European immigrants who arrived in America at the turn of the twentieth century. Born in 1888, he arrived from Hungary in 1906 and did factory work as a tailor and a presser in New York City. He worked to survive, but his dream from age ten was to write plays. He made a breakthrough in 1927 with *Rapid Transit,* an inventive play in which all the crazy energy of the industrial age is compressed in a twenty-four-hour time frame. He was an active playwright and teacher until his death in 1967.

Egri studied books on the craft and found them unsatisfactory. That is often an incentive to write your own, and Egri produced a guidebook, illustrated by examples of classical drama, which has stood the test of time.

In his *Poetics,* Aristotle argues that action—not character—is the driving force in the creation of dramatic literature. A man unwittingly kills his father and marries his mother. That action defines the character of Oedipus (and would eventually make Freud a rich and happy man!). Egri politely flips the switch on Aristotle. It is *character* that drives drama, he argues, not action. The author shows the kind of man, say, Macbeth is (brave, ambitious, vulnerable to suggestion, and easily influenced by his ruthless wife), and shows how those characteristics generate his seduction by the witches and his murder of the king.

This argument is persuasive but, as we shall see, has inherent flaws. Egri builds his case by describing what he feels is the essential creative act of effective storytelling. That act, he argues, is framing a *premise*. Before action, he says, there is character. And before character, there is the premise. In Egri's conception, the premise is a brief statement that captures the essence of the story. Brevity is crucial. It can be spoken in seconds. It rarely extends beyond five or six words. By example, Egri looks at classic works and distills for each a premise.

Romeo and Juliet: "Great love defies even death."
King Lear: "Blind trust leads to destruction."
Macbeth: "Ruthless ambition leads to its own destruction."
Othello: "Jealousy destroys itself and the object of its love."

Egri writes, "Every good play must have a well-formulated premise. There may be more than one way to phrase the premise, but, however it is phrased, the thought must be the same."

You can't plagiarize a premise, he writes. The premise is a deep story pattern, not a stereotype but an archetype, so it has the ability to generate an infinite number of plays. Any aspiring playwright, then, could take the *Romeo and Juliet* premise and create characters and actions to show that great love defies even death.

"A good premise is a thumbnail synopsis of your play," writes Egri and lists some of his favorites:

- Bitterness leads to false gaiety.
- Foolish generosity leads to poverty.
- Honesty defeats duplicity.
- Heedlessness destroys friendship.
- Ill-temper leads to isolation.
- Materialism conquers mysticism.

These remind me of the "moral of the story" that might appear at the end of folktales or beast fables. Of the fifteen examples on Egri's list, ten use *lead/leads* as the verb, as in "Extravagance leads to destitution."

The power of the premise is such that it can serve as a microcosm for the entire play. A three-act play, his favorite genre, creates a dialectic: thesis, antithesis, synthesis. More practically, a first act might dramatize or embody in a character the elements of, say, extravagance. A second act shows the actions that derive from that character flaw. A final act reveals where it all leads.

As an aspiring playwright, this feels right to me. For several years I have been working on a modernization of a medieval English work called *The Second Shepherds' Play*, created in the fifteenth century by an unnamed cleric known to us as the Wakefield Master. As part of a cycle of plays performed on religious holidays in cathedral towns, he tells the story of three lowly shepherds who become the first humans (besides Mary and Joseph) to experience the presence of the Christ Child. In my opinion, it is the best English play before Shakespeare. It also happens to be hilarious, which might seem to contradict the piety of its final action.

It goes like this: Three shepherds appear, one at a time, to the audience on a cold and stormy night. Each one addresses the audience in a soliloquy complaining about his lot in life. One complains about the horrible weather. Another about the rich aristocrats who keep him down. Another about a shrewish wife. These are affecting, funny, universal complaints. The shepherds finally meet and greet one another, sing a song, and warn one another about the danger of sheep stealers. Enter Mak, a great villain, armed with a little bit of magic. He casts a spell that puts them to sleep, and then he steals their best sheep and takes it home to his wife, Gil, for a great meal. Gil, who is a chronic complainer, has recently given birth to a child and sleeps with a cradle next to her. She worries that the shepherds will come and kill them for sheep stealing.

The shepherds wake up, realize their loss, and head to Mak's house with vengeance on their minds. But Gil has a plan. She hides the sheep in the cradle next to her bed, making believe it is her newborn babe (notice already the comedic foreshadowing of the birth of the Lamb of God!). When the shepherds arrive, there is no sight of their sheep, and they begin to feel guilty about disturbing the family. They leave but return to give the baby a gift. When they look into the cradle, they see the ugliest baby ever born. While the law would allow them to kill the thieves, the shepherds pull their punches and toss Mak in a blanket, making sure he hits the ground with each toss. They leave and are visited by a beautiful angel with a wonderful song, which they imitate. She points them to a star over Bethlehem, where they greet the Holy Family, give the baby some simple gifts, and go on their way singing of the glory of God and of a life of hope and redemption.

My dream is one day to produce a modernization that will help restore the play to a high place in the canon of English drama. But I wonder: When the Wakefield Master wrote *The Second Shepherds' Play*, was he working from a premise? Maybe so, and maybe it came from scripture: "The humble shall be exalted." My version might be "With good hearts, the lowly shall be led to glory."

If we return to Egri's structural notion that "premise precedes character," and that "character generates action," we have to deal with the tension in the argument. For, if my reading is correct, a premise, though it contains the seeds of character, is primarily a statement of action. Remember those examples that contain the verb *lead*? Or how about another of his favorites: "Craftiness digs its own grave." This will create a play with a character whose craftiness is discernible only through actions. He admits as much: "Let us examine '*Frugality leads to waste.*' The first part of this premise suggests character—a frugal character. The second part, '*leads to,*' suggests conflict, and the third part, '*waste,*' suggests the end of the play."

Egri admits that good premises have resulted in bad plays and that good plays have been constructed without benefit of an energizing premise. He also offers examples of authors using language other than "premise" to express the same strategy. "Others, especially men of the theater, have had different words for the same thing: theme, thesis, root idea, central idea, goal, aim, driving force, subject, purpose, plan, plot, basic emotion." At Poynter, over four decades, we have challenged writers to explain, "What is your story really about?" "Can you say it in six words?" "Can you say it in one word?" So, yes, by all means, try writing a premise. See where it leads.

LESSONS

1. The premise is a short statement that generates the action in a play. As a test, go back and read examples of your own work. Can you describe in ten words or fewer what that work is about?

2. Think about the writing ideas now on your mind. Can you encapsulate them in a tentative premise? Mine would be "Opponents and advocates of legal abortion occupy invisible common ground." Or "Privileged parents game system to get kids into elite colleges." Each of those is ten words. Try it for your work.

3. Go back and review the traditional premises favored by Egri. Can you think of fresh, new stories that might fit those same premises? Try "with good hearts the humble shall be exalted."

4. Egri favors the three-act play. One reason might be that it erects an architecture of beginning, middle, and ending. As an experiment, think of any piece of writing you produce as a three-act play. Can you identify those parts of the work, where each begins and ends?

20

———✦·

Add dimension to characters. Flat ones are useful; round ones feel more human.

Aspects of the Novel
By E. M. Forster

Toolbox: *Novelist E. M. Forster became famous among teachers
of literature for drawing a distinction between "flat" characters
and "round" ones. The more complex, the more crazily human
characters feel, the rounder they are. Flat characters are easy
to recognize: they are types—at worst, stereotypes—but at best
compelling embodiments of a single trait. Any character details
that add a degree of tension or ambiguity—the chef who loves
fast foods, the feminist addicted to pornography, the pacifist who
owns a gun—drives us and the reader toward roundness.*

Some writing books would be worth the purchase if they offered you one great lesson among several minor ones. You will
find lots of lessons in *Aspects of the Novel*, written in 1927
from a series of university lectures by E. M. Forster. Known to
his friends as Morgan (his middle name), Forster spent twenty

years (1905 to 1924) writing important novels. Americans may know his stories such as *A Room with a View* and *A Passage to India* from the movies they inspired. Oddly, the flow of novels mostly stopped, although Forster led a rich literary, civic, and university life at Cambridge until his death in 1970.

Even a brief outline of his biography reveals the complexity of his character: His father died when he was one, and he was doted on by his mum and aunties. His experience of secondary school was a cold one (that seems a universal experience for British children even if they wind up at Hogwarts!). He found his calling as a creative writer at Cambridge and became a member of a discussion group known as the Apostles, which included some of England's most brilliant minds. He traveled through Greece, Italy, and Germany, gaining experiences that would come to life in his novels. He traveled to India, where he came to despise British imperialism. He wrote what would become a famous novel, *Maurice*, about a gay man. Because homosexuality was a crime in England until 1967, the novel was not published until after his death. During World War I, he joined the Red Cross.

In an introduction to a collection of Forster's novels, Neil Felshman describes the years after the famous author stopped churning out novels:

For the next forty-odd years, E. M. Forster lectured and wrote essays and criticism on literature and politics. He became active in the international writer's organization PEN and lobbied for greater freedom of expression for writers, decrying the suppression of Radclyffe Hall's lesbian novel

The Well of Loneliness and D. H. Lawrence's *Lady Chatter-ley's Lover.*

The financial legacy of a rich aunt sustained him. Interestingly, as Felshman tells us, "He refused a knighthood in 1949, but twenty years later, on his ninetieth birthday, he accepted the Order of Merit, the highest non-political distinction, from Queen Elizabeth II."

When it came to literature, Forster knew what he liked. From reading *Aspects of the Novel*, it is clear that he *loves* Jane Austen. Charles Dickens? Not as much. Why? Because Forster understands, describes, and promulgates an important literary distinction: the difference between flat characters and round ones. This distinction is so clear, so rich, and so purposeful that it was adopted as a lesson by creative writing teachers everywhere. The great critic F. R. Leavis, perhaps with a bit of jealous mischief, noted that all the English teaching mistresses in all the girls' schools in all of England had pounced on the distinction. (Not everyone is a fan: James Wood takes issue with Forster's distinction and preferences in *How Fiction Works*.)

As I think of my own attempts to write fiction, I have Forster's distinction in my head. Are my characters flat? Are they round? Do I need both? Why does it matter? So, Morgan, you are clearly a round character in your own right—fully human. Why would you or I be interested in flat characters at all? *Flat* has such a negative connotation. His answer, in *Aspects of the Novel*:

Flat characters were called "humours" in the seventeenth century, and are sometimes called types, and sometimes caricatures. [In the morality plays of the Middle Ages, depictions of the battle between good and evil, the characters actually had the names of virtues and vices: Pride, Humility, Lechery, Chastity....] In their purest form, they are constructed round a single idea or quality: when there is more than one factor in them, we get the beginning of the curve towards the round....

One great advantage of flat characters is that they are easily recognized whenever they come in—recognized by the reader's emotional eye, not by the visual eye, which merely notes the recurrence of a proper name....

A second advantage is that they are easily remembered by the reader afterwards. They remain in his mind as unalterable for the reason that they were not changed by circumstances; they moved through circumstances, which gives them in retrospect a comforting quality, and preserves them when the book that produced them may decay.

The most successful perpetrator of the flat character, argues Forster, is Charles Dickens. While he gives the author his due—his talent at making flat characters memorable—he nonetheless holds Dickens as less an artist than Jane Austen, whose characters may represent certain personality traits: sense, sensibility, pride, prejudice. But when set in motion—in plot or dialogue—those characters exhibit conflicting traits that reveal their full, round humanity.

A good example, not mentioned by Forster, might come

from perhaps the most successful short novel in the history of English literature, *A Christmas Carol*. Leaving the ghosts aside—Marley is perhaps a bit rounder than the Christmas spirits—let's focus on three main characters. Enter Ebenezer Scrooge. His change comes about not in a human way but by a supernatural conversion. He is a type. The grouch. The miser. The cheapskate. The...well, the scrooge. We remember one thing about him—his scroogeness, his humbugability.

The next type is Bob Cratchit: He is a foil for Scrooge. The hardworking father who is so good-hearted that he is willing to toast the health of his mean-spirited boss because, well, because it is Christmas. He works so hard to sustain his family, and to care most particularly for the health of his crippled son Tiny Tim. But what, besides his bad health and good spirit, do we know about Tim? He plays one note. He is there to be pitied, and then to become the beneficiary of the converted Scrooge's largesse. Flat, flat, flat. And somehow still great, great, great.

I can cite a more contemporary example, the musical *Hamilton* created by Lin-Manuel Miranda, which I attended in March 2019, while I was revising this chapter. With Forster in mind, I could not help noticing the flatness of characters such as the two Georges. George Washington is portrayed as thoroughly uncomplicated, a pillar of bravery, nobility, and leadership. Then there is King George, full of pomp and foppery, whose interludes provide the comic relief in a modern Shakespearean tragedy. The flatness of such characters provides the round characters—Alexander Hamilton, Aaron Burr, Angelica Schuyler—the opportunity to step forward in all their human complexity. According to Forster,

A novel that is at all complex often requires flat people as well as round, and the outcome of their collisions parallels life more accurately....Dickens's people are nearly all flat....Nearly every one can be summed up in a sentence, and yet there is this wonderful feeling of human depth. Probably the immense vitality of Dickens causes his characters to vibrate a little, so that they borrow his life and appear to lead one of their own. It is a conjuring-trick.

As for round characters:

The test of a round character is whether it is capable of surprising in a convincing way. If it never surprises, it is flat. If it does not convince, it is a flat pretending to be round. It has the incalculability of life about it—life within the pages of a book.

Of the round characters he cites, the one that stands out is Flaubert's Madame Bovary. We can try to capture her in a single statement, maybe something like this: A romantic young woman who dreams of Paris is stuck in a marriage with a provincial bore. The words *romantic* and *provincial* are often repeated in describing the story, but you can't get anywhere near Emma Bovary without the narrative in action. Like Hamlet, she is so complex, so multifaceted, so vulnerable, so hungry for change that she comes out round, round, round.

A big question for you fiction writers, new or experienced: Is your character flat, a type you can capture at a glance—that grumpy police lieutenant who never smiles, who shouts into the police room so everyone can hear his displeasure? He is flat, and you may need him to be.

Or is your character a high-school chemistry teacher dying of cancer, who comes up with the idea of selling crystal meth in order to raise money so his family can prosper after his death, and whose cancer goes into remission, but who can't stop cooking meth and making money and going up against the cartels, because he prefers to be a drug kingpin than Mr. Chips. If you have seen the television series *Breaking Bad*, although there are flat characters in it, you have experienced the power of roundness.

LESSONS

1. As you write fiction or nonfiction, remember that characters can be flat or round. Use the flat ones to represent a single virtue or attitude, a type—especially one we have seen before.

2. Because of their familiarity, flat characters may give pleasure to the reader, but they fail to reflect the complexity of human life.

3. Begin to pay attention to the difference between flat and round characters in your television viewing. You may find that some genres—situation comedies come to mind—may not require much roundness. In *Seinfeld,* Jerry, George, Elaine, and Kramer each seem to manifest an exaggerated version of 1990s-style New York neuroses. The minor characters—the soup Nazi, the library cop—may not be common types, but they are nonetheless one-dimensional.

4. One strategy feature writers use to create roundness in their characters is to identify "the bruise on the apple." Editor Mike Wilson would use that phrase to make sure that his writers were not seduced by the likeability of characters being profiled. Surely they had a negative trait that would humanize them. Villains benefit from roundness, too: the tax cheat who is caregiver for a parent with dementia. Complexity in narrative comes from round characters such as Madame Bovary and Hamlet and maybe even Spider-Man.

21

Report for story. Gather what you need to make nonfiction read like a novel.

Frank Sinatra Has a Cold: And Other Essays
By Gay Talese

The New Journalism
Edited by Tom Wolfe and E. W. Johnson

Toolbox: *A gift of language lets us fabricate stories, describing actions that never happened by characters who never existed. Most of us associate words like* story, yarn, tale, *or* fable *with making things up. Authors of nonfiction can take the stuff of everyday life and weave it into something that is experienced as a novel is. The most effective—and ethical—method to create this "reads-like-fiction" effect is immersive research or reporting. Spend a day with a gravedigger. Collect character details, scenes, dialogue, points of view. Together they create that experience we call "story."*

When Gay Talese was asked to contribute something to the 2005 anthology *This Is My Best,* he chose a profile he wrote in 1966 for *Esquire,* "Frank Sinatra Has a Cold." To those who know Talese's nonfiction, this comes as no surprise. In an anniversary edition of *Esquire,* the editors once declared the story on Sinatra to be the best work ever to appear in the magazine. *Esquire* republished the essay with remarkable images of Talese's elaborate outlining.

Oddly, the author preferred to work on cardboard slabs, the type that used to be tucked into shirts you brought home from the dry cleaner. He could fold these in a way he found comfortable in his pocket. When the reporting—taking weeks and weeks—was completed, other cardboard slabs could then be used to construct a storyboard. He would outline the story, scene by scene.

From that outline, Talese would write a draft, which he would pin, page by page, across his office wall. From the back of the room, he could examine the global structure of the story, and then, with binoculars, read the fine print, word by word.

(I just realized how much the photos of this "story wall" have influenced my own process. As I look over the top of my computer at this moment, I see a bulletin board. In the top corner is the working title of this book, *Murder Your Darlings.* Across the bulletin board—the dimensions are 8′ by 4′—there are currently forty-one index cards, each representing a possible chapter in this book. The colors are yellow, lilac, pink, and green. Those colors signify nothing, but they make the wall pretty and brighten my day. The cards are numbered 1 to 41, revealing only the order in which they were written, not the order they will appear in the book, if they appear at all. But after I finish a "zero draft" and then a legitimate first draft, I will begin to step back, à la Talese, and look at the global structure of the work, the larger thematic categories, the connections among chapters, some idea of flow. The cards, I know, will come down, where I can study them, make notations on the back, maybe find a comfortable table, or even a nice rug—with a nearby dog—to turn the tiles into a mosaic.)

The lessons from the Talese story are wide and deep. You can get to them via a quick look at the opening passage:

> Frank Sinatra, holding a glass of bourbon in one hand and a cigarette in the other, stood in a dark corner of the bar between two attractive but fading blondes who sat waiting for him to say something.

This is an oft-quoted story lead, studied, praised, and criticized. Talese wrote a famous book about sex in America, and, at a writing conference later in his career, caused a stir when he appeared unable to name a woman nonfiction author whose influence he had felt. Those "two attractive but fading blondes" evoke an earlier era of *Mad Men*–style sexism, when it was common to identify men by their role (two pals or two cronies) and women by their hair color.

Here are the lessons I draw from a close reading of that sentence:

1. In nonfiction, there is nothing more important than access.
2. The best access is called being "a fly on the wall."

3. Immersive reporting is the lens through which scenes are observed and reconstructed.

4. Specific character details are crucial, but they need not be too specific to get the job done.

5. Although brand names could be used as what Tom Wolfe calls "status details"—and Talese often uses that trick—here, *bourbon* and *cigarette* are good enough. If he had given us *Maker's Mark* or *Marlboro,* it would have focused the light away from the central theme.

6. Writers can use imagery to send direct but also subliminal messages. Here it's all about tension and contrast: blonde hair in a dark corner, conversation stifled by silence, the downer/upper simultaneity of alcohol and nicotine.

While "Frank Sinatra Has a Cold" is worth close study down to the last bits of punctuation, writers must realize that Talese, at that moment in time, writing for *Esquire,* had at his fingertips the elements of success that so many writers these days lack. He could spend as much time trailing Sinatra as he needed to do the job, with an expense account to support his efforts.

In his collection of essays under the Sinatra title, Talese includes one that he wrote in 1997, titled "Origins of a Nonfiction Writer." His story begins in 1932 when he was born into an Italian-American family, his father a tailor, and his mother the operator of the family dress business. As a young man in this shop, he says he learned to listen, to pay attention without intruding, a skill that became handy when he became a professional observer and interviewer. He writes:

The shop was a kind of talk show that flowed around the engaging manner and well-timed questions of my mother; and as a boy not much taller than the counters behind which I used to pause and eavesdrop, I learned much that would be useful to me years later when I began interviewing people for articles and books.

This next paragraph needs to be read by anyone who aspires to become a public writer, not just so he or she can show off a style, but to find powerful voices in everyday people, who, if given a chance, might have something to say:

> I learned to listen with patience and care, and never to interrupt even when people were having great difficulty in explaining themselves, for during such halting and imprecise moments...people often are very revealing—what they hesitate to talk about can tell much about them. Their pauses, their evasions, their sudden shifts in subject matter are likely indicators of what embarrasses them, or irritates them, or what they regard as too private or imprudent to be disclosed to another person at that particular time.

Before Talese wrote about Frank Sinatra, he wrote about former heavyweight champion Joe Louis. Although Talese denies that he was trying a "new" form of nonfiction, he recounts how his colleague Tom Wolfe interpreted Talese's work as part of a literary movement called "The New Journalism." In a 1973 anthology by that name, Wolfe and E. W. Johnson compiled twenty-three essays, a collection that holds up nicely, thanks to the selection of authors who continue to be key figures in the study and debate of nonfiction writing. In addition to Talese and Wolfe, we can turn to the likes of Joan Didion, Norman Mailer, Truman Capote, Hunter S. Thompson, Joe McGinniss, Robert Christgau, and Garry Wills.

That's a great starting lineup, but the value of these collected pieces in part two of the book is overshadowed by Wolfe's essay in part one. If you are going to declare a literary movement, you need not just the evidence of examples; you need a manifesto. What is so new about New Journalism? Is it any different from the Old Journalism? Aren't you scribes just making stuff up like beat reporters did in the old days? Maybe you should call it the New Fiction! No, argued Talese, he was producing the "Literature of Reality."

But how is it accomplished? Wolfe had the recipe, and he passed it along until the end of his life in 2018. He describes his mission and purpose in the book's preface:

Namely, what is it precisely—in terms of technique—that has made the New Journalism as "absorbing" and "gripping" as the novel and the short story, and often more so? This led, eventually, to two discoveries that I think are crucial for anyone interested in writing. One: There are four specific devices, all of them realistic, that underlie the emotionally involving quality of the most powerful prose, whether fiction or nonfiction. Two: Realism is not merely another literary approach or attitude. The introduction of detailed realism into English literature in the eighteenth century was like the introduction of electricity into machine technology.

It raised the state of the art to an entirely new magnitude. And for anyone, in fiction or nonfiction, to try to improve literary technique by abandoning social realism would be like an engineer trying to improve upon machine technology by abandoning electricity.

But what about the four devices? I will explain them to you as I have come to understand them and use them in my own writing and teaching:

1. Stories need characters, and characters have characteristics. Next time you are in a coffee shop, look around. You are a fly on the wall. Pay attention to how people look, what they are wearing, the slogans on their T-shirts. Check out the tattoos. Count the piercings. Focus on one barista. Write down a list of details, gestures, habits that together help you understand the personality, character, or, to use Wolfe's term, "status" of the person.

2. Stories, expressed in all genres, require a sequence of scenes. A scene is a unit of narrative. You have been experiencing action in scenes since you were a toddler. When I was a toddler, I was afraid of walking, but I could walk if I held my mother's hand. "Step, step, step" she would say in a one-bedroom apartment on the Lower East Side of New York City. When she pulled her hand away, I would look up, and then fall down on my diapered little behind. One day, my mother handed me an old-fashioned wooden clothespin. I held one end. She held the other. She let go, but I kept walking...until I

looked up, realized she was not at the other end, and fell down. That's a scene!

3. Traditional journalists traffic in quotes—things that are said about people and events of the day. Storytellers may use quotes, but their more powerful strategy is the gathering of dialogue. Remember Gay Talese listening to the people in the dress shop? They were probably not even aware of his presence. He was listening in. As he grew into a writer, he might interview a character, even asking them what they were thinking at a moment of action, but he might also be not just listening to, but listening in. Does a fly on the wall have ears? Narrative dialogue does not even require two people talking. One person may just be listening, or the main character may be yelling at someone across a noisy bar.

4. The fourth technique is often called point of view. Storytellers show us not just what they are seeing, but what their characters are perceiving from their positions in the setting. As a young reporter, I was formed by an experience I had at a rock concert in downtown St. Pete, Florida, featuring the New York punk group the Ramones. They played in a venue called Jannus Landing, and in front of the stage the punky fans were doing their thing. That stage was right up against a retirement hotel. If I joined the dancers and looked up, I would have seen surprised older ladies, some with blue hair, looking down at the mosh pit, gazing upon hair bluer than theirs, some fashioned into a mohawk.

The main criticism I've heard of the New Journalism was that some authors—Truman Capote, for example—really were making things up. Nonfiction, claimed John Hersey in a famous essay titled "The Legend on the License," is a discipline in which distortion by subtraction is tolerated, but not distortion by addition. Both Wolfe and Talese proclaimed the need for an approach to reporting and research that was more rigorous than the standard, not less. Reporters covering City Hall collected quotes, numbers, who said what at the meeting today. Those practicing the Literature of Reality needed to collect more: character details, observed scenes, dialogue, points of view: a regimen most difficult to master. When practiced at the highest level, it creates stories that can be amazing to behold, that reach for the level of art.

LESSONS

1. In writing nonfiction, seek eyewitness access to events. Be a fly on the wall, but the ceiling works, too, and in some cases the windowsill or toilet tank.

2. Remember that most stories are not witnessed directly. They are reconstructed from sources who were on the scene. The best reporters seek multiple sources, who may see the same event from different points of view. Consider that diversity a strength, not a weakness.

3. Learn to interview for story. Practice the questions that will lead to narrative opportunities: What happened out there? What did it look like? What did you see, hear, smell? What did she say to you? But even: What were you wearing? Your dog ran off in the storm? What is its name? Do you have a photo of Fido?

4. In writing nonfiction narrative, keep your standards high. Anticipate questions from editors or teachers: "How do you know that?" A good answer is "I saw it with my own eyes." Another is "I got there an hour after it happened, and the minister walked me through the church." Another is "I got it from this police report (or court transcript)." Another is "You can see it on this video."

V

Rhetoric and Audience

One definition of rhetoric is the use of language to persuade. Many writers claim that they write to please themselves. But the word *persuasion* has built into it the idea of "another," the audience. The word *audience*—think of *audio*—denotes a group of listeners, those who are moved by a message. I just found out the root of the Latin word for *persuade* means "sweet." As in the orator offering something tasty to the crowd, an idea embedded in the proverb that it's easier to catch flies with honey than vinegar. The Roman orator and teacher Quintilian built a foundation for all writers and speakers with strategic advice on how to move audiences for the common good.

Over the two millennia since Quintilian, few scholars were as attentive to how audiences respond to texts as Louise Rosenblatt. She divided the experience of reading into two dynamic categories: the "efferent," in which readers carry away important practical information; and the "aesthetic," in which readers linger over a text to appreciate its artistry. Reports, it turns out, are different from stories, so writers can choose between utility and beauty when they begin to type.

From the 1940s through our own time, practical scholars and teachers looked for ways to measure the readability of prose. Champions of this movement toward civic clarity were Rudolf Flesch and Robert Gunning, each of whom created an index that attempted to match things like word and sentence length to ease of reading.

From the civic to the literary, we find a long history of theories designed to help us understand the effects of stories and dramatic literature on audiences ancient and modern. What happens in a theater when an audience witnesses a tragic death? They experience a catharsis, argued Aristotle, a purgation of emotions.

When it comes to what audiences should expect, authors Vivian Gornick and Mary Karr, both practitioners of memoir, disagree. Where is the line between fact and fiction? Is there an implied contract between the reader and writer about transparency of method, poetic license, and whether the search for a higher truth allows the writer of memoir to invent events that never happened?

22

Anticipate the needs of readers. Deliver urgent
information or compelling narratives.

Literature as Exploration
  and
*The Reader, the Text, the Poem: The Transactional Theory of the
Literary Work*
By Louise M. Rosenblatt

Toolbox: *Good writers anticipate the needs of readers. In an
emergency, a reader may need "just the facts." Another reader
may benefit from an elaborate narrative that offers pleasure as
well as wisdom. At times the writer stays in the background so
as not to distract the reader from urgent information. At other
times, the writer steps forward in a way that calls attention to
the writer's craft. Ask yourself: What is my reader looking for: to
carry away information, or to experience something richly aesthetic? Each need calls for a different set of tools.*

I never met her, but Louise Rosenblatt is one of my literary heroes. When I first discovered her work, I learned that she was

ninety-nine years old, still engaged in matters of the mind. She died in 2005 at the age of one hundred years and six months.

It was only in preparing this chapter that I learned of her full history, a century of life that magnifies her literary theories. She was born in Atlantic City, New Jersey, in 1904. Her parents were Jewish immigrants. She attended Barnard, the women's college of Columbia University. Her roommate, the editor in chief of the college newspaper, was a young woman named Margaret Mead, yes, *that* Margaret Mead, who encouraged her younger friend Louise to study anthropology and follow her to Samoa. Instead, after succeeding her friend as editor in chief of the school paper, Louise headed not to the South Sea Islands, but to France. There she got to hang out with French authors and American expats of the Lost Generation.

She completed her literary education in French universities and in 1931 finished her first book, returning to America to teach at her alma mater, Barnard, then at Brooklyn College and New York University. An admirer of John Dewey, the philosopher of democracy, she remained politically and socially active throughout her life. In World War II she used her French-language skills to help the United States Office of War Information analyze reports and information coming in and out of Nazi-controlled France. She lent her support to the NAACP, and at the end of her life was a strong advocate of reforming the education policy known as No Child Left Behind. What a life!

Somewhere amid this broad range of experience, Rosenblatt asked herself a question she spent her career trying to answer. Imagine a teacher of high-school literature in New York City. She, like many other teachers, introduces the works of William

Shakespeare to her students by assigning them *Romeo and Juliet*. Why does reading the play, in which the star-crossed lovers take their lives, make one student cry, another laugh, and still another bored to death?

Long before academic critics began to focus on readers' responses to literature, Rosenblatt pursued the idea that reading is "transactional." The author might create a text, but, in the end, it is the reader who turns those words into a poem. The author and text remain—with key exceptions—sturdy and steady. But the poem is a different experience for each reader. Why? Because each student brings to the reading a set of experiences—an autobiography—that filters the meaning of the work.

This theory carries great implications for the author: It means, for example, that no author can determine the response of any reader—say, make one cry—but he or she can certainly influence it. Are there some writing moves that influence reader responses—fear, outrage, desire, satisfaction—more fully? Is there a reliable set of author tools? And it means something else: It invites the question of whether all reader responses are created equal. If Joe thinks *Measure for Measure* is a tragedy, and Joan thinks it is a comedy, could they both be right? It became a tricky question for Rosenblatt, who argues that, no, not all readings are equal; to be taken seriously, the reader has to pay very close attention to all aspects of the text.

These insights led Rosenblatt to a profound and practical literary distinction, one that has led me to one of the more influential writing lessons of my career. She determined through her study and her teaching that there are two distinctive types of reading experiences produced by two different writing intentions. It isn't an either/or distinction, but one that exists on a spectrum. She calls one type of reading "efferent" and the other type "aesthetic."

The word *efferent* derives from a Latin verb meaning "to carry away." Most reading is utilitarian. We read the side of the cereal box to find out how many calories we will be pouring into our bowls. We check the TV listing to find out when the broadcast of the Yankees/Red Sox game will begin. We go to Wikipedia or other online sources to read on our computers or smartphones whether Louise Rosenblatt was 100 or 101 years old when she passed away. Our purpose is to "carry away" knowledge we were seeking and other information that took us by surprise. It is the practical writer's purpose to deliver such knowledge without confusion, ambiguity, or delay. When I read in the efferent style, the *last* thing I look for is a metaphor.

Rosenblatt's key example is that little-used but critically important genre known as the warning label. If in error you drink from a little bottle that contains poison rather than bourbon, you need information that might save your life. You have these desperate questions: Should I stick my finger down my throat? Should I drink milk? Should I call poison control? You need answers, and now.

What would happen, instead, if you looked at the label and encountered this bit of business from Romeo, who is buying poison from the Apothecary:

There is thy gold, worse poison to men's souls,
Doing more murder in this loathsome world,

Than these poor compounds that thou mayst not sell.
I sell thee poison. Thou hast sold me none.
Farewell. Buy food, and get thyself in flesh.—
Come, cordial and not poison, go with me
To Juliet's grave, for there must I use thee.

As you were dying from the poison, at least you would be the beneficiary, lacking an efferent text, of an aesthetic one.

Here, instead, taken from the Swedish Chemicals Agency, is the kind of reading experience you might be looking for:

General tips when using and storing chemicals:

- Keep chemicals in their original packaging. Do not pour into lemonade bottles, mugs or the like.
- Look for any danger symbols and read the information given. Follow the instructions on the label.
- Avoid skin contact, eye contact, and inhalation of the chemicals.
- Keep them out of reach of children.
- If a poisoning accident occurs, call…the Poison Centre…. You will find further information on the Swedish Poisons Information Centre website.
- Consider the environment when you dispose of leftover chemicals or empty packaging.

Not a metaphor in sight. To find one, you might need to travel from the efferent end of the spectrum to the aesthetic. At that end, we are looking beyond the practical and instrumental, the information we can carry away. At the aesthetic end we gain pleasure from watching the author dance, from lingering within the language, from being conscious of forms of enlightenment and surprise during the experience of the text.

An efferent text is "good" if we can read it once. A good aesthetic text proves its goodness when readers desire to read it over and over again, deriving insight and pleasure with each reading.

Let's return to the speech from Romeo:

There is thy gold, worse poison to men's souls,
Doing more murder in this loathsome world,
Than these poor compounds that thou mayst not sell.
I sell thee poison. Thou hast sold me none.

What makes this aesthetic? It is a piece of dialogue, an experience, overheard by the audience or reader. It does not just point us to a place; it puts us there. It is in story form, a narrative. A character, the apothecary, sells helpful chemicals that cure us, but also forbidden ones that can harm us. He is willing to part with these—for a price. Romeo argues that the real "poison" in human life is not this chemical, but greed, in the form of the gold he pays for it. What has value? The poison he will take to Juliet's grave, or the money-poison he pays for it. The gold, argues Romeo, corrupts more completely.

I am sure there is more to be experienced from that scene than my summary provides, which is Rosenblatt's point. There is little practical learning about the danger of certain chemicals to be gleaned from Shakespeare. What matters is an experience of literature that leads us closer to an understanding of the mysteries of human nature.

Inspired by Rosenblatt's distinction, I gained the confidence to craft my own for practical use by journalists and other public writers. For them, I thought, Rosenblatt's terms might be too esoteric. Instead I took language directly from the writer's toolbox. On one end of the spectrum is the genre called the report; at the other end is the story. Most of the texts in, say, the *New York Times* or the *Tampa Bay Times* are reports, constructed upon the answers to questions such as *who, what, where, when, why,* and *how*. Who spoke at the council meeting? What happened to the proposal to fix the potholes? When will the new museum open? Where along the waterfront will the new pier be constructed? Why were so many air conditioners in the public schools not functioning on the first day of school? How will the money be raised to repair them? The writers who create reports have a special responsibility to make them accurate, clear, and as free from bias as possible.

Stories are different. The purpose of stories is not to convey information, but to create a vicarious form of experience. To show what it was like for children to experience a hot Florida classroom in August without the benefit of air-conditioning requires the special power of stories, only possible through the instrument of eyewitness reporting. What was it like to run out of gas along Interstate 75 while trying to find a safe haven from Hurricane Irma?

Stories, even fictional ones, require research and reporting, but the traditional questions require an unfreezing process until *who* becomes character, *what* becomes action, *where* becomes setting, *when* becomes chronology, and *why* becomes motive. I apologize, Louise Rosenblatt, if my translation of your theory for my students and colleagues leaves something to be desired. I can assure you that it has helped countless writers understand the distinction between texts that point you there and ones that put you there.

LESSONS

1. Anticipate the needs and interests of readers and their possible responses to texts. Understand the rhetorical differences between writing for efferent as opposed to aesthetic effects. In short, the more urgent the need for information, the less literary the text should sound.

2. Remember that a key difference between reports and stories involves both the purpose of the text and the mission of the writer. A report delivers information upon which people can act. A story delivers scenes that readers can vicariously experience. A report "points you there." A story "puts you there."

3. Historian Paul Kramer offers cogent advice: "Alongside whole pieces being on the story-to-report spectrum, there can be sections of pieces that are further to one end than others, so that the spectrum exists both between texts and within them. As long as the oscillation is done subtly, that combination can make for the richest reading experience."

4. Think more about how *your* collective experiences—your autobiography—influence the ways in which you interact with a text. What are you seeing in a poem or story that only you can see?

23

Embrace rhetoric as the source of language power. Use it to move your best words out of hiding.

Quintilian: On the Teaching of Speaking and Writing
Edited by James J. Murphy

Toolbox: *Anytime you hear what strikes you as a great speech, ask yourself "What makes it great?" The answer requires examining a text, whether it is a sermon, lecture, campaign speech, eulogy, or TED Talk. From the ancient to the modern, teachers of rhetoric offer reliable tools for making meaning and being persuasive. They have a million names for these strategies (like* hyperbole!*). You need only a few to build your writing muscles: establish a parallel pattern, then give it a twist; juxtapose elements that don't easily sit together; and place the most emphatic word or phrase at the end of a sentence, or, better yet, of a paragraph.*

I love names that begin with the letter Q, and this chapter includes two of them. Let me reintroduce to you the British man of letters Sir Arthur Quiller-Couch and his forebear, Roman rhetorician Marcus Fabius Quintilianus, better known as

Quintilian. Sir Arthur often used *Q* as a pen name. I now refer to the Roman dude as the Q-man.

Q and the Q-man.

In the first chapter we noted that it has been more than a hundred years since Quiller-Couch delivered a series of lectures to his students at Cambridge University in England, talks that have been anthologized in the book *On the Art of Writing*. The book you hold, *Murder Your Darlings*, is titled after the most famous bit of Quiller-Couch advice. Inspired by Samuel Johnson, Q encourages writers to cut from a draft those darling phrases that seem the most self-consciously elegant. In other words: stop showing off.

In one lecture, Q encourages his students, saying that with a couple of powerful tools "you can go a long way." One such tool is emphatic word order, and to describe it Quiller-Couch invokes Quintilian, who wrote this (in Latin, of course) before his death around the year 100 C.E.:

> There is sometimes an extraordinary force in some particular word, which, if it be placed in no very conspicuous position in the middle part of a sentence, is likely to escape the attention of the hearer and to be obscured by the words surrounding it; but if it be put at the end of the sentence is urged upon the reader's sense and imprinted on his mind.

To illustrate this advice, Quiller-Couch offers his students an example of the Roman's Q-tip, arguing that "The wages of sin is Death" is more powerful than "Death is the wages of sin."

This strategy differs from the "arrangement of words" described earlier in the work of George Campbell. The great Scot was more interested in the beneficial arrangement of clauses within long complex sentences and the purposes best fulfilled by certain types of sentence structures.

The Q-men (Quintilian by way of Quiller-Couch) offer a more practical rhetorical move, one that can be used in any sentence for any genre. When I teach this strategy, I use a line from a speech by Michelle Obama, who reminded a convention of Democrats: "I live in a house that was built by slaves." The White House. Not "Slaves built the house I live in." While both sentences are grammatically correct, her version is much more rhetorically powerful. Thank you, Michelle Obama, and thank you, Quintilian. If you practiced the craft of vaudeville, you were called a vaudevillian. If I practice the craft of Quintilian, am I now a Quintilian-ian? I certainly hope so.

I once mourned the shift of the word *rhetoric* from something powerful and purposeful toward something pejorative: fancy but empty discourse. I wished for a resurgence in rhetoric, the classical understanding of how the best speakers and writers communicate and persuade. Quintilian could be our patron.

On his behalf, I am about to do you a favor. Rather than send you to Quintilian's most significant body of work, the *Institutio Oratoria*, I will offer you highlights from a translation edited by James J. Murphy. Here are Quintilian's greatest hits, the ideas and strategies that make him as relevant now as he was in the days of the Roman Republic. You won't want to murder any of these darlings:

1. Let a text cool off before revision. In a letter to Trypho, an eminent bookseller in Rome, the Q-man writes that he prefers not to rush his works into print: "I allowed time for reconsidering them, in order that, when the ardor of invention had cooled, I might judge of them, on a more careful reperusal, as a mere reader." I've heard the same advice from many writers, that even under deadline pressure they need to get away from the text so that it can cool off. The cooler the text, the more clear-eyed the revision.

2. Connect reading, writing, and speaking. Quintilian started a school to train the leading citizens of Rome and is as well known for his theories on education as he is for rhetoric. For example, "Not only is the art of writing combined with that of speaking, but correct reading also precedes illustration, and with all these is joined the exercise of judgment." Stanford scholar Shirley Brice Heath once asked me to describe the behaviors of the most literate Americans. I was stumped. She said, "They read, they write, and they know how to speak about reading and writing." It follows that students must practice these behaviors every day, acts of literacy that will lead to good judgment.

3. Study writers of all kinds. Quintilian argues, "Nor is it sufficient to have read the poets only; every class of writers must be studied, not simply for matter, but for words, which often receive their authority from writers." Two millennia later, the British author David Lodge would put it this way: "That is why a novelist...must have a very keen ear for other people's words...and why he cannot afford to cut himself off from the low, vulgar, debased language; why nothing linguistic is alien to him, from theological treatises to backs of cornflakes packets."

4. Gain knowledge from all fields of study. "Nor can grammar be complete without a knowledge of music," writes Quintilian, "since the grammarian has to speak of meter and rhythm." He goes on to make a case for knowledge of astronomy and philosophy as well, thinking of grammar, not in a narrow sense, but as the strategic use of language in all disciplines.

5. Strive for a reliable voice. "By speakers, as well as writers, there are certain rules to be observed. Language is based on reason, antiquity, authority and custom....Custom, however, is the surest preceptor in speaking: we must use phraseology, like money, which has the public stamp." It seems that Quintilian anticipates a kind of reconciliation between prescriptive and descriptive forms of grammar and usage. There are rules to follow, but it turns out to be common usage that lends the ring of truth. We think of Latin as a dead language, but for Quintilian it was very much alive, enriched by new words, influenced by travel, conquest, technology, all aspects of Roman imperial culture. George Orwell made a similar argument during World War II: that efforts to rally the English people to make sacrifices for the war effort should be made in the language of common Brits (he called it "demotic" speech), and not dressed in the finery and education of the upper classes and BBC.

6. Over-the-top is better than under-the-bottom. Writing by students should not be "dry and insipid," nor should it be "wantonly adorned with far-fetched descriptions." In other words, good writing is neither underwritten nor overwritten. But here is the key for Quintilian: "Both these kinds of narratives are faulty, yet that which springs from poverty of mind is worse than that which comes from exuberance." I take him to mean that it is easier to tone down the exuberance of the young overwriter than to light a fire under those who lack creativity and imagination.

7. Work toward being a fluent writer. "The sum of the whole matter, indeed, is this: that by writing quickly we are not brought to write well, but that by writing well we are brought to write quickly." Do I see here the use of a linguistic inversion known as a *chiasmus,* one of my favorite rhetorical moves, as in "It's not the dog in the fight that matters but the fight in the dog"? Or, more craftily: "I'd rather have a bottle in front of me than a frontal lobotomy."

8. Use your craft for the common good. The sharpest arrow in Quintilian's quiver is the notion that rhetoric requires the merger of craft and character, of method and purpose: the good citizen equipped to serve others with the power of the spoken and written word. This should be the idea that inspires all public writers most of all. It is an idea that should be at the heart of civic education, even from childhood. "Care is to be taken, above all things," wrote Quintilian, "that tender minds...may learn not only what is eloquent, but, still more, what is morally good."

LESSONS

1. Too often in modern discourse, the word *rhetoric* carries a negative connotation, signified by the accompanying adjective *empty*. Words to fool the audience. Embrace instead the original meaning of *rhetoric*, a discipline of language attached to education, literacy, and public life.

2. On deadline you may have to hand in a text right after drafting. The longer you can let the writing cool off, the more you can return to it with the eyes of the average reader. This works even if you have a cooling period of only a few minutes.

3. Don't hide your best words or phrases in the middle of a sentence or paragraph. Move them to the beginning or, better yet, the end. The reader will see them; the audience will hear them with more emphasis.

4. The word *grammar* has many confusing meanings. There is "prescriptive" grammar, which seeks to direct us toward proper usage; there is "descriptive" grammar, which tries to understand how people actually use the language. Quintilian gives us "rhetorical grammar," the tool of language that creates meaning with a purpose, whose strategies can be learned over a lifetime.

24

Influence the emotional responses of your audience. Drive readers and viewers to the conflicting emotions of pity and fear.

Poetics
By Aristotle (translated by Gerald F. Else)

Aristotle's Poetics for Screenwriters: Storytelling Secrets from the Greatest Mind in Western Civilization
By Michael Tierno

Toolbox: *If you have ever sat in a dark movie house with tears in your eyes, you have experienced a feeling that Aristotle describes as catharsis. Yes, people have been crying in theaters for more than 3,000 years. Where do those tears come from? Aristotle argues that a catharsis is the purging of emotions— a physiological venting of pity and fear. It's easy enough for a writer to bring tears to your eyes. Just allow a child to go missing, or instead, to be reunited with her mother. Tragedy requires more. At the beginning we must move closer to the character, admiring his virtues, hoping he survives and triumphs. When terrible things happen to that character, we can pity him. But* *we must also realize that the forces that threaten the hero threaten all of us. There is fear in our tears.*

The subtitle of *Murder Your Darlings* is "And other gentle writing advice from Aristotle to Zinsser." We honored the Z-man in an early chapter, so to keep a promise, it's time to find our way back to the A-man, the alpha dog of ancient civilization, the philosopher who built an intellectual foundation for just about everything, including literary criticism.

This book is about writing, not ontology or metaphysics, so I confess to being ill-equipped to summarize the ways Aristotle differs from his famous mentor, Plato. Except for this: Plato did not care much for poets. He is specific about his aversions in *The Republic,* his work on creating an ideal polis, a well-functioning and well-led civic society. While he would elevate the philosophers to positions of leadership (as Ronald McDonald would be inclined to elevate the clowns), Plato thought of exiling the poets, or at least minimizing their influence. The poets were purveyors of what ideological critics of the press would call "fake news." In Plato's eyes, they were double fakers. They created in words not the real world, but copies or imitations of it. And the things they copied did not even have to exist, like the Minotaur, or mischievous gods, or the Cyclopes, a race of giants each with one eye in the middle of their forehead, as featured in *The Odyssey.*

But even if the poets were writing a poem about a Grecian urn, that urn, the one you could hold in your hand or spit into, was not really real. It was a copy of the essential urn that existed in some higher sphere, the world of "urn-ness." In other words, the poets were making copies of copies. (Philosophy majors may lodge their complaints or correct my description at rclark@poynter.org.)

Here is Robin Waterfield, who translated and commented on *The Republic*:

> What Plato has to say about poetry is mostly transparent, although his *reasons* for saying it are not. But the most important suggestion I can make to a reader at this point is to try to avoid the natural tendency to mitigate Plato's words. When he claims that representational poetry can deform minds…, he means it; when he says that avoiding such poetry is critical if one wants to be a good person…, he means that too.

And this:

> Why this hostility to poetry? Why is it the enemy? Because the poets were the educators of Greece…. They were used as such in the schools and played a central role in a Greek's general cultural conditioning. The poets (even the comic poets) thought of themselves as teachers, and their audience took them to be teachers.

Enter our man Aristotle. He rebels from Plato's negativity and applies his own philosophical analysis to all aspects of language use: from rhetoric, to poetry, to satire, and, for my purposes here, to Greek tragedy. You can discover a long list of useful thoughts about language from reading Aristotle, but I want to focus on one literary effect that has retained its power and utility. It explains why a scene in a tragedy might move someone in the audience to tears.

Literary critics of the twentieth century accelerated interest in the audience, the receivers of texts. I do not know enough to declare that Aristotle invented reader-response criticism, but he gave it a giant push by trying to answer the question as to why audiences react the way they do to dramatic tragedy. Dreadful things happen in tragedy, which by classic definition ends with the death of the tragic hero, a great but flawed character whose suffering has a deep meaning, revealing the darker corners of human existence. Sitting in the Globe Theatre in Shakespeare's London offers the audience a vicarious experience, a virtual reality. Members of the audience weep at the suffering of those star-crossed lovers Romeo and Juliet, or they gasp at the death of King Lear, and sit forlornly at the death of his one true, loving daughter, Cordelia. (When we saw *Hamilton,* the audience wept bitterly through the second act as Eliza Hamilton mourned the deaths of her son and her husband, both killed in duels.)

Aristotle predated Shakespeare by more than a millennium. But he was blessed with the likes of Aeschylus, Euripides, Aristophanes, and Sophocles, who gave Aristotle (and eventually Freud) the play *Oedipus the King* to ponder. Using Oedipus as a critical case study, Aristotle analyzes the accidental meeting and killing of Oedipus's father at a crossroads, along with the shocking realization that Oedipus's wife, Jocasta, is also his mother. In short, without realizing it, the hero kills his father and marries his mother. What must the audience have felt when

Oedipus returns to the stage, having blinded himself when he "sees" what he has done? The common critic—like me—would notice the play is all about blindness and seeing—with the character of Tiresias, the oxymoronic blind seer, revealing to King O the consequences of his crimes.

When the audience "sees" and is moved by these events, they undergo an experience Aristotle describes as catharsis, a Greek word that survives to our day. He defines *catharsis* as the purging of the emotions of pity and fear. These emotions exist in some contradiction, or at least tension. Pity drives us closer to the protagonist. His or her suffering becomes ours. We might do something to ameliorate the suffering if we could. We imagine what we would feel if the suffering happened to us. (We want the best for Alexander Hamilton, admire him, and root for him.)

Enter fear. If pity draws us to the protagonist, fear drives us away. The fates, or destiny, or the gods have created the circumstances for the hero's suffering and death. If it could happen to Oedipus or Antigone, it could happen to us. We worry that we are nothing but props in the hands of angry gods. The character Gloucester, who has his eyes plucked out for his loyalty to King Lear, says it best, a powerful insight from his blindness: "As flies to wanton boys are we to th' gods; / They kill us for their sport." In summary: To create pity, draw the audience closer to the character; to create fear, drive the audience away.

Greek scholar Richard Janko writes about catharsis as an experience of physiology, psychology, and moral education:

The purpose of the catharsis of pity and fear...is not to drain our emotional capacities so that we are no longer able to feel

224

these emotions; instead it is to predispose us to feel emotion in the right way, at the right time, towards the right object, with the right motive, and to the proper degree....

How, then, does the cathartic process operate? By representing pitiful and fearful events artistically, it arouses pity and fear in the members of the audience, each according to his own emotional capacity, and by a homoeopathic process so stimulates these emotions as to relieve them by giving them moderate and harmless exercise; and with relief comes pleasure.

To create the transaction that results in catharsis, the author or playwright must characterize the protagonist in a way that attracts us, as in Cordelia's steadfast loyalty to her father in light of the dreadful treachery of both her sisters. We want to embrace or support Cordelia in her determination to stay with King Lear to the bitter end—unto death. Their mutual suffering and their death upon death was experienced as so excruciating for the audience, so unbearable, that a seventeeth-century playwright, Nahum Tate, reworked the play to give it a happy ending.

Death may be the final word in tragedy, but it has an antidote. We get to walk out of the theater. The hero is dead, but we are very much alive, "seeing" human experience in a more complex and dramatic way.

In the book *Aristotle's* Poetics *for Screenwriters,* veteran filmmaker Michael Tierno simplifies—perhaps oversimplifies—Aristotle (as do I) for the working writer. For our purposes, his best chapter title is: "A Movie Gave You a Bad Case of Pity and Fear? The Doctor Recommends a Catharsis."

Here is Tierno's description of catharsis as it applies to the moviegoer:

> In the final moments of a movie, the audience experiences the moment that allows them to purge themselves of pity and fear built up through the plot structure. Through this "catharsis," the audience releases not just the emotions the movie has stirred up in them, but they also dump other psychic garbage they've been carrying around. Catharsis leaves the audience with a renewed sense of mental clarity and better able to function in life. According to Aristotle, catharsis works best if *everything* in the story builds toward creating this one experience. The key is to understand that catharsis doesn't just "happen" in the final moments of a movie; it builds throughout the story up until the final *release*.

Now comes the fun part, and perhaps an opportunity for practical debate:

> One of the most cathartic movies ever made is *Titanic*, if the scores of young girls who watched it at least ten times and wept each time is any indication. [No need to be sexist about it, Mike; I tried not to, but I cried, too.]
>
> …Jack not only dies to save Rose, but suffers intensely in doing so. The combination of physical suffering and emotional suffering helps intensify the emotions of the audience, who, feeling the tragedy in their very bones, are swept away. This intense physical suffering allows the audience to experience a deeper catharsis when it comes.

It comes when the much older Rose finally lies down in her cabin bed and dies, joining Jack in heaven. *This* is where the audience releases their burden of pity and fear and finally experiences catharsis.

I agree with this take, but it raises a centuries-long debate about tragedy. You may remember that Hamlet has this crucial moment of indecision when he can kill his treacherous uncle and avenge his father's murder. Why does he hesitate? Because the usurper king is on his knees in prayer. Hamlet does not want to accidentally send him to heaven. He prefers a hellish destination. A universe that imagines an afterlife in which sinners can be forgiven undermines the effects of tragedy. Tragedy is better experienced when an earthly death leads not to paradise, or even hell, but extinction.

The deaths in *Titanic* are nothing like these, but there can be no doubt that the action of the movie builds and builds to a moment of intense catharsis. If Romeo and Juliet were star-crossed, I am willing to describe Jack and Rose as sea-crossed. Cue the singing diva from Canada.

LESSONS

1. Pay more attention to your own emotional reactions to literature. I remember rereading *To Kill a Mockingbird* not long ago, tears coming to my eyes at the final scene. Where was that emotion, which I had not felt in earlier readings, coming from? Such questions as a reader will enrich your sensibilities as a writer.

2. Draw a distinction—in art and life—between the sentimental and the tragic. Both spark an emotional response, but in different ways. We cry at weddings—that's sentimentality. When we cry at funerals—especially when the death is untimely and the result of cruelty and violence—the catharsis is more profound.

3. When Aristotle writes about the purging of emotions of pity and fear, he is describing human reaction to a story—a work of art. In catharsis, the audience experiences a kind of contradiction, that in mourning the suffering of others—characters in stories—we experience a kind of pleasure. This requires that we create for the reader sympathetic characters and then make them suffer so we can feel their humanity.

4. This can be difficult for a writer: If you are writing about someone who is admirable and heroic, humanize this character by identifying a flaw. Or, if you are writing about a morally reprehensible person, can you show a redeeming character trait?

25

Sign a social contract with the reader.
Be transparent about your methods, especially
with memoir and the personal essay.

The Situation and the Story: The Art of Personal Narrative
By Vivian Gornick

The Art of Memoir
By Mary Karr

Toolbox: *What constitutes responsible practice in genres such as the personal essay or the memoir? The answer is wrapped in controversy. Many writers think of these as hybrid genres, real-life stories distorted by the limitations of memory. A strict interpretation holds the memoirist to the same standards as the journalist. There is an implied social contract between the writer and the reader. Yes, memory may be faulty or inadequate, but there is a difference between the failures of memory and intentional fabrications. The best way to reconcile these differences is through the strategic virtue we call transparency. At the beginning of a work— not at the end—let us in on your techniques: Composite characters? Conflated scenes? Invented dialogue? If you don't want your* *reader to know what you're up to, avoid that strategy—or label your work fiction.*

I once wrote a personal essay that appeared in the *St. Petersburg Times* about an archnemesis from my boyhood. I will call him Bobby. That's kind of a joke, because his name was actually Bobby. He was a neighborhood kid who, when we were about eight years old, hit me in the face with a rock. It was probably the only time he ever hit his target. He hit me just below the right eye. I felt an unknown sensation, blistering pain and then dripping blood, and I am sure I ran up the hill to our house crying, OK, screaming.

Revenge is a dish best served cold, and it was a cold snowy night about six years later. We were both Boy Scouts, and after a meeting at Searing Memorial Church—where Bobby had punched me in the back for no reason at all—the kids stopped at the top of Shafter Avenue, across the street from an old cemetery. The markers went back to the Civil War. A friendly snowball fight ensued, and, in my essay, I described how, out of nowhere, Bobby's hobgoblin head came into view, and, against the backdrop of the necropolis, I flung a snowball that flew like an icy comet and exploded against his cheekbone with a sound like a tire iron smashing a pumpkin. He screamed at the impact and went galumphing home.

Certain personal narratives—like mine above—broadcast their hyperbole. That said, when I wrote the essay, I believed the essential elements were true. I got hit with a rock. I was in the Boy Scouts (Troop 177). It was in that church. Next to the church was an old cemetery. The markers did go back to the 1800s. I nailed him with a fully packed snowball upside the head. And he ran home, as I watched, triumphant.

Except for this: Years later I returned to the Long Island village where this happened, walked to the spot where the snowball fight took place, and, to my dismay, noticed that, while the church steeple rose above the corner, you could not see any of the grave markers in the cemetery. Do not believe that I lost any sleep from this slightly fictionalized tilting of the earth to make the event more Mephistophelian. But I did ask myself this question: "Roy, if you had known beforehand, say from a photograph, that the geometry of the streetscape was skewed, would you have included the cemetery anyway?" My answer: maybe.

Now let me ask you, my readers, this question? What if I were thinking, *For the sake of the story, it would be so cool to put a cemetery next to the church,* even if a playground is there instead? The problem of finding the line between fiction and nonfiction is ancient, and persistent. Even with the passage of centuries, even with the adoption of literary standards and practices, there are authors who cannot resist the temptation to "pipe" the story. That old newspaper word derives from writers covering police raids on opium dens. The reporter, inhaling the smoke—went the gag—would hallucinate the story onto the page.

Does it matter whether elements in your story are literally true or are the product of creative license? It depends on whether you are consulting a strict or loose constructionist in the enduring battle over the standards regarding genres we call "the personal essay," "the memoir," and "creative nonfiction."

There are books aplenty on the topic, and I have selected two of them by two outstanding practitioners of personal writing and storytelling.

One, Vivian Gornick, wrote *The Situation and the Story;* Mary Karr has given us *The Art of Memoir.* In spite of their philosophical differences about whether the memoir is a non-fiction genre or, perhaps, a hybrid, both authors offer aspiring memoirists practical and worthy advice.

I love useful distinctions, and here, from Gornick, is a beauty:

Every work of literature has both a situation and a story. The situation is the context or circumstance, sometimes the plot; the story is the emotional experience that preoccupies the writer: the insight, the wisdom, the thing one has come to say.

She offers these examples:

In *An American Tragedy* the situation is Dreiser's America; the story is the pathological nature of hunger for the world. In Edmund Gosse's memoir *Father and Son* the situation is fundamentalist England in the time of Darwin; the story is the betrayal of intimacy necessary to the act of becoming oneself. In a poem called "In the Waiting Room" Elizabeth Bishop describes herself at the age of seven, during the First World War, sitting in a dentist's office, turning the pages of *National Geographic,* listening to the muted cries of pain her timid aunt utters from within. That's the situation. The story is a child's first experience of isolation; her own, her aunt's, and that of the world.

If I had had the benefit of this distinction—situation and story—I would have done a better job of reporting and writing my twenty-nine-part serial narrative "Three Little Words." The situation was the spread of AIDS across the globe in the early 1990s and the fear and stigma attached to the disease. The story was of a well-respected educator, Mick Morse, the married father of three children, who was dying of AIDS and denying his identity as a closeted gay man.

Here is more from Gornick:

> The subject of autobiography is always self-definition, but it cannot be self-definition in the void. The memoirist, like the poet and the novelist, must engage with the world, because engagement makes experience, experience makes wisdom, and finally it's the wisdom—or rather the movement toward it—that counts.

She quotes a nameless gifted writing teacher: "Good writing has two characteristics. It's alive on the page and the reader is persuaded that the writer is on a voyage of discovery." Gornick adds:

> The poet, the novelist, the memoirist—all must convince the reader they have some wisdom, and are writing as honestly as possible to arrive at what they know. To the bargain, the writer of personal narrative must also persuade the

reader that the narrator is reliable. In fiction a narrator may be—and often famously is—unreliable....In nonfiction, never. In nonfiction the reader must believe that the narrator is speaking truth. Invariably, of nonfiction it is asked, "Is this narrator trustworthy? Can I believe what he or she is telling me?"

It is at this point that the argument gets tricky, as it depends upon how you understand the reader. Is the reader "willfully ignorant," as one author argues, or a skeptic, always attuned to the false note, sniffing for fabrication in what is purported to be "the way it was"?

The debate on the nature of nonfiction narrative played out in a dramatic way one summer at Goucher College in Towson, Maryland, outside Baltimore. Goucher is a school that offers an MFA with an emphasis on narrative nonfiction. Some of the best authors and teachers of the craft in America have visited the program, either as instructors or tutors. Gornick was one of those visitors. (Full disclosure: On August 7, 2011—on my fortieth wedding anniversary—I received an honorary degree from Goucher and gave the summer commencement speech.)

I was not there the summer of Gornick's visit, but my best friend was: Tom French, who won a Pulitzer Prize in Feature Writing in 1998. So was Walt Harrington, a veteran of immersive reporting and narrative writing with years at the *Washington Post*, now an influential writing teacher at the University of Illinois.

A kerfuffle erupted after Gornick read from her memoir, which presented conversations with her mother, encounters,

Gornick admitted, that characterized honestly her relationship with her mom but that had never actually occurred in the way they were presented. (I have not met or interviewed Gornick but have talked to witnesses and read her comments about the ensuing debate.) Like many defenders of the "fourth genre," Gornick sees memoir as an act of the imagination. Based on memory (which has its own fictionalizing effects), memoir, it is said, represents not literal truth but a higher truth—reality as it is experienced, not as it is documented.

Over time, as news of the debate got out, the antagonists seemed to harden their stances. The loose constructionists surrounded Gornick with support, and the hard-liners began to draw harder lines, declaring more demanding standards and practices.

In 2006 the controversy was dramatized and became national on one of the most famous episodes of *The Oprah Winfrey Show*. For her influential book club, she had chosen *A Million Little Pieces*, a memoir of alcoholism and dissolution, by author James Frey. Originally imagined as a novel, the bestseller was published as nonfiction. It had been based upon Frey's personal experiences, but investigative reports revealed that key scenes had been either fabricated or exaggerated. Several authors, including this reporter, wrote columns criticizing Winfrey's continued support for the book. Three of us were invited to her show to air our concerns. What we did not realize is that Winfrey would disavow Frey and cross-examine him in front of a national audience until the opening cheers for him eventually turned to boos.

I argued, with others, that an implied social contract exists between the reader and an author of nonfiction and that the contract reads, "Please believe me, my memory of events may be flawed, but none of this was intentionally made up." If the author decides to veer from this standard, say, by using composite characters, the author must be transparent, revealing the strategies *before* the story begins, not in a footnote at the end.

I found the best articulation of this approach in *The Art of Memoir* by Mary Karr (2015). Her authority on the subject derives from her experience as writer and teacher. She is a poet, an essayist, and an author of three prizewinning memoirs, notably *The Liars' Club*, about her tough childhood in East Texas, which the *New York Times* praised as "Astonishing...one of the most dazzling and moving memoirs to come along in years."

When it comes to the contract between reader and writer, she begins: "When I think of all the stiff pronouncements I've made demanding truth in memoir over the years, I'm inclined to hang my head. I sound like such a pious twit, the village vicar wagging her finger at writers pushing the limits of the form. Forgive me, I am not the art police."

She continues:

No writer can impose his own standards onto any other, nor claim to speak for the whole genre. I would defend anybody's right to move the line for veracity in memoir, though I'd argue the reader has a right to know. But my own humble practices wholly oppose making stuff up.

Karr finds her antagonist in none other than Vivian Gornick, who was interviewed by *The Believer* magazine:

I embellish stories all the time. I do it even when I'm supposedly telling the unvarnished truth. Things happen, and I realize that what actually happens is only partly a story, and I have to make the story. So I lie. I mean, essentially—others would think I'm lying. But you understand. It's irresistible to tell the story. And I don't owe anybody the actuality. What is the actuality? I mean, whose business is it?

Mary Karr's riposte remains my favorite statement on the subject:

Well, if I forked over a cover price for nonfiction, I consider it my business. While it's great she owned up to her deceits, it's hard to lend credence to any after-the-fact confession, especially one as vague or self-justifying as this one. It's as if after lunch the deli guy quipped, "I put just a teaspoon of catshit in your sandwich, but you didn't notice it at all." To my mind, a small bit of catshit equals a catshit sandwich, unless I know where the catshit is and can eat around it.

(You can see from the bold humor in her style why Mary Karr is one of my favorite writers on Twitter.) If I could find any summarizing piece of that thought that would fit on my tombstone, I'd be tempted to ask Karr's permission. Though I side with Karr on this topic, in no way does this disqualify the sharp and helpful distinction made by Gornick in *The Situation and the Story*.

LESSONS

1. Treat the personal essay and the memoir as nonfiction forms. Accept that your memory is not perfect but also that you should not intentionally add things to your story that did not happen in real life.

2. Respect the implied contract that exists between writer and reader when it comes to nonfiction. Be transparent. Whatever your standards, disclose them at the beginning of the work.

3. If you use in memoir strategies associated with fiction—composite characters, invented dialogue, conflated scenes—use an author's note to let the reader in on them.

4. The limitations and distortions of memory should not give you license to "make stuff up." Use historical records, old newspaper clippings, and photo albums to test your memory. You will find details that enrich both the story and what Gornick defines as "the situation."

26

———✦———

Write to the level of your reader—and a little higher. Learn the tricks that make a text easy to read or, if you prefer, hard.

The Art of Readable Writing
By Rudolf Flesch

How to Take the Fog Out of Writing
By Robert Gunning

Toolbox: *Since the 1940s, certain writers and teachers have tried to make prose more comprehensible to readers at different educational levels. I might write differently for a kindergarten class than I would for a law school seminar. That said, some great prose— Charlotte's Web comes to mind—can be read with pleasure and insight by readers who are eight years old or eighty. The algorithm of comprehensibility is not difficult to learn and requires no calculator. Shorter words and shorter sentences slow down the pace of information in a good way. Each period is a stop sign. While useful to some with technical knowledge, jargon—niche language used by experts—and long words delivered in long sentences and paragraphs clot the flow of meaning for a general audience.*

I remember teaching my first composition classes in 1972, when I stumbled upon a collection of essays titled *Speaking of Rhetoric*. When you keep a book nearby for forty-five years of writing and teaching; when you mark up its pages with underscores, stars, and checkmarks; when you decide *never* to loan it out, even to a trusted friend: then you can declare to the world that you have discovered a book that is truly useful.

In fewer than two hundred pages, we get more than twenty essays on various categories of language and rhetoric, written by authors as influential and popular as Mark Twain, James Thurber, Malcolm Cowley, John Kenneth Galbraith, and H. L. Mencken. It was in this volume that I first read Orwell's "Politics and the English Language." Sadly, only one featured writer is a woman (not a surprise in a 1966 book). Marchette Chute, an American author, was a distinguished biographer of English literary figures. Her essay, "Getting at the Truth," is a doozy, as timely on the issues of nonfiction evidence as Orwell is on language abuse in politics.

E. B. White is represented in two essays. Relevant here is the one titled "Calculating Machine." It takes a hard crack at an author, editor, and teacher named Rudolf Flesch, a man both loved and reviled because of his beliefs that texts should be comprehensible and that certain tests could measure their readability. White was clearly on the side of most writers when he dismissed the work of Flesch and his fellow travelers with this quotable sentence: "It is our belief that no writer can improve his work until he discards the dulcet notion that the reader is feeble-minded, for writing is an act of faith, not a trick of grammar."

White's understanding of Flesch is that: "[He contends] that the 'average reader' is capable of reading only what tests Easy, and that the writer should write at or below this level. This is a presumptuous and degrading idea. There is no average reader, and to reach down toward this mythical character is to deny that each of us is on the way up, is ascending."

In short: Don't write down to the reader, write up. E. B. White is a literary hero to generations of writers. The rhetoric in his dismissal of Flesch is persuasive, but it also calculates as somewhere between unfair and wrong.

For as long as I can remember, there have been ambitious efforts to make American prose more comprehensible. They have come from journalism organizations such as the Associated Press, from pockets of legal education, from citizen groups and consumers who think contracts or terms of service should be easier to grasp. There is a tug of war in the academy, down to the high-school level, on the function of literacy education. Should students be taught to write in a more theoretical way—in literary criticism, for example—or would they be better off to learn to lay it out straight in businesses, crafts, and professions?

A hilarious example of this effort to make texts easier to understand came from a group of public writers devoted to civic clarity. It was more than a group. It was a squad. And it had ground rules. For example, if members communicated with one another in writing, they were required to use words of only one syllable. This stricture helped them avoid polysyllabic gobbledygook and esoteric jargon—like the kind I just used. When the *Wall Street Journal* got their nose on that news, they knew it was worth coverage, earning a spot on the creative middle of the paper's front page.

I have misplaced my copy of the story but remember this: The entire column was written in words of one syllable. Let's just say it was a tour de force. To accomplish this the writers had to make some accommodations:

- The word "syllable" was replaced by "pulse."
- Editors had to change the first name of the writer of the column from Joseph to "Joe."
- His byline described him not as "staff writer" but as "staff scribe."

I remember that in the last paragraph, it was as if the writer could not contain his word hoard any more, leading to a climax of polysyllables.

While countless teachers and editors have espoused clear writing, some champions stand above the crowd. In our decade it is Bryan Garner. His books define what good writing looks like when it comes to the law, a body of work expanded upon in writing workshops for wigged-out pettifoggers. But in my mind, Garner stands on the shoulders of trailblazers. The two most prominent are Rudolf Flesch and Robert Gunning. Each wrote practical guidebooks; each consulted with businesses, schools, and government agencies. And each created a gadget, a device, a rubric, may I say an algorithm, to measure the readability of a text—work, we have seen, dismissed by the likes of E. B. White as a "calculating machine." Flesch's "Readability

Formula" became widely known as the Flesch Test, while Gunning became influential with his Fog Index.

Rudolf Flesch migrated with his family from Austria in 1938, just in time to escape the ravages of Nazi Germany. As part of his doctoral dissertation at Columbia University, Flesch developed his theories and practices around the issues of language use and reading comprehension. By 1946 he had turned his ideas on reading and writing into a first book, *The Art of Plain Talk,* followed in 1949 by *The Art of Readable Writing.* He spent the rest of his life teaching people (and organizations) how to write with a particular audience in mind. By the time he had written the influential book *Why Johnny Can't Read—and What You Can Do about It,* he was serving as a readability consultant to the Associated Press and to various publishers, government agencies, educational organizations, and corporations.

Having done that kind of consulting myself, I remember a welcome I received from an administrator in a government agency. She showed me her business card, which listed her name, followed by a twenty-seven-word title. "Welcome, Dr. Clark, to the place where language goes to die." Wow, I thought, that's a really good sentence. This person has what it takes to lead her staff toward clear and interesting writing.

So how did Dr. Flesch measure readability?

His grading rubric had seven degrees of reading ease, each tied to educational grade levels:

Very Easy—4th grade
Easy—5th grade

Fairly Easy—6th grade
Standard—7th or 8th grade
Fairly Difficult—some high school
Difficult—high school or some college
Very Difficult—college

He would begin his calculation by taking a sample text. He would then measure:

1. Average sentence length.
2. Average number of syllables per 100 words.

A Very Easy text, for example, would average 8 words or fewer per sentence. It would have an average of 123 syllables for every 100 words.

For a Very Difficult text, the reader would encounter sentences averaging 30 or more words, with more than 200 syllables for 100 words.

A sentence of 8 words is pretty short. (That last sentence has 8 words.) A sentence of 30 words starts to feel long, testing the reader's ability to comprehend it as rolling phrases of information begin to pile up toward the period. (29 words there.)

When it comes to syllable count: Flesch's numbers make the case that a text filled with one-syllable words is easier to read than one filled with two- or three-syllable words. There are asterisks here galore. Logic and experience teach us that some short sentences might be hard to comprehend ("The eater craves existence"); while some short words may be difficult:

angst, sprag, or *zouk.* Flesch and his colleagues tinkered with the test over the years, trying to account for additional variables in texts that make them harder or easier to read. He tried to counter arguments against his idea that you could (or should) equate the ability to read certain texts with educational grade level.

The Flesch tool may have been misused over the years, to the discouragement of some writers whose work was judged too difficult for their readers. That is unfortunate because I now believe that Flesch's theory is true. Sentence length and syllable count are key factors in influencing the readability of a text.

As evidence, I would like to test two short texts that appear in my book *Writing Tools.* The first is a single sentence from a newspaper editorial titled "Curb State Mandates."

To avert the all too common enactment of requirements without regard for their local cost and tax impact, however, the commission recommends that statewide interest should be clearly identified on any proposed mandates, and that the state should partially reimburse local government for some state imposed mandates and fully for those involving employee compensation, working conditions and pensions.

That single sentence contains 59 words. It also contains 102 syllables. Extrapolated to 100 words (using my calculating machine) would require 173 syllables. By both measures, we have a Flesch calculation of Very Difficult.

But wait, you say, I did not need your stinkin' measurements to tell me this editorial was Very Difficult to read. I could tell by trying to read it! Then why didn't the writer make it easier for you? And what would that look like if he did?

Here is my "translation":

> The State of New York often passes laws telling local governments what to do. These laws have a name. They are called "state mandates." On many occasions, these laws improve life for everyone in the state. But they come with a cost. Too often, the state doesn't consider the cost to local government, or how much money taxpayers will have to shell out. So we have an idea. The state should pay back local governments for some of these so-called mandates.

Okay, Dr. Flesch, here we go again. This passage contains 8 sentences and 81 words, an average of 10 words per sentence. It contains 110 syllables. At that rate, 100 words would generate 136 syllables. By connecting words per sentence with syllables per 100 words, I learn I have created a text that is "Very Easy" to read. I must add that "Very Easy" is rarely my goal as a writer. But certain civic purposes are best achieved by clarity and plainness.

While I have never before submitted my texts to Flesch's measurements, I have translated the concept in my writing and teaching, guided by the mantra of Donald Murray, who advised writers to use "Shorter words, shorter sentences, shorter paragraphs at the points of greatest complexity." I advise students, for example, to use sentences such as "Here's how it works" to introduce explanations that might be hard to grasp.

In spite of four decades of study and writing on a wide diversity of issues, Flesch's reputation and legacy are built on his comprehensibility algorithms. It happens. The great baseball player Roger Maris is known for hitting 61 home runs in 1961, beating the record of Babe Ruth, and not for wonderful seasons of all-around play.

In the same way, the creator of the Flesch test (a more recent version of which is the Flesch-Kincaid Grade-Level metric) turns out to be quite fond of long sentences, and displays passages from Joseph Conrad and Alexander Hamilton to reveal their flowing strength and beauty. To my surprise, he leaned a bit more toward the descriptive side on issues of grammar and usage. He begins a delightful chapter, "Did Shakespeare Make Mistakes in English?" with this quote from W. Somerset Maugham: "It is well to remember that grammar is common speech formulated. Usage is the only test. I would prefer a phrase that was easy and unaffected to a phrase that was grammatical."

Flesch writes: "There's hardly a rule in English usage that holds good in all possible situations; in fact, wherever there is a choice, the mechanical application of a rule-of-thumb will be more often bad than good."

He is transparent about his goals as a scholar and an author:

I am sure you realize by now that this book is not dealing with what usually goes by the names of grammar, usage, composition, or rhetoric. On the contrary. If you want to learn how to write, you need exact information about what kind of language will fit what kind of audience. And scientific data about the psychological effects of different styles.

And handy, usable facts and figures about common types of words, sentences, and paragraphs. And knowledge of the results achieved by various writing techniques. In short, you need a modern scientific rhetoric that you can apply to your own writing.

(Copyeditor Kathryn Rogers informs me that by running a spelling and grammar check on Microsoft Word, writers can check a document's readability stats. It's right there, in the Flesch.)

THE FOG INDEX

I have noted that one of the best independent bookstores in America is Haslam's, and it happens to be on Central Avenue in my hometown of St. Petersburg, Florida. I tend to visit the writing section to see how my own books are doing. Along the way, on countless occasions, my eyes caught sight of an old and odd-looking book. So for $4.95 I purchased a modest work of 46 pages with the title *How to Take the Fog Out of Writing*. The author was a man named Robert Gunning, who, out of the delightfully named Blacklick, Ohio, revised the work of Rudolf Flesch, and monetized it into something called the Fog Index.

He is a clear-writing warrior who argues that in spite of the rise of industrial America during the 1950s and '60s, the lack of clear communication was costing businesses a fortune. Each page of this slim volume contains advice worth putting into practice. He is especially good at taking dense, jargon-filled writing from reports and letters and translating it into clear prose.

He begins with his "Ten Principles of Clear Writing," and because this text is so difficult to find, I am listing all of them:

1. Keep Sentences Short.
2. Prefer the Simple to the Complex.
3. Develop Your Vocabulary.
4. Avoid Unneeded Words.
5. Put Action into Your Verbs.
6. Use Terms Your Reader Can Picture.
7. Tie In with Your Reader's Experience.
8. Write the Way You Talk.
9. Make Full Use of Variety.
10. Write to Express, Not to Impress.

In my reading, writing, and teaching, I find myself placing more attention than ever on how the text looks on a page or screen. I have often bragged that I can look at a text written in a language I do not understand—say, Danish—and tell if it is easy or hard to read.

The chief evidence is white space. "Please begin to think of white space as a form of punctuation," I tell my students. If the period is a stop sign for the sentence, white space does the same work for the paragraph. The white space is a visual form of ventilation for the text. It invites the reader in, sending the message that you can glide—rather than struggle—through a report.

Robert Gunning was on the case in 1964:

When a reader picks up the letter or report you have written, part of his energy goes toward recognizing your words. Then he expends even more energy in combining those words to get your ideas and the *relationships* between them.

For an illustration of this, recall how you act as a reader. Suppose two letters come to your desk at the same time. One is a solid block of tightly spaced type. The other is generously broken into paragraphs, and includes indentation, enumeration, and possibly sub-heads. Which will you pick up first?

We always choose the page that is lightened with white space. We do this because we know from long experience that a letter or report so written is better organized. The writer has tried to make the relationship between his ideas clearer. And every step he takes in this direction makes reading easier for us.

Of course, I prefer reading the work of E. B. White to that of Rudolf Flesch and Robert Gunning. Most of White's work is literary, while that of the Clarity Twins is more explanatory. We need both. Stuart Adam, Canada's most influential journalism teacher, once wrote that public writing crosses a spectrum from the civic to the literary. In a community, in a democracy, we desperately need stories and the vicarious experience they afford us. But we also need reports in the public interest to inform us so that we can make the most important and practical choices imposed upon us. Yes, writing is an act of faith and not a trick of grammar. No, we cannot just make information available to the public, even if it is technically accurate. Instead, we must take responsibility for what readers know by delivering hard facts in language they can understand.

LESSONS

1. Write up to your readers, not down. Never underestimate your readers. But learn enough about them so you can serve them well.

2. Word length and sentence length affect comprehension. To make hard facts easy reading, use shorter words, sentences, and paragraphs where the going gets toughest.

3. Remember, a text ventilated by white space will be easier to read.

4. To make texts more comprehensible: Imagine a conversation with a specific reader; slow down the pace of information; translate jargon; lift data out of text into charts and graphs; emphasize the impact.

VI

Mission and Purpose

A number of artistic breakthroughs in the field of cinema were created or advanced by a German filmmaker named Leni Riefenstahl. Alas, her genius was dedicated to the elevation of Hitler's Germany. Art is good. Craft is good. But they will be judged, in the end, by their service to humane, even noble, purposes. When semanticist S. I. Hayakawa came to understand the vicious nature of Nazi propaganda, he was inspired to teach his students how to direct their use of language to the public good.

Another Roman author, Horace, steps into the light with a sense of mission that is both public and aesthetic, arguing that the purpose of great literature is to delight and instruct or, on the good days, to do both!

In a conversation full of insight and humor, Kurt Vonnegut and Lee Stringer explore the relationship between personal and public tragedy and the most powerful forms of writing. Authors, especially those who suffer greatly, can use their pain as fuel, finding redemption in the darkest experiences.

Novelists of passionate purpose often offer visions of the future that are dystopian. Instead of a perfected future, they show us a world poisoned by tyranny and oppression. Orwell imagines such a future in the novel *1984*. Before him Aldous Huxley created his *Brave New World*. Years later, Huxley revisited his dire predictions, including one in which forms of propaganda would lead human beings against their enlightened self-interest. All the more reason for writers to be inspired by their better angels, appealing not to fear and intolerance, but to the greater good.

All good writers should be "in search of light," the title of a collection of radio broadcasts of Edward R. Murrow, arguably the greatest American journalist of the twentieth century. His reports from Europe during the Battle of Britain and the liberation of the Buchenwald concentration camp reveal what is possible when the eyewitness lends testimony on crucial events in a resounding public voice—the marriage of craft to mission and purpose.

Finally, works by Natalie Goldberg and Charles Johnson showcase writers who find their creativity in a rich variety of sources, encouraging all of us to devote our whole selves to the writing enterprise.

27

Learn the strategies that make reports reliable.
Monitor your bias and unload your language.

Language in Thought and Action
By S. I. Hayakawa

Toolbox: *When it comes to communication, reports are the build-ing blocks of democratic life. Self-government and responsible en-terprise depend on the report. A report differs from a story or an essay or a letter to the editor. To understand how best to write a report, consider its opposite: a text that spins or shapes the truth. Subjectivity, partisanship, and bias can never be eliminated from a report, but they can be tamed in the interest of impartiality. There are methods to build reliable reports in every field of endeavor. Pay attention to the connotations as well as to the denotations of words; learn how to unload the language; offer a variety of points of view—not just two; avoid false equivalence. In an era of misinformation, propaganda, and vicious conspiracy theories, we need reports.*

If I had to choose just one book on language that all American college students should read, it would be this one: *Language in*

Action. Written in 1939 and published in 1941, it was expanded after World War II with the title *Language in Thought and Action.* Think of those dates and their historical significance: 1939 and 1941. The author, S. I. Hayakawa, wrote early versions of this language book for his students at the Illinois Institute of Technology, where he was a young faculty member.

In an introduction, he left no doubt that this book was written not just to help students read and write, but for a higher purpose:

> The original version of this book, *Language in Action,* published in 1941, was in many respects a response to the dangers of propaganda, especially as exemplified in Adolf Hitler's success in persuading millions to share his maniacal and destructive views. It was the writer's conviction then, as it remains now, that everyone needs to have a habitually critical attitude towards language—his own as well as that of others—both for the sake of his personal well-being and for his adequate functioning as a citizen. Hitler is gone, but if the majority of our fellow citizens are more susceptible to the slogans of fear and race hatred than to those of peaceful accommodation and mutual respect among human beings, our political liberties remain at the mercy of any eloquent and unscrupulous demagogue.

That statement rings as true in the politics of 2020 as does Orwell's "Politics and the English Language," written in 1946. Aldous Huxley joined the club with a series of essays in the mid-1950s, published as *Brave New World Revisited.* Twenty-five years after publication of his dystopian novel *Brave New World,* Huxley was willing to admit which of his fictional predictions had gone nowhere, and which ones had hit the mark.

His most telling chapter is the one on propaganda. The Nazis had taken a still mostly neutral term—*propaganda*—and made it vicious. Their euphemism for the genocide we now call the Holocaust was the "final solution" to the "Jewish problem." Huxley distinguishes between slogans that inflame the passions of the masses and language that speaks to human reason and to humankind's attraction to the good. That distinction, I believe, also motivated Hayakawa to try to translate the field of general semantics from a set of abstract principles of language into a workbench of practical tools students could use. In a foreword he wrote:

> I have long known that the task of a student of semantics who would help others cannot simply be that of enunciating general propositions, however true they may be. His task is to live and act, in as many situations as possible, with the semantic principles always in the back of his mind, so that, before he recommends them to others, he may see how they may (and may not) be applied to actual human problems.

Before we get to the content of this important book, let me share the details of an exciting intellectual and political life, one that created for Hayakawa countless personal challenges and case studies of effective communication. The big arc: He was born and educated in Canada, studied and taught at American universities at a time when people of Japanese descent were despised, built his reputation as a practical scholar, became the president of San Francisco State University, and was elected to the U.S. Senate to represent California. Along the way, he worked as a delivery boy, traveling salesman, taxi driver, and advertising copywriter. (You can be sure that his expertise in semantics came in handy in crafting ad copy!) As a political outsider, he faced controversy and also relished a quirky reputation. He was often photographed wearing a tam o'shanter or nodding off at a hearing.

Which leads to the question: Why study semantics?

Even with my advanced degree in English literature and experience as a teacher of composition, I knew little of that field of language study. When I heard the word *semantics,* it had a negative connotation, much like *rhetoric.* When President Obama made an effective speech, some political opponents, including at one time Hillary Clinton, would dismiss it as "just rhetoric," that is, tricks of language. In a debate, someone might fend off an argument by saying, "Oh, that's just a matter of semantics," that is, more tricks of language.

I have come to think of semantics—along with rhetoric—as two of the most important categories of practical language knowledge. Semantics describes how words make meaning, or how they fail to do so. Why do some words seem loaded with opinion or bias? Why are some words considered taboo? Where do words come from? Why do words change meaning over time, sometimes making a word more positive, sometimes more negative? What is the difference between using "idea" words vs. "thing" words? What is the "ladder of abstraction"? In the dictionary, the words *nude* and *naked* are shown as synonyms, so why do they feel so different in common usage?

All these questions fall under the category of general semantics, a field of language study invented by another immigrant, a Polish American scholar named Alfred Korzybski. Speaking of immigrants, what is the difference between an "illegal" one and an "undocumented" one? What is the difference between a "civil war" and "sectarian violence"? What is the difference between an "invasion" and an "incursion"? The arguments may be political, but, if you want to study the language differences, folks, you must walk through the field of semantics. Semantics. Language in thought. Language in action.

I have chosen to summarize one chapter in Hayakawa's book, to explain its contents and also to explore its rich implications for communicating within a democratic order. Here is how Hayakawa begins a chapter called "The Language of Reports":

> For the purposes of the interchange of information, the basic symbolic act is the *report* of what we have seen, heard, or felt: "There is a ditch on each side of the road." "You can get those at Smith's hardware store for $2.75." "There aren't any fish on that side of the lake, but there are on this side." Then there are reports of reports: "The longest waterfall in the world is Victoria Falls in Rhodesia." "The Battle of Hastings took place in 1066." "The papers say that there was a big smash-up on Highway 41 near Evansville." Reports adhere to the following rules: first, they are *capable of verification;* second, they *exclude,* as far as possible, *inferences* and *judgments.*

For those of you who may be reading this, say, in the year 2030, let me offer a brief overview of America in 2020. The country feels polarized politically. The left and the right seem capable of little compromise on hot-button issues such as abortion, immigration, gun control, and climate change. Not only do people disagree on policies, but they can't seem to agree on what a fact is. To use a philosophical term, we are in an epistemological morass. Terms like "truthiness" and "alternative facts" have surfaced in political culture. Voters seem to care more about ideology than practical truth and reliable evidence. Politicians and pundits have been known to tell lie after lie after lie with no significant consequences. Propagandists and conspiracy theorists have used social media to magnify the untrue narratives they like and to attack the people they hate. Antagonists across the globe seek to undermine American institutions, even messing with our election process. Teams of journalists around the globe—many of them attached to the school where I work—have devoted themselves to fact-checking.

If that, in a nutty nutshell, describes 2020, consider this single paragraph from Hayakawa, written seven decades ago:

Reports are verifiable. We may not always be able to verify them ourselves, since we cannot track down the evidence for every piece of history we know, nor can we all go to Evansville to see the remains of the smash-up before they are cleared away. But if we are roughly agreed on the names of things...and on how to measure time, there is relatively little danger of our misunderstanding each other. Even in a world such as we have today, in which everybody seems to be quarreling with everybody else, *we still to a surprising degree trust each other's reports.* We ask directions of total strangers when we are traveling. We follow directions on road signs without being suspicious of the people who put them up. We read books of information about science, mathematics, automotive engineering, travel, geography, the history of costume, and other such factual matters, and we usually assume that the author is doing his best to tell us as truly as he can what he knows. And we are safe in so assuming most of the time. With the emphasis that is being given today to the discussion of biased newspapers, propagandists, and the general untrustworthiness of many of the communications we receive, we are likely to forget that we still have an enormous amount of reliable information available and that deliberate misinformation, except in warfare, still is more the exception than the rule. The desire for self-preservation that compelled men to evolve means for the exchange of information also compels them to regard the giving of false information as profoundly reprehensible.

And yet, in 2020 political antagonists dismiss anything that contradicts their worldview as "fake news," and those who deliver it as "the enemy of the people." In the years leading up to this antagonism, we have seen, in many expressions of culture, a denial of the possibility of objectivity. No one, it is argued, is a blank slate. Everyone who delivers a message carries the anchor of their own experience. The best argument on the topic comes in the book *The Elements of Journalism*. Without naming Hayakawa, the authors, Bill Kovach and Tom Rosenstiel, stand solidly beside the semanticist on the importance of reports. Journalism, they write, is a discipline of *verification*, not assertion. There are many talking heads on cable news programs. There are fewer dedicated reporters who understand the importance of finding things out, checking things out, and *then* reporting things in the public interest. In this sense, objectivity is not a neutral state of being, but a process by which reporters try to recognize their bias and filter it from reports.

How to strengthen the reliability and credibility of the reports we create? Hayakawa's chapter is filled with specific tips:

- As much as possible, avoid inferences. This requires that "we make no guesses as to what is going on in other people's minds." This may mean showing rather than telling; not "he was angry," but "he pounded his fist on the table" and "swore."
- Avoid judgments, that is, any expression of the writer's approval or disapproval. Not "the senator was defiant," but "the senator's vote was the only one against the bill."
- Exclude words that "snarl" (such as "murderous immigrants"); or words that "purr" (such as "freedom-loving gun owner").
- Avoid judgments and conclusions that "stop thought." By calling a neighborhood "tidy" or "untidy," you keep the reader from having to draw conclusions from specific evidence.
- Slant both ways at once. With this advice, Hayakawa argues that a slant to a story that extends in only one direction abandons impartiality in favor of advocacy. If I call attention to a character's white teeth but not his dirty fingernails, I am slanting the text. Using both details restores some impartiality.

- Discover your bias. From Hayakawa: "When a newspaper tells a story in a way that we dislike, leaving out facts we think important and playing up unimportant facts in ways that we think unfair, we are often tempted to say, 'Look how they've slanted the story! What a dirty trick!'"

Many readers argue that news organizations intentionally slant information for some secret ideological purpose. In fact, the slant may be unintentional, based on the general experiences of the people who produce the story. Awareness of one's biases and preferences—not just in secret, but transparently—allows the stakeholders to make reports solid. It is a tribute to reporters and editors at the *Boston Globe,* for example, a number of them Catholics, that they were able to expose the cover-up of child abuse by priests—as portrayed in the movie *Spotlight.*

LESSONS

1. Recognize that verifiable reports provide the foundation for self-government and democratic institutions. They are crucial to all social and economic enterprises that depend upon reliable information to take action.

2. A good report does not require the writer to be free of biases, preferences, or opinions. It does require the writer to follow a process that filters, as much as possible, these from the final product, a difficult but necessary path toward fairness and neutrality.

3. In revision, test your language for signs of loaded words. In referring to the words of a speaker, you may be tempted to use *admitted, conceded, implied, argued, retorted,* or even the much-maligned *opined,* when the word *said* says it best.

4. Writing solid reports requires a mental discipline that may conflict with daily routines in which we make many assumptions. To assume, says an old caution, is to make an "ass" out of "u" and "me." Don't assume that a person who wears a wedding ring is married. If it matters, check it out.

28

Write to make your soul grow. Transform the
disadvantage of suffering into the redemptive
advantage of powerful writing.

Like Shaking Hands with God: A Conversation about Writing
By Kurt Vonnegut and Lee Stringer

Toolbox: *A teacher met an author who had just published a book
about his time in prison. "You're so lucky," said the teacher. "How's
that?" "You have such interesting experiences to write about. A
bad experience for me is forgetting where I parked my minivan at
the mall." For the writer, disadvantage becomes advantage. Kurt
Vonnegut makes sense: To write a good story, take a sympathetic
character and place him in horrible circumstances to see what
he's made of. If you need models, look no further than the holy
books—from Job to Jesus. Righteousness never means escape from
suffering.*

I have vivid memories of 1969, the year of my twenty-first
birthday. I spent the summer working at Rockefeller Center in
New York City. I was dumped, not by one but by two wonderful young women. I thought I was doomed to bachelorhood,

but met another wonderful young woman who wore her hair very long and her skirts—in the fashion of the day—very short, as short as a Hemingway sentence. Married her. Forty-eight years.

In that same year, Kurt Vonnegut Jr. was a popular author of the day, having written quirky semi-sci-fi dark comedies such as *Cat's Cradle* and *Slaughterhouse-Five*. I attended Providence College in Rhode Island, and Vonnegut was giving a lecture across town at Brown University. I remember sitting on the floor of a large auditorium to hear him. The making of the 1960s' counterculture was at its height, and Vonnegut was a grown-up with a sensibility that pleased us, critical of his own time as a former publicity writer for General Electric, a rebel against some of the Hoosier norms that helped create him.

I remember a student asking him a question about science-fiction superstar Isaac Asimov. The question, asked in a somewhat snooty tone, was something about Asimov's theory that human evolution would be tied to space travel; as humans populated other moons and planets, the experience would radically change human nature. Vonnegut's response was polite—initially. He spoke of how he admired Asimov's productivity as a writer, and his imagination. But when it came to stuff like exploration of the universe, Asimov, he opined, was "full of shit." The audience gasped with surprise. "THERE'S NO AIR UP THERE!" he said, and we roared with laughter. "IF YOU TRY TO BREATHE, YOU'LL DIE!!"

On November 14, 1969—it may have been the day after we heard Vonnegut—large groups of students piled onto buses in downtown Providence for a trip to Washington, D.C., where we would participate in a massive march against the Vietnam War. Thousands upon thousands of us from around the nation would make that trip. Just before we settled in for what would turn out to be a long journey on a cold night, the doors opened, and a tall lanky man with scruffy hair and a goatee boarded the bus and made his way to the last seat in the back. It was Vonnegut.

I was surprised and amazed. An author who had seen some of the worst fighting in World War II was acting in solidarity with an army of young dissenters. If a writer of such experience and insight could see the world through our eyes, who knows, maybe we were right to protest this war.

War is hell. But somehow, for writers like Vonnegut, the hell of war can be mitigated, even redeemed, by writing. Critic Peter Reed offers this summary of Vonnegut's war experience in the preface to Vonnegut's short-story collection *Bagombo Snuff Box:*

> This collection includes stories that draw on Vonnegut's World War Two experiences. The events on which *Slaughterhouse-Five* was based are by now widely known: how Vonnegut was captured by the Germans at the Battle of the Bulge, was held as a prisoner of war in Dresden, was sheltered in an underground meat storage room when that city was incinerated in massive air raids, and after the Nazi defeat wandered briefly in a Germany awash in refugees before he was reunited with American forces.

In his own introduction to that collection, Vonnegut adds:

> I returned to Dresden, incidentally, the setting for *Slaughterhouse-Five*, on October 7th, 1998. I was taken down into the cellar where I and about a hundred other American POWs survived a firestorm that suffocated or incinerated 135,000 or so other human beings. It reduced the "Florence of the Elbe" to a jagged moonscape.
>
> While I was down in that cellar again, this thought came to me: "Because I have lived so long, I am one of the few persons on Earth who saw an Atlantis before it disappeared forever beneath the waves."

In that same introduction, Vonnegut identifies with the simple yet magical act of making meaning out of a written text: "With my brains all fired up, I do the nearly impossible thing that you are doing now, dear reader. I make sense of idiosyncratic arrangements, in horizontal lines, of nothing but twenty-six phonetic symbols, ten Arabic numerals, and perhaps eight punctuation marks, on a sheet of bleached and flattened wood pulp!"

I don't remember many exclamation marks in Vonnegut's prose, so that one has the force of a hundred emoticons. That energy of reading propelled him toward his craft:

> Then I took to teaching creative writing, first at Iowa, then at Harvard, and then at City College in New York. Joseph Heller, author of *Catch-22*, was teaching at City College also. He said to me that if it hadn't been for the war, he would have been in the dry-cleaning business. I said to him that if

it hadn't been for the war, I would have been garden editor of *The Indianapolis Star.*

So, yes, war is hell, unless you're a great writer, in which case, war is hell in a handbasket filled with royalty checks. I thought of my college roomie Fred Day, who spent the early 1970s in Vietnam, an experience that gave him lots of compelling things to write about upon his return. Me, I was in graduate school reading Homer on the Trojan War and Shakespeare on the Wars of the Roses. Grad school was hell, man. Some of those library shelves could be really dusty.

Vonnegut had the opportunity and the ability to transform terrible life experiences into vicarious experiences for the reader. He could grab me by the shirt and drag me into the firebombing of Dresden. That is the transportational power of narrative. Through the words of the author, I am able to travel to another time and place, and in the comfort of my easy chair, experience what it might be like.

There is a short section in Vonnegut's introduction that he describes as "Creative Writing 101." I won't quote all of his strategies (I encourage you to find his list and read it for yourself), but here are the ones I found most cogent to my craft:

2. Give the reader at least one character he or she can root for.

3. Every character should want something, even if it is only a glass of water.

6. Be a sadist. No matter how sweet and innocent your leading characters, make awful things happen to them—in order that the reader may see what they are made of.

For the writer, then, disadvantage becomes advantage. That theme became central to a thin, elegant volume titled *Like Shaking Hands with God*. It contains the edited transcript of a public conversation between Vonnegut and a writer named Lee Stringer, which took place on October 1, 1998, at a New York City bookstore. The chat was moderated by Ross Klavan and focused on the writing craft. In a fascinating exchange, the two authors—from radically different backgrounds—agree that hard times can be a reliable incubator of good writing.

Klavan asks them to comment on their common ground.

Kurt Vonnegut: The common ground? Well, you have identified it. We have written out of our own lives, and being writers was easier for us because we had something to write about. Thank God I was in Dresden when it was burned down....

Lee Stringer: You know, the subject of *Grand Central Winter*, which involves homelessness, has been seen by a lot of people as a tragedy. But usually at the end of a tragedy somebody dies, and being alive right now I can't think of it as a tragedy. What I've taken away is a certain brand of optimism. Even the bad stuff is an opportunity. There are possibilities there. In fact, I see more possibilities in adversity than in, say, lying on satin pillows. So, in that respect, I guess I am an optimist. I think there's reason for optimism—at least for personal optimism. I don't know if the world is going to survive, but I'm going to go as long as my heart beats.

He later describes how he discovered that he was a writer:

Lee Stringer: I was just sitting there with a pencil, I'll say that much. A pencil that I was using as a drug implement, to push the screens in my pipe. And one day I didn't have any drugs and I decided to use it as a pencil. I'm sort of smart that way. Because I was going to use that pencil some way or another, I guess. And I started writing. And the extraordinary thing was that it was five hours later before I stopped. I don't think I had done anything for five hours in a row during that time *except* to get high or try to outrun the effects of getting high. I don't think there was anything else that I did with that much concentration. It was a real moment.

Kurt Vonnegut: There's a swell book that's out of print now....It's called *The Writer and Psychoanalysis* by a man who's now dead named Edmund Bergler. He claimed he had treated more writers than anyone else in his field, and being that he practiced in New York, he probably did. Bergler said that writers were fortunate in that they were able to treat their neuroses every day by writing....And I have said about the practice of the arts that practicing any art—be it painting, music, dance, literature, or whatever—is not a way to make money or become famous. *It's a way to make your soul grow.*

LESSONS

1. Use writing to transform suffering, yours or that of someone you know or learn about.

2. As you choose characters to write about, remember Vonnegut's advice that it is best to write about someone who wants or needs someone or something—who has something important at stake.

3. A sympathetic character—say, Harry Potter—must suffer a lot, so that we can see what he's made of and so his triumph can feel more satisfying.

4. People who suffer often suffer twice—or more. They suffer during an event—a war, a plague, a hurricane—and suffer again months or years later, what we now call post-traumatic stress. Think of storytelling as a way to mitigate this "second suffering." The writer calls it up and creates a story. Or the writer tells the story of another sufferer. While this is no substitute for psychotherapy or medication, telling the story of suffering has its own therapeutic benefits.

29

Write to delight and instruct. Often you can accomplish one or the other, but you are at your best when you can do both.

The Epistles of Horace
"Ars Poetica" (or "Art of Poetry")
Translated by David Ferry

Toolbox: *Perhaps you are a poet. Or you write headlines for a big-city tabloid newspaper: "Headless Man in Topless Bar." Better still, maybe you are both. Poets and headline writers both compress language for meaning. They also play with words. The higher purposes of good writing are ancient and enduring: to delight and instruct. One effect can exist without the other, but when they are combined the writer climbs to the top of the mountain. For your most public stories, look for subjects that are both interesting and important. Do not try to fool readers into thinking that all interesting things are important. But do try to make important things interesting so readers will pay attention and, when needed, take action.*

Sometimes a versatile and productive writer has become known for a single work—maybe even one cool idea. When

I think of my mentor, Donald Murray, I think of the phrase "writing process" and the idea that good writing is produced not by magic but by a series of rational steps. When I think of my friend William Zinsser, I think of the word "clutter" and the good tips he shared on how to cut it from your writing. Screenwriter Robert McKee teaches that every good story needs an "inciting incident," a moment that disturbs the normal rhythm of the day.

When I think of the Roman poet Horace (and, yes, I sometimes do), I think of not just one cool idea, but one *great* idea, so great that every writer in every genre should pin it near her or his writing space. It is great not because it is technical, but because it is inspirational and aspirational. It deals with the mission of writers and the purposes of their tasks. I now realize that, somewhere in my undergraduate education, I was presented with this bit of wisdom. I understood it, but, more reader than writer, I did not appreciate its strategic importance. The idea is that the purpose of literature is "*delectare et docere*": to delight and instruct. In other words, the best piece of writing should offer pleasure and wisdom, the sweet and the useful. Thank you, Quintus Horatius Flaccus, better known by his Roman street name Horace.

If you envision Italy as a boot, the heel is where Horace entered the world in 65 BCE His family could not escape the political turmoil that led to the assassination of Julius Caesar and the elevation of Caesar Augustus. Horace, under the guidance of the poet Virgil (now that's what I call a writing coach), found his way into favor and, before his death in 8 BCE, became one of Rome's most honored poets, playwrights, critics, and rhetoricians.

Modern readers of Horace are fortunate to have David Ferry as translator of his odes and epistles. While Horace wrote in a tight Latin verse—six beats to the measure—Ferry liberates the English version in iambic meters, capturing the energy of the original. Ferry offers this favorite passage from Horace:

My aim is to take familiar things and make
Poetry of them, and do it in such a way
That it looks as if it was easy as could be
For anybody to do it (although he'd sweat
And strain and work his head off, all in vain).
Such is the power of judgment, of knowing what
It means to put the elements together
In just the right way; such is the power of making
A perfectly wonderful thing out of nothing much.

I laughed when I read this, and if you too are a fan of the sitcom *Seinfeld* you will understand why. It was, after all, the ambitious mission of Jerry and George to create a comedy show "about nothing."

Ferry offers this appreciation of his Latin muse: "It's the voice that's the life of these poems: so free, so confident, so knowledgeable about himself, and about work, so contemptuous of pretense, so entertaining, so joyful." Writers and writing teachers (and writing books!) often try to explain the "voice" of the writer: what it means, what it sounds like, where it's found, how to judge its authenticity. Horace and Ferry understand—with two millennia separating them—that voice is a made thing. Ferry explains:

In the Epistles, Horace perfected the hexameter verse medium in which his voice performs, always as if conversationally, speaking in these letters with such directness, wit, and urgency, to young writers, to friends, to his patron, to the Emperor Augustus himself. It is the voice of a free man talking about how to get along in a Roman world full of temptations, opportunities, and contingencies, and how to do so with your integrity intact.

To the extent that poetry and oratory are delivered through the ear rather than the eye, voice becomes even more important.

One of the letters composed by Horace was delivered to a wealthy family named Piso. At least one of their sons was an aspiring poet and playwright, so Horace feeds his interest in a work that comes down to us as "Ars Poetica," that is, "The Art of Poetry," a brave and more entertaining forerunner of Sir Philip Sidney's "Defence of Poesy," which was written almost 1,600 years later, when the wisdom of ancient Greece and Rome was being reborn in Elizabethan England.

Horace provides great practical advice throughout. When it comes to writing plays, Horace prefers five acts, not more nor less; showing over telling; keeping gruesome acts offstage; and a plot that does not require the appearance of a deus ex machina: "Don't call upon a god to come in and solve it." On other writing matters, he suggests that you pick material you can handle; not be discouraged if you aim and miss; not be afraid to coin new words as long as "you don't attempt to *over*do it." When it comes to correct usage, Horace seems willing to stand astride, like the Colossus of Rhodes, the prescriptive and descriptive schools: "Words now in honor may fall, if Use, which is / The governor of our language, should decide."

All such wisdom derives from a governing idea:

Poetry wants to instruct or else to delight;
Or, better still, to delight and instruct at once.
As for instruction, make it succinct, so the mind
Can quickly seize on what's being taught and hold it;
Every superfluous word spills out of a full mind.
As for delight, in what you invent stay close
To actuality; your fable shouldn't
Feel free to ask your audience to credit
Just anything whatsoever, no matter what:
Produce no human babies from monsters' bellies.

Shakespeare, through Hamlet, will offer the same advice a millennium and a half later when the prince urges players to hold a mirror up to nature.

Journalists spend years developing a type of literacy known as "news judgment," but I would argue that all writers who seek to publish need to develop something similar: a public judgment. That phrase describes the ability to take the experiences, events, happenings, triumphs, and dangers of the day, sort through them, select those that are most significant, and make them available to an audience through a variety of genres and media platforms.

When I began a career in journalism in 1977, computer technology in the newsroom, along with word processing, were recent innovations. There was still something called a wire room, glass enclosed, filled with noisy machines. The newswires of the day—AP, UPI, Reuters, New York Times—spat out dozens of stories. Men and women called news editors or wire editors worked into the night, sorting through these dispatches, dumping some, cutting or collating others. We will get to *how* they decided in a minute.

But let's move ahead forty-three years to 2020, and now we have a revolutionary technology, the internet, that has become an important source of news, information, and entertainment (featuring cute children, dogs, kittens). People who work for websites and social networks use different language to describe their craft, but it is not much different from what Mike Moscardini and Bob Jenkins did on the night desk of the *St. Pete Times* in the 1970s. Today, tech-savvy producers "aggregate" material from a variety of sources and then "curate" it for their audience.

To understand how they make these decisions, I turn back to Horace. To delight and instruct. News judgment, or public judgment, or just writer's judgment, when well honed, includes the capacity to select and publish material upon two criteria:

- What is interesting?
- What is important?

Can we agree that in the digital age we have lots of stuff available to us that calls out for our attention and quite a lot of it is interesting? That does not make it important. Cable news stations, for example, will cover a criminal trial for weeks or months. People watch it like a soap opera. The sources of attraction are familiar: sex, violence, scandal, the fall of someone rich and powerful. But none of this makes those stories of great public value.

Many writers, editors, and producers spend too much time and effort trying to create the illusion that something interesting is important. The most responsible public writers flip the switch. They know that important news or information—an increase or decrease in the money supply, for instance—may not be inherently interesting, but they feel a social duty to work at it, to make the important interesting enough that people will pay attention.

I don't know what Horace thought about the use of adverbs, but he might have written "Delight instructively." Or "Instruct delightfully." History proves that most of the great stories of all times—in all cultures, in all genres—arrive at the intersection of the interesting and important: the assassination of JFK, the moon landing, the destruction of the Berlin Wall, the events of 9/11.

Inspired by Horace, I return the mic to him for the final words: "Poetry wants to instruct or else to delight." But wait, there's more: "Or, better still, to delight and instruct at once."

LESSONS

1. Consider what makes something interesting to you. It will differ from person to person, but the answer is not completely subjective. Here, from news, entertainment, and literature, are ten things humans seem to find interesting.

- the actions of adorable children and cute animals
- conflict, at almost every level
- various expressions of human sexuality
- athletic achievement
- victory by an underdog
- the downfall of hypocrites
- how people behave or misbehave at ceremonies, such as weddings
- music and dance
- mysteries solved
- nature at its best and worst
- [Add your own to this list.]

2. Create the same kind of list for what makes something important:

- something that happens to me or someone I know
- something that affects the place where I live
- something that dramatically transforms the routines of life
- disasters such as storms and floods
- things that involve the expenditure or waste of money and resources
- war, actual (Vietnam) and metaphorical (war on drugs)
- threats to the environment
- beneficial scientific discoveries

- death tolls
- acts of heroism

3. Make a list of the biggest news stories you can remember within the span of your life. They are likely to be both interesting and important, imparting types of wisdom and pleasure, in the spirit of Horace.

4. Make a list of things you find interesting and important—stories that could delight and instruct—that you believe are underemphasized by the media.

30

Become the eyes and ears of the audience.
Write from different visual and aural
perspectives, from a distance and up close.

*In Search of Light: The Broadcasts of Edward R. Murrow,
1938–1961*
Edited by Edward Bliss Jr.

Toolbox: *More than ever, writers write with sound and visual
elements—from photographs to videos to spreadsheets. This multimedia versatility has been more than a century in the making.
One hero of the craft is Edward R. Murrow, who helped invent
broadcast news on both radio and television. Even without pictures, he would write to help listeners "see," in both the visual and
cognitive sense. One of his best strategies was to vary the distance
between himself as a narrator and what he was witnessing. He
could stand atop an urban landscape and describe what he was
seeing in the sky, or he could walk into a concentration camp and
describe the smell of a prisoner, the tatters of his clothes. The camera on your smartphone is a valuable writing tool. Or turn your
notebook into that camera. Write down what you see.*

I admit that *In Search of Light* may seem an odd choice for a book about writing books. It is, after all, a collection of the spoken words of a broadcast journalist. You will not find any specific writing advice—nothing about subjects and verbs, nothing about how to create a storyboard for nonfiction narrative, nothing, even, about how to write for the ear, or how to write with moving images.

But Edward R. Murrow was not just any broadcast journalist. I have argued that he was *the* broadcast journalist of the twentieth century, having invented the form for CBS News, not once, but twice: first for radio and then for television. He faced his challenges, prone, in spite of his apparent confidence, to panic attacks. And I am not sure I have ever seen a photographic or film image of the man when he was not smoking a cigarette, a habit that led to his early death.

I have included his book here because it will inspire you to become a better writer. Not only was Murrow inventing a craft—writing for broadcast—but, from the get-go, he became one of its best practitioners. To read his radio dispatches from World War II is to understand the power of delivering stories that were written for the ear but that appeal to the eye—making us see. As he became a leader in broadcast journalism, he also understood that the technology of radio and, especially, television, could be used for trivial commercial purposes or for profound ones, a dilemma now magnified in the digital age.

Here is why Murrow was the outstanding journalist of his time:

1. Edward R. Murrow exhibited for radio the power of eye-witness reporting, especially from dangerous locations: delivering radio dispatches from the Battle of Britain—as the city of London suffered under the barrage of bombings from the German Luftwaffe—and from the liberation of the Buchenwald concentration camp.

2. He demonstrated what it takes to excel at writing and reporting in the middle of a revolution in information technology. After establishing a new standard for reporting for CBS radio, he carried those standards and practices into television news in its infancy.

3. He brought to television long-form investigations to hold the powerful accountable. This included his practice of correcting the record, an influential early example of what has now grown into a discipline of political fact-checking. Most notably, Murrow used this strategy to expose the vicious propaganda and Communist "witch hunting" made infamous by Senator Joseph McCarthy.

4. Just as powerful writing and reporting can be used to afflict the comfortable, it can be used to comfort the afflicted. One of Murrow's most compelling works was *Harvest of Shame,* the heartbreaking narrative of migrant workers laboring under excruciating poverty and horrific conditions across America.

5. Murrow was not only the greatest American reporter of his day, but also the greatest American journalism leader. Such was his commitment to excellence that he argued against the values of his own employer in a speech to his television colleagues about the responsibility to transcend entertainment values and profits.

Those achievements are grand, but they would not exist without Murrow's perfection of the writing craft—especially the narrative style of eyewitness reporting. Here are two excerpts from radio dispatches, the first from London on September 22, 1940:

I'm standing again tonight on a rooftop looking out over London, feeling rather large and lonesome. In the course of the last fifteen or twenty minutes there's been considerable action up here, but at the moment there's an ominous silence hanging over London. But at the same time a silence that has a great deal of dignity. Just straightaway in front of me the searchlights are working. I can see one or two bursts of antiaircraft fire far in the distance. Just on the roof across the way I can see a man wearing a tin hat, a pair of powerful night glasses to his eyes, scanning the sky. Again, looking in the opposite direction, there is a building with two windows gone. Out of one window there waves something that looks like a white bed sheet, a window curtain swinging free in this night breeze. It looks as though it were being shaken by a ghost. There are a great many ghosts around these buildings in London. The searchlights straightaway, miles in front of me, are still scratching that sky. There's a three-quarter moon riding high. There was one burst of shellfire almost straight in the Little Dipper.

This is gripping stuff, a story delivered in the moment, live, without script. He is our eyes and ears. We cannot see over radio, unless the narrator provides us with the details: the man with the tin hat scanning the sky, the window curtain shaken as if by a ghost, searchlights scratching the sky, shellfire in the Little Dipper. In other examples, he adds, of course, the natural sounds breaking the silence—not special effects for radio adventures, but what you would hear were you there. In a way, you *are* there.

That dispatch came from the Battle of Britain at the beginning of the war. Near the war's end, it will be Murrow who, on April 15, 1945, presents to the world the first evidence of what we have come to call the Holocaust, which he sees with his own eyes, of course, at the liberation of the Buchenwald concentration camp.

Permit me to tell you what you would have seen and heard, had you been with me on Thursday. It will not be pleasant listening. If you are at lunch, or if you have no appetite to hear what Germans have done, now is a good time to switch off the radio, for I propose to tell you of Buchenwald. It is on a small hill about four miles outside Weimar, and it was one of the largest concentration camps in Germany, and it was built to last. As we approached it, we saw about a hundred men in civilian clothes with rifles advancing in open order across the fields. There were a few shops; we stopped to inquire. We were told that some of the prisoners had a couple of SS men cornered in there. We drove on, reached the main gate. The prisoners crowded up behind the wire. We entered.

And now, let me tell you this in the first person, for I was the least important person there, as you shall hear. There surged around me an evil-smelling horde. Men and boys reached out to touch me; they were in rags and the remnants of uniform. Death had already marked many of them, but they were smiling with their eyes....

[Murrow reports on his encounter and conversations with several prisoners, who tell him their stories. Then this:]

We proceeded to the small courtyard. The wall was about eight feet high; it adjoined what had been a stable or a garage. We entered. It was floored with concrete. There were two rows of bodies stacked up like cordwood. They were thin and very white. Some of the bodies were terribly bruised, though there seemed to be little flesh to bruise. Some had been shot through the head, but they bled but little. All except two were naked. I tried to count them as best as I could and arrived at the conclusion that all that was mortal of more than five hundred men and boys lay there in two neat piles.

[To this day, there are those who try to deny that the Holocaust ever happened. It's as if Murrow anticipates such pernicious denial in this closing passage:]

I pray you to believe what I have said about Buchenwald. I have reported what I saw and heard, but only part of it. For most of it I have no words.... If I've offended you by this rather mild account of Buchenwald, I'm not in the least sorry.

There are similarities and differences between the first dispatch from the rooftops of London and this one from inside a concentration camp. Both are created from the accumulation of details, witnessed directly by the narrator. The main difference has to do with the distance of the reporter from the subject matter, a crucial strategic concern for all writers. From the rooftop, the point of view moves mostly across the sky and to an adjacent building. Now remember the perspective from inside the camp. The narrator is so close that he can smell the dying. He sees naked bloodless bodies stacked like cordwood.

Different, as well, is the pace of information. The sentences from the Battle of Britain roll along in a smooth variation, depending upon the content. Notice, though, in Buchenwald, how the sentences get shorter and shorter. Tom Wolfe says that readers accept very short sentences as "the gospel truth." When Murrow transmits the awful truth of what has been executed, it takes ten short sentences in a single paragraph to get the job done. He does not want the listener (now reader) to rush through this experience. In a carefully crafted script, he makes the reader stop ten times (remember, the Brits refer to a period as a full stop).

The diction in the second passage has a familiar ring to it, different from that in the first. I would argue it has a biblical quality to it—something ancient—both prophetic and apocalyptic: "all that was mortal of more than five hundred men and boys lay there in two neat piles." That crushing detail captures, as well as anything I can think of, the efficiency of the Nazi genocide machine. Tell when you have to, writers, but show when you can.

On October 15, 1958, Murrow gave perhaps the most famous speech ever delivered by a working journalist. It was a speech about journalism, television, and the future of news. It was delivered in Chicago at a meeting of the Radio-Television

News Directors Association. More than any statement from Murrow, it got at that place where craft connects with mission and purpose:

> I have no technical advice or counsel to offer those of you who labor in this vineyard, the one that produces words and pictures. You will I am sure forgive me for not telling you that the instruments with which you work are miraculous, that your responsibility is unprecedented, or that your aspirations are frequently frustrated. It is not necessary to remind you of the fact that your voice, amplified to the degree where it reaches from one end of the country to the other, does not confer upon you greater wisdom than when your voice reached only from one end of the bar to the other.

Here is Murrow's famous conclusion, quoted countless times by journalists who care about their public mission, even quoted in 2019 by Norah O'Donnell on her first night as anchor of the *CBS Evening News*:

> This instrument [television] can teach, it can illuminate; yes, and even it can inspire. But it can do so only to the extent that humans are determined to use it to those ends. Otherwise it's nothing but wires and lights in a box. There is a great and perhaps decisive battle to be fought against ignorance, intolerance, and indifference. This weapon of television could be useful.

There are some books that, when you finish them, make you want to read more. *In Search of Light* has that power and something else—it makes you want to write more.

LESSONS

1. All texts can be read aloud, but some—radio reports, podcasts, audiobooks—are designed to be delivered to the ear. When an audience listens to a story, it is important that they be able to "see," in the visual and cognitive senses. Include details or images that stimulate the visual senses.

2. From Murrow's war dispatches, learn the ability to report and write from multiple distances, from a wide cityscape where you can see lights in the sky to dramatic close-ups where you can see ragged clothes hanging from a prisoner's body.

3. Most texts appeal to the visual sense of the reader. Other senses—such as smell, sound, touch, and taste—are too often underappreciated or ignored. Consider other senses beyond the Big Five: temperature, motion, pain, balance, hunger, thirst, ecstasy—all offering opportunities to writers to make experiences feel "real." Check your notebook. Are you writing details that appeal to multiple senses—at least more than one? If a smell or sound is not in your notebook, it is unlikely to reach the text.

4. Now that you have the chance to read Murrow from the page, search online for the many examples of his radio dispatches and television broadcasts. Describe the difference between the sound of his actual voice and the voice that comes off the page.

31

Choose advocacy over propaganda.
Never appeal to readers' base instincts, and
challenge those who do.

Brave New World Revisited
By Aldous Huxley

1984
By George Orwell

Amusing Ourselves to Death
By Neil Postman

Toolbox: *Learn the difference between advocacy and propaganda. One appeals to rational self-interest, the other to emotion and the baser instincts, such as fear of the stranger. This does not mean that emotion is out of bounds for the advocate. Stories—about child abuse, for example—ignite righteous anger and a desire for reform. Here is the key: Stories filled with emotion must be based on fact. Check every fact. Develop a BS detector that helps you sense when a message or messenger is trying to exploit you.*

As a high-school student I had three literary heroes: One was American: J. D. Salinger; two were Brits: Aldous Huxley and George Orwell. Like many other students of my generation, I wanted to be a catcher in the rye, following Holden Caulfield and his red hunting hat through high school. For numerous reasons, my affection for Salinger has faded with age while my attachment to the British dystopians has grown and grown.

To a sixteen-year-old boy, Huxley's vision of the future was compelling, a view of a society in which powerful forces kept the common man and woman from rebellion through a combination of drugs ("soma") and porn (not "movies" but "feelies"). What followed was Orwell's political beast fable, *Animal Farm*, leading to, perhaps, the most famous year in literary history: *1984*.

In the aftermath of Hitler's Germany, in the shadow of Stalin's Soviet Union, Orwell's *1984* was terrifying, a dictatorship where an all-knowing, all-seeing Big Brother controlled your actions by exploiting your darkest fears. For protagonist Winston Smith it was not kill or be killed. That was too easy. It was rat on your own true love or have your face gnawed off by rats.

In a foreword to a new edition of *Brave New World and Brave New World Revisited*, the late Christopher Hitchens—a literary heir to both Huxley and Orwell—reveals their shared history. For example, Huxley, whose vision deteriorated almost to blindness, once taught French language and literature at Eton. Literary luck would have it that one of his students was a young man named Eric Blair. In the not-too-distant future, little Eric would become George Orwell.

Huxley wrote *Brave New World*. Orwell wrote *1984*. Since then, readers and critics have argued about which vision of the future was most prophetic. For Huxley, the masses will be lulled into submission by drugs, pleasure, and entertainment. For Orwell, citizens are slaves, their minds controlled by fear and intimidation, the leaders of the ruling party distorting every aspect of human life, including language.

The late critic Neil Postman offered his take in a 1985 lecture that became the book *Amusing Ourselves to Death*. You can tell by the title that he would have voted for Huxley's dystopia as closer to the emerging truth. Even now, in 2020 we can see versions of *1984* in places like North Korea and in groups such as ISIS in the Middle East. Postman is more interested in stiletto heels than jackboots. Americans, he argues, are addicted to television and its enduring distractions, modern versions of Huxley's soma. If Postman, Orwell, Huxley, and Hitchens—and I would add Susan Sontag—were revived for a nice lunch at the Algonquin Round Table, it would be interesting to hear them discuss the distractions of the day, from smartphones to video games to streaming videos to pornography everywhere, soon to be delivered more realistically through the platforms of virtual reality.

Huxley understood this game of peering into the future and took the remarkable step of holding himself accountable for his 1932 predictions. In a series of newspaper essays turned into a book, *Brave New World Revisited*, he lists the major categories of his futuristic predictions and grades himself without a curve. He logs his concerns as overpopulation (with hints of eugenics as a solution), overorganization, propaganda, advertising, brainwashing, chemical persuasion, subconscious persuasion, and what might be called "aversive conditioning," bending the natural healthy affinities of children to the will of their overlords.

Huxley defends some of his predictions, and in a letter to Orwell makes a case for them:

> Infant conditioning and narco-hypnosis are more efficient, as instruments of government, than clubs and prisons, and ... the lust for power can be just as completely satisfied by suggesting people into loving their servitude as by flogging and kicking them into obedience.... The nightmare of *Nineteen Eighty-Four* is destined to modulate into the nightmare of a world having more resemblance to that which I imagined in *Brave New World*.

Pleasure, argues Huxley, is more efficient than pain.

But this is a book about writing books. What do the works of Huxley and Orwell tell us about the use of language? Both Huxley and Orwell conjure up forms of tyranny that depend upon the manipulation of language and the persuasive use of propaganda to enslave the mind. In his essay "Politics and the English Language," Orwell argued famously that political corruption leads to language corruption, which leads to further political corruption.

Huxley's lesson is equally compelling, a distinction crucial for any writer who seeks to work in the public interest. That distinction concerns the art of selling, whether persuasion for commercial interests or for political ones. One name for this is advertising. Another is propaganda. From Huxley's point of view, we might call one form of propaganda good and the other bad. The good kind appeals to human reason; the bad kind only to the baser instincts.

According to the OED, the word *propaganda*—derived from *propagate*—was used by the Catholic Church for a committee that would spread the faith through foreign missions, a meaning that goes back to the late 1600s. Later its meaning expanded to the support of ideas beyond the religious: "Any association, systematic scheme, or concerted movement for the propagation of a particular doctrine or practice." Notice the neutrality of that definition, making no distinction between messages in support of bad practices or good ones.

That neutrality extended into the twentieth century. When the meaning of a word changes from neutral to something negative, we say it has taken on pejorative connotations. Hayakawa described that semantic shift, pointing to Nazi propagandists as among the culprits. It was then that propaganda began to be associated with vile purposes—genocide, the persecution of minority groups, the elevation of tyrannical power. Along the way, we lost a name for *good* propaganda. The best we can do in 2020 is the word *advocacy*. If I am an advocate for solar energy, people understand my posture and the nature of my messages. If I declare myself a propagandist for that cause, I only raise suspicion among the as yet unpersuaded.

Here is Huxley in the chapter "The Arts of Selling":

The survival of democracy depends on the ability of large numbers of people to make realistic choices in the light of adequate information. A dictatorship, on the other hand, maintains itself by censoring or distorting the facts, and by appealing, not to reason, not to enlightened self-interest, but to passion and prejudice, to the powerful "hidden forces," as Hitler called them, present in the unconscious depths of every human mind.

Looking at the political movements in 2020 across national boundaries, it is difficult to read that paragraph and not think it prescient. Huxley unpacks the distinction between good and bad propaganda, which he argues has two faces even in Western democracies:

There are two kinds of propaganda—rational propaganda in favor of action that is consonant with the enlightened self-interest of those who make it and those to whom it is addressed, and non-rational propaganda that is not consonant with anybody's enlightened self-interest, but is dictated by, and appeals to passion.... If politicians and their constituents always acted to promote their own or their country's long-range self-interest, this world would be an earthly paradise. As it is, they often act against their own interests, merely to gratify their least creditable passions; the world, in consequence, is a place of misery.

Here is what pornographers in *Brave New World* might have called the "money shot":

Propaganda in favor of action that is consonant with enlightened self-interest appeals to reason by means of logical arguments based upon the best available evidence fully and honestly set forth. Propaganda in favor of action dictated by the impulses that are below self-interest offers false, garbled or incomplete evidence, avoids logical argument and seeks to influence its victims by the mere repetition of catchwords, by the furious denunciation of foreign or domestic scapegoats, and by cunningly associating the lowest passions with the highest ideas, so that atrocities come to be perpetrated in the name of God and the most cynical kind of *Realpolitik* is treated as a matter of religious principle and patriotic duty.

Shakespeare was among the poets who argued that the lines of poetic praise in his sonnets could make his lover immortal. Readers would read them for generation upon generation. I was going to end this chapter with the preternatural wish that Huxley and Orwell might be restored to life. We need them so badly. But wait. No need for a Lazarus miracle. They are still with us after all. Their words, their ideas, their ideals—right here at our fingertips.

LESSONS

1. In your reading and your consumption of news and information, be alert to the differences between good and bad propaganda. Does the message aim high—to reason—or low—to the baser instincts?

2. In your writing, attend more carefully than ever to verifiable fact and reliable evidence. Even if you are an honest writer, it is easier to get things wrong than to get them right. Before you hand in a draft of your story, go through it and put a check mark on every fact, asking "How do I know this?"

3. Have a discussion with your friends and colleagues as to whether your world seems more Huxleyan or Orwellian or something else. If you were to write a dystopian novel set in the year 2084, what challenges would it contain?

4. Orwell's most practical writing advice comes at the end of his essay "Politics and the English Language." Among his lessons:

- Never use a metaphor, simile, or other figure of speech that you are used to seeing in print.
- Never use a long word where a short one will do.
- If it is possible to cut a word out, always cut it out.
- Never use the passive where you can use the active.
- Never use a foreign phrase, a scientific word, or a jargon word if you can think of an everyday English equivalent.
- Break any of these rules sooner than say anything outright barbarous.

32

———+———

Be a writer—and so much more. Use all your
resources to see the whole sky.

Wild Mind: Living the Writer's Life
By Natalie Goldberg

The Way of the Writer: Reflections on the Art and Craft of Storytelling
By Charles Johnson

Toolbox: *Accept that you are a writer. But being a writer is only
one of the roles that you play. You may also be a musician, a pho-
tographer, a mechanic, a yoga instructor, a bartender, a chaplain,
a baker, or—what the heck—a candlestick maker. Of all these and
many more, writing is the craft into which you can incorporate the
others. The more you draw from your various experiences, the more
integrated and authentic your writing voice will become. You will
experience life more intently, you will see with more insight, you
will feel with more empathy. Like Jimi Hendrix, you will kiss the sky.*

This is my final chapter because both my agent and editor told
me it was time to stop writing. It would not be wise or practical

for me to include *everything* I want to say about writing books. My contract called for 75,000 words. When I counted words in a completed draft, they totaled 125,000. I have on my shelves another 100 books that deserve chapters of their own. What was I going to do next?

By now it's clear that I am a putter-inner. I write down what I think I want to say and exercise no restrictions when it comes to length. I write a tweet this way, sometimes even a text message, laying it out until the character counter alerts me, like my toaster-oven buzzer, that I am burning the bagel. The most egregious example came with *The Glamour of Grammar*. After missing a deadline, I wrote for three months without stopping, turning in a hundred chapters, twice as many as the contractual target of fifty.

I hope what I am about to say fills you with hope. I face the same writing problems you do, maybe with added anxiety because I am supposed to be a writing coach, someone licensed to help other writers. I don't want to be the dentist with bad teeth. My problem is that I forget—or ignore—my own writing advice. Even though solutions and strategies fill my books, I have to relearn them. I know, for example, that I cannot boil down a draft by word editing, squeezing out the useless words in a chapter. There is clutter in my drafts, to be sure, but not 50,000 words of it. Yes, I know, brevity comes from selection and not compression.

I will apply that lesson to my final draft, but not until I complete this final chapter. I will go back to my first chapter and reread the advice of Professor Q, that I may have to murder at least a few of my darlings, those elements where I sing too loud, or where I squeeze in a turn of phrase or an anecdote I dote on (like that one!), even if it has little to do with a theme or my main point.

I realized I could not fulfill my mission for this work without including a book by Natalie Goldberg, *Wild Mind,* and another by Charles Johnson, *The Way of the Writer.* Each book deserves a chapter, and my plan was to write two chapters and slip them into the appropriate thematic sections. But something magical happened at the last second. I found a common theme embodied in their work. This meant I could include them in a single chapter. Not only that, but each book expresses and exemplifies the wisdom of craft that feels most appropriate for a final lesson.

I will express that wisdom in brief: A writer needs a main craft, but also an associated one. It could be cooking. It could be playing poker. It could be dance. It could be sculpture or architecture. For Natalie Goldberg, it is the art of painting and the study of Zen Buddhism. For Charles Johnson, it is philosophy and visual arts. It delighted me when I discovered that Goldberg and Johnson both draw writing power from their ability to create visual representations, something they have in common with the likes of William Blake, G. K. Chesterton, and William Hazlitt.

I cannot draw a lick, but that doesn't leave me empty-handed. I am sustained by music, popular culture, and sports. I am no expert on music theory, but I have been playing the piano since I was eight years old. I have played in rock bands since I was sixteen. I own a hundred-year-old upright piano, three electric keyboards, a Taylor acoustic guitar, a bass guitar, two ukuleles, twelve harmonicas, and an Italian-made accordion purchased at a yard sale in New Jersey. I have learned the shared language of music and writing: from composition, to rhythm, to cadence, to voice, to repetition. A story can build to a crescendo or have a coda. There is a type of musical chord called "suspended," a group of notes that contain a bit of discord, the light friction of anticipation. You can't end a musical piece on a suspended chord. It must be resolved. Narratives do not usually end with suspense; maybe with a cliffhanger, yes, but not in the final chord. That suspense, like the chord, must be resolved.

I've argued that when it comes to writing books, popularity counts. I am happy for Natalie Goldberg and her readers. Over thirty years, her book *Writing Down the Bones* has reached a million copies in print, a mark shared by the likes of William Zinsser for *On Writing Well*. Her subtitle is "Freeing the Writer Within." Her path toward liberation can be traced to her practice of Eastern religion in places like Sante Fe and Taos, New Mexico.

As I researched her life, I was struck by certain experiences we share. Born in Brooklyn in 1948 (check), raised on Long Island (check), Jewish relatives (check), runs workshops and retreats for writers (check), likes to write in coffee houses (check), has written more than a dozen books (check). Where I learn most from her, though, is in our differences. Raised as a Roman Catholic, I am sustained by the stories of the Old and New Testaments, and by the liturgies and sacraments that impart grace and a sense of the miraculous and transcendent. When a child is baptized, the minister pours the water then recites the words and something wonderful happens, felt by a community of believers. I find parallels in my own writing—rituals of language that are transformative, for me, and, I hope, for those who read me.

For Goldberg it is Zen Buddhism, and, at least indirectly, she is our Zen master. The moment that this worked most powerfully for me was when I encountered her phrase *Wild Mind,* which is also the title of the sequel to *Writing Down the Bones.* To live the writer's life requires a way of seeing. But what is Wild Mind, and what makes it wild?

Here is part of a wonderful chapter:

I am on a backpacking trip in Frijoles Canyon, part of Bandelier National Monument in New Mexico. We followed a trail along a stream that cut through pink-and-orange cliffs. In the morning we saw deer—mule deer, I am almost certain that's what they were—first one and a little later two. When they saw us, they didn't run so much as hop away.

Goldberg is doing something I am not very good at, re-creating a sense of place, making me see it, with the feeling of real time and direct observation, with the delight of colorful beauty and surprise, the gift of the vision of the deer.

Now I am leaning against a boulder. The stone cools my back. Reader, even though you are not here with me, I want you to look up at the sky. Do you see it? It is a big sky. If you've never been this far west, then imagine standing beneath the sky in Ohio: a two-lane highway, the day gray, you can see the horizon all around. Nothing disturbs that view but an occasional farmhouse with a row of Russian olives as a windbreak or a white square building on the side of the road that says EAT in thin neon. The bottom line of the E and the left branch of the A are broken off.

She is working some kind of mojo on me, and I am not sure whether to give in or resist. How can I see both the big sky and that detail of the broken sign? Is she pointing my nose, like the headlights of a car, toward New Mexico, or Ohio, or Florida, where I am sitting now?

So, either in New Mexico or Ohio, we are under a big sky. That big sky is wild mind. I'm going to climb up to that sky straight over our heads and put one dot on it with a Magic Marker. See that dot? That dot is what Zen calls monkey mind or what western psychology calls part of conscious mind. We give all our attention to that one dot. So when it says we can't write, that we're no good, are failures, fools for even picking up a pen, we listen to it.

Talking directly to the reader, Goldberg then uses the word *you* fifteen times in a single paragraph, creating a composite character of a frustrated writer, someone who wants so much to be a writer, but who gives up at the first sign of frustration.

This goes on endlessly. This is monkey mind. This is how we drift. We listen and get tossed away. We put all our attention on that one dot. Meanwhile, wild mind surrounds us. Western psychology calls wild mind *the unconscious,* but I think *the unconscious* is a limiting term. If it is true that we are all interpenetrated and interconnected, then wild mind includes mountains, rivers, Cadillacs, humidity, plains, emeralds, poverty, old streets in London, snow, and moon. A river and a tree are not unconscious. They are part of wild mind.

Her conclusion lifts me up every time I read it, and I feel a moral duty to dip you in it, a literary baptism by immersion:

So our job as writers is not to diddle around our whole lives in the dot but to take one big step out of it and sink into the big sky and write from there. Let everything run through us and grab as much as we can of it with a pen and paper. Let yourself live in something that is already rightfully yours— your own wild mind....

This is what Zen, too, asks you to do: to sit down in the middle of your wild mind. This is all about a loss of control. This is what falling in love is, too: a loss of control.

Can you do this? Lose control and let wild mind take over? It is the best way to write. To live, too.

I would love to listen in on a conversation between Natalie Goldberg and Charles Johnson. So many similarities, yet so many differences, the duality of a Zen koan. You should easily recognize what they have in common. In addition to being a prolific writer and an influential writing teacher, Charles Johnson is a practitioner of the visual arts and Buddhism. In the cover photo of his book *The Way of the Writer,* we see Johnson in his office, clearly a writer's workspace, with shelves full of books, a desk topped with notebooks, a lovely child—perhaps a grandchild—nearby, and two dogs behind him on the rug. I wish I knew their names. On the corner of his desk is an ebony statue of a sitting Buddha. His book is alive with allusions to Buddhist philosophy and literature. As Johnson's former student Marc C. Conner says in the book's afterword, Johnson seems especially fond of a Zen proverb about "the sculptor whose main task is to see the stunning statue that resides within the unworked piece of wood or stone." For the writer, then, it is not a matter of "conscious creation," but of finding the story hiding in the stone of experience.

The difference between Goldberg and Johnson rests in his passion for merging philosophy and literature. While these fields of study have long been antagonists—the High Truth vs. the low truth—Johnson draws from the well of logic and abstraction a way to reconcile them with feelings of passion and emotion.

Whenever we discuss literature, it is likely that at some point we find the conversation turning to its sister discipline, philosophy. Both forms of expression offer interpretations of our experience delivered through the performance of language. Moreover, the relationship between philosophy and literature is reinforced by the obvious but seldom-stated fact that philosophers are not just thinkers; they are also writers. And our finest storytellers, the ones who transform and deepen our understanding of the world, are not just writers;

they too are engaged in the adventure of ideas.... But, unfortunately, our conversation on this important subject is often clouded by prejudices and misconceptions about the nature of philosophy and literary art—for example, that writers tell stories (mere fiction) but philosophers tell the truth. However, I think the very creative process that characterizes literary art of the highest order may, if viewed from the *inside,* clarify some aspects of this relationship, and demystify the algorithms of creativity in composition that apply to both fiction and philosophy.

Both philosophy and literary art are ways of thinking, ways of clarifying our understanding of the world and human experience. While some kinds of writing can be created and published quickly, both philosophy and literature benefit from a long process of theorizing, of argument, of success that becomes failure and vice versa. Some philosophers avoid anecdote and exemplification. An example might at one moment strongly convey a larger abstraction but at another seem dated, narrow, or just a bad fit.

When it comes time to illustrate storytelling as a form of truth telling, Johnson reverts not to syllogisms, but to a remarkable anecdote. It begins with a reunion with a fraternity brother; their daughters were competing in a talent contest, and the brother tells Johnson that he enjoyed his novel *Middle Passage.*

I thanked him, and mentioned that I appreciated his reading the story, because over a period of six years I threw away

3,000 pages to arrive at the 250-page book he experienced. I watched his eyes grow wide. When I said my ratio of throwaway to kept pages is often 20:1, I saw his mouth fall open. Then I realized that he probably thought that pages he read sprang almost fully formed from my brain like Athena from the head of Zeus. He might even have imagined, wrongly, that when I started writing *Middle Passage*, I knew how the story would turn out.

There was no way he could know that for me a novel is a very special thought experiment, because I've always seen the literary as a potential site for philosophical agency. And I've never seen ideas as existing in some abstract realm floating high above human experience. Rather, I see ideas as originating in the historical muck and mud of our daily experience cloaked in the immediate particulars of this world, and only later do we abstract them for the purpose of study and reflection. So what does this philosophical novelist do? I simply try to return those ideas to the palpable world of experience from which they first sprang.

A student of the late John Gardner, author of *On Moral Fiction*, Johnson became obsessed not just with the *how* of writing fiction but with the *why*. In the afterword, Conner says of Johnson, "'Why do we write fiction?' he asks. 'Why do we read it?…Why are stories so important to us?'"

Such questions fuel Johnson's writing and his teaching of writing. "The goal is to help students understand the majesty and magic of deep reading experiences," writes Conner.

Johnson argues that the true practice of reading has much in common with the phenomenological practice of bracketing one's experience and focusing only on the present moment— much as the Buddhist turns all attention to this present spot of existence and resists the allure of the illusionary past and future. Johnson blocks out all extra-literary concerns— critical ideas, reputations, literary theories, and so on—and seeks only "the same innocent enchantment I had when I was a reader of twelve or thirteen...the experience of mystery and wonder, and needing to know *what happens next.*"

In the end, the work of Goldberg and Johnson—and the work of all the authors highlighted in *Murder Your Darlings*— demonstrates a simple but profound truth: writers use everything. They use their imaginations, their instincts, their reason, their many senses, their experiences, their relationships, their words, every story they have ever absorbed since childhood. For you, writing may be a profession, a hobby, or an aspiration. Whatever your path, writing will help you know more and feel more. It will magnify and intensify the experience of being human.

LESSONS

1. Without reference to your notes or the book, list three things you best remember from reading *Murder Your Darlings*.

2. Of all the books mentioned here, list three you would like to read for yourself. Write about why you have selected those.

3. Besides being a reader and a writer, make a list of other roles you play. Consider how you might draw from those experiences to enhance your writing.

4. If this book has helped you, consider reading my others: *Writing Tools, The Glamour of Grammar, Help! For Writers, How to Write Short,* and *The Art of X-Ray Reading,* all published by Little, Brown.

AFTERWORD

It takes me, from conception to publication, about three years to write a book. It was a clever and useful idea, I thought in 2017, to write a writing book about writing books.

Now, as I write these final words of *Murder Your Darlings*, I find myself in a much different place than where I was when I sat down to write the first chapter. Don Murray taught me to be ready for the surprises in my writing, and I am startled by a big one: This book took me higher and deeper in my craft than I thought possible.

My subtitle contains the A-to-Z trope: writing advice from Aristotle to Zinsser. That range happens to be alphabetical but is more important in its chronological trajectory. Aristotle's birth in 384 BCE to Zinsser's death in 2015 covers 2,399 years, a collective effort of more than two millennia to figure out how stories work and how language creates meaning.

I know a party game—there must be social media versions—in which you list the three people from history you would like to invite for a meal. (How about Shakespeare, Lincoln, and Mary, mother of Jesus, with Mozart in the corner on a keyboard?)

In real life, the people you bring together matter. Your choices say a lot about them, and even more about you. I've spent my career organizing writing seminars and conferences, some for three people, some for thousands. Among these were the National Writers Workshops, in which aspiring writers would descend on a city to work with masters of the craft. It occurred to me in a daydream that this book has the spirit of those learning encounters.

How about a panel featuring Horace, Hayakawa, and Murrow on eyewitness reporting and storytelling? How about Aristotle in conversation with Louise Rosenblatt on how readers respond to stories? And imagine what you might overhear in the hallway from a fervent chat between Kurt Vonnegut and Mary Karr about the line between fact and fiction.

"In the largest sense," wrote my historian friend Paul Kramer about this book, "you're hosting what's likely to be the liveliest gathering of word nerds history has ever assembled."

It has been my honor to host this party and invite you to attend. An author can receive no greater gift than the attention of readers. From this day forward, keep the conversation going with George Orwell and E. B. White and Anne Lamott. Take that good talk into your daily writing life and share it with your writing friends. Learn something new about the craft every day. And get ready for that next surprise.

ACKNOWLEDGMENTS

Please judge this book by its cover. It is the work of Keith Hayes, the artist who designed covers for all six books I have done with Little, Brown. When Keith announced he was leaving LB to become art director at Flatiron Books, he must have heard out of Florida a wail of grief so profound it made its way up Interstate 95 to the Big Apple. When Keith learned of my despair, he vowed to return one more time to provide me with cover—and with a cover. Love that dagger.

At the center of the LB team is Tracy Behar, the best editor I have ever had or would hope to have. My legendary agent, Jane Dystel, promised in 2006 that Tracy and I would prove to be a productive pair, and our six books together in little more than a decade are evidence of Jane's sound judgment. Tracy, thanks for helping me find some darlings to murder—and some to save. Thanks also to Michael Pietsch and Reagan Arthur, and to Betsy Uhrig and her team of copyeditors. Special credit goes to Kathryn Rogers, who, with a keen eye and a deep cultural literacy, sharpened my sentences and fact-checked my mistaken assumptions. (It turns out Billy Welu was a right-handed bowler. I could have sworn he was a lefty.)

Murder Your Darlings will be published in 2020, my fortieth anniversary as a teacher at the Poynter Institute, the school that owns the *Tampa Bay Times,* a news organization that has won twelve Pulitzer Prizes. My dad worked for the United States Customs for forty great years, and following his model, I am honored to have found a supportive, creative, and principled home in which to live my professional life. To all my colleagues at Poynter and the *Times,* to all the students there who have grown into my teachers, I offer my thanks.

To the City of St. Petersburg, my home since 1977, thank you—not just for the sunshine and the sea but for working hard to transform yourself from a sleepy Florida town to one of America's most dynamic and creative cities. Call if you need me. To the Pinellas County Public Schools and its language-arts teachers—especially Mary Osborne and Holly Slaughter: You are champions of literacy. Thank you for leading the effort to turn our classrooms into laboratories of reading, writing, and speaking.

To my best American friend, Tom French, a Pulitzer Prize–winning writer who has turned Indiana University into the home of national championship writers and storytellers. To my best Canadian friend, the late Stuart Adam, the brightest and most dignified journalism scholar I have ever known.

To Paul Kramer, historian and author, for his encouragement and insightful reading of my manuscript.

To booksellers everywhere. Especially to the team at Haslam's Bookstore, home to the ghost of Jack Kerouac and two great bookstore cats, Beowulf and Teacup. Also to Wilson's, 321 Books, and Lighthouse Books. And to Laura Taylor at the Oxford Exchange, my literary home in Tampa.

All writers need a coffee shop where they can rest and recharge, and over the last decade, mine has been the Banyan in St. Pete. Thanks to Erica Allums for her hospitality, charm, and devotion to writers.

To the memory of Jamie Hawkins-Gaar, who left behind at a young age a legacy of creativity, humor, and decency that inspires all of us who knew him.

I feel a need, without naming a particular person, to thank my Facebook friends and Twitter followers. In a social media environment that is too often antisocial, I have been blessed with people who have supported my work, helped sell my books, celebrated my birthdays, and were sad with me the day my dog Rex went to heaven.

Something quite remarkable happened to me during the writing of this book. I was honored by my alma mater, Providence College, and asked to give the commencement speech at the end of its centennial celebration. From that full scholarship in 1970 to this honor a half century later, I can only promise, to paraphrase the Beach Boys, to be true to my school because my school has been so true to me.

I often teach writers to save their best for last, so I conclude my nineteenth book with gratitude to my brothers Vincent and Ted. To my three daughters (in alphabetical order), Alison, Emily, and Lauren, for coaching me in how to be a good man. Oh, yeah, I almost forgot. To their mom, Karen. Keep up the good fight. I'm right here.

APPENDIX

Books by Roy Peter Clark

Free to Write: A Journalist Teaches Young Writers. Portsmouth, N.H.: Heinemann Educational Books, 1987. In the early 1980s, I spent many days as a volunteer writing teacher in Florida public schools. For twenty-nine consecutive summers I conducted writing camps for students and teachers. This book describes what I learned.

America's Best Newspaper Writing (second edition). With Christopher Scanlan. New York: Bedford / St. Martin's, 2006. Since 1979 the Poynter Institute has helped the American Society of Newspaper Editors conduct their Distinguished Writing Awards. This is a collection of the best work over three decades, with accompanying essays and commentary.

The Changing South of Gene Patterson: Journalism and Civil Rights, 1960–1968. With Raymond Arsenault. Gainesville: University Press of Florida, 2002. For eight years during the civil rights movement, Gene Patterson wrote a signed column for the *Atlanta Constitution* every single day. This collection reveals what happens when a master writer—with moral and physical courage—attaches himself to a noble cause.

Coaching Writers: Editors and Reporters Working Together across Media Platforms. With Don Fry. Boston / New York: Bedford / St. Martin's, 2003. Perhaps the first book to take editing beyond the technical aspects of craft to include the human element. Editors may have to fix broken stories, but more important is the mission of encouraging aspiring writers.

Journalism: The Democratic Craft. With G. Stuart Adam. New York: Oxford University Press, 2006. An annotated anthology of more than forty seminal essays on journalism and democracy, focusing on news judgment, the gathering of evidence, the appropriate use of language and narrative strategies, and the importance of critical thinking and interpretation.

Writing Tools: 55 Essential Strategies for Every Writer. New York: Little, Brown, 2006. The first of six books I wrote for Little, Brown, all edited by Tracy Behar. A tenth-anniversary edition, published in 2016, adds five writing strategies to the original fifty. More than 200,000 copies have been sold in several formats. It has been translated into eight languages, including Mandarin and Arabic. It offers practical writing wisdom, from nuts and bolts to special effects to blueprints to useful habits.

The Glamour of Grammar: A Guide to the Magic and Mystery of Practical English. New York: Little, Brown, 2010. Fifty chapters on aspects of rhetorical grammar, that is, using technical aspects of language to make meaning in powerful ways. Sections include words, punctuation, standards, meaning, and purpose. The *New York Times* dubbed it "a grammar manual for the twenty-first century."

Help! For Writers: 210 Solutions to the Problems Every Writer Faces. New York: Little, Brown, 2011. Based upon the theory that most writers follow a similar process and face the same challenges, this book sets out seven steps of the writing process, three problems for taking each step, and ten practical solutions for each problem: 210 in all. I describe the steps as getting started, getting your act together, finding focus, looking for language, building a draft, assessing your progress, and making it better. A final word concerns "keeping the faith."

How to Write Short: Word Craft for Fast Times. New York: Little, Brown, 2013. With writers of the digital age in mind, this book looks back on the enduring power of short writing from the beginning of written texts. Looking at both the craft and purposes of short writing—the how and the why—I offer hundreds of examples of the best short writing, from sonnets, proverbs, aphorisms, marginalia, and song lyrics to blog posts, text messages, and tweets.

The Art of X-Ray Reading: How the Secrets of 25 Great Works of Literature Will Improve Your Writing. New York: Little, Brown, 2016. This book explores how writers read. Revisiting great works of literature—from Chaucer to Toni Morrison—I examine powerful texts with a kind of X-ray vision, looking down into the master texts to see and share the strategies that created them.

BIBLIOGRAPHY

This bibliography contains books featured in *Murder Your Darlings*. Books mentioned but not featured are also included. I also list, on occasion, the work of an author who has inspired a particular insight. Each citation comes from a book that I own or that I have access to through a nearby library. I am not always working from the most recent edition, which is easily accessible to the reader via an online search. I have learned to love these books and have come to think of them as among my darlings. When using excerpts from these texts, my intention is always to adhere to the standards of fair use, to honor the texts and their authors, and to strive for an educational purpose, useful and inspirational to aspiring writers of all ages. Here they are, as promised in my subtitle, from Aristotle to Zinsser:

Aristotle. *Poetics*. Translated by Gerald F. Else. Ann Arbor: University of Michigan Press, 1967.

Barthes, Roland. *Camera Lucida: Reflections on Photography*.

Translated by Richard Howard, foreword by Geoff Dyer. New York: Hill and Wang, 2010.

———. *Writing Degree Zero*. Translated by Annette Lavers and Colin Smith, preface by Susan Sontag. New York: Hill and Wang, 1968.

Berg, A. Scott. *Max Perkins: Editor of Genius*. New York: Dutton, 1978.

Bishop, Stephen. *Songs in the Rough: From "Heartbreak Hotel" to "Higher Love."* New York: St. Martin's Press, 1996.

Blair, Hugh. *Lectures on Rhetoric and Belles Lettres*. Edited by Linda Ferreira-Buckley and S. Michael Halloran. Carbondale: Southern Illinois University Press, 2005. (Originally published London: W. Strahan, 1783.)

Bliss, Edward, Jr., and John M. Patterson. *Writing News for Broadcast*. Foreword by Fred Friendly. New York: Columbia University Press, 1971.

Bloom, Harold. *Shakespeare: The Invention of the Human*. New York: Riverhead Books, 1998.

Boyd, Brian. *On the Origin of Stories: Evolution, Cognition, and Fiction*. Cambridge, Mass.: The Belknap Press of Harvard University Press, 2009.

Brande, Dorothea. *Becoming a Writer*. New York: Harcourt Brace & Co., 1934. (Reissued twice with forewords by John Gardner and Malcolm Bradbury, respectively.)

Brody, Jennifer DeVere. *Punctuation: Art, Politics, and Play*. Durham: Duke University Press, 2008.

Brown, Rita Mae. *Starting from Scratch: A Different Kind of Writers' Manual*. New York: Bantam Books, 1988.

Burnett, Whit, editor. *This Is My Best*. New York: The Dial Press, 1942.

Campbell, George. *The Philosophy of Rhetoric*. Condensed by

Grenville Kleiser. New York and London: Funk & Wagnalls, 1911.

Coates, Ta-Nehisi. *Between the World and Me*. New York: Spiegel & Grau, 2015.

Conner, Jack E., and Marcelline Krafchick, editors. *Speaking of Rhetoric*. Boston: Houghton Mifflin Company, 1966.

Cronin, Doreen. *Click, Clack, Moo: Cows That Type*. Pictures by Betsy Lewin. New York: Simon & Schuster, 2000.

D'Agata, John, and Jim Fingal. *The Lifespan of a Fact*. New York: W. W. Norton, 2012.

Egri, Lajos. *The Art of Dramatic Writing: Its Basis in the Creative Interpretation of Human Motives*. New York: Touchstone Books, 1960. (Published in 1942 as *How to Write a Play*.)

Elbow, Peter. *Writing Without Teachers*. New York: Oxford University Press, 1973.

_____. *Writing with Power: Techniques for Mastering the Writing Process*. New York: Oxford University Press, 1981.

Espenshade, A. Howry. *The Essentials of Composition and Rhetoric*. Boston: D. C. Heath, 1904.

Evans, Harold. *Do I Make Myself Clear? Why Writing Well Matters*. New York: Little, Brown, 2017.

Felski, Rita. *The Limits of Critique*. Chicago: The University of Chicago Press, 2015.

Fish, Stanley. *How to Write a Sentence: And How to Read One*. New York: Harper Perennial, 2011.

Fiske, Robert Hartwell. *To the Point: A Dictionary of Concise Writing*. New York: W. W. Norton, 2014.

Flesch, Rudolf. *The Art of Plain Talk*. New York: Harper and Brothers, 1946.

_____. *The Art of Readable Writing*. New York: Harper and Brothers, 1949.

Forster, E. M. *Aspects of the Novel.* London: Hodder & Stoughton, 1974. (First published by Edward Arnold in 1927.)

Fowler, H. W. *Modern English Usage.* Oxford: Clarendon Press, 1927.

Frye, Northrop. *Fables of Identity: Studies in Poetic Mythology.* New York: Harcourt, Brace & World, Inc., 1963.

Gardner, John. *On Moral Fiction.* New York: Basic Books, 1978.

Garner, Bryan A. *Garner's Modern English Usage,* 4th edition. Oxford: Oxford University Press, 2016.

Garvey, Mark. *Stylized: A Slightly Obsessive History of Strunk & White's* The Elements of Style. New York: Touchstone, 2009.

Gilligan, Carol. *In a Different Voice.* Cambridge: Harvard University Press, 1982.

Goldberg, Natalie. *Wild Mind: Living the Writer's Life.* New York: Bantam, 1990.

———. *Writing Down the Bones: Freeing the Writer Within,* 30th-anniversary edition. Boulder, Colorado: Shambhala, 2016.

Gornick, Vivian. *The Situation and the Story: The Art of Personal Narrative.* New York: Farrar, Straus and Giroux, 2001.

Graff, Gerald, Cathy Birkenstein, Russel Durst. *"They Say / I Say": The Moves That Matter in Academic Writing, with Readings.* New York: W. W. Norton, 2015.

Gunning, Robert. *How to Take the Fog Out of Writing.* Chicago: Dartnell Corporation, 1964.

Hale, Constance, and Jessie Scanlon. *Wired Style: Principles of English Usage in the Digital Age.* New York: Broadway Books, 1999.

Hall, Donald. *Writing Well.* Boston: Little, Brown, 1973.

Hart, Jack R. *A Writer's Coach: An Editor's Guide to Words That Work.* New York: Pantheon Books, 2006.

Hayakawa, S. I. *Language in Action* (later expanded to *Language in Thought and Action*). New York: Harcourt, Brace, 1941.

Hazlitt, William. "On Familiar Style," in *Types of Prose Writing*, edited by Clark H. Slover and DeWitt T. Starnes. Boston: Houghton Mifflin, 1933.

Hearn, Lafcadio. *Talks to Writers*. New York: Dodd, Mead, 1920.

Horace. *The Epistles of Horace* (including "Ars Poetica"). Translated by David Ferry. New York: Farrar, Straus and Giroux, 2015.

Hutchins, Robert M. *A Free and Responsible Press: Report of the Commission on Freedom of the Press* (also known as the report of the Hutchins Commission). Edited by Robert D. Leigh. Chicago: University of Chicago Press, 1947.

Huxley, Aldous. *Brave New World and Brave New World Revisited*. Foreword by Christopher Hitchens. New York: Harper Perennial, 2004.

James, Henry. *The Art of the Novel*. New York: Charles Scribner's Sons, 1934.

Janko, Richard. *Aristotle on Comedy: Towards a Reconstruction of Poetics II*. Berkeley and Los Angeles: University of California Press, 1984.

Johnson, Charles. *The Way of the Writer: Reflections on the Art and Craft of Storytelling*. New York: Scribner, 2016.

John-Steiner, Vera. *Notebooks of the Mind: Explorations of Thinking*. Albuquerque: University of New Mexico Press, 1985.

Karr, Mary. *The Art of Memoir*. New York: Harper Perennial, 2015.

Kenner, Hugh. "The Politics of the Plain Style" in *New York Times Book Review*. Sept. 15, 1985. Republished in *Mazes: 64 Essays*. New York: North Point Press, 1989.

Kenyon, Jane. *A Hundred White Daffodils*. St. Paul, Minn.: Graywolf Press, 1999.

Kerrane, Kevin, and Ben Yagoda, editors. *The Art of Fact: A Historical Anthology of Literary Journalism*. New York: Scribner, 1997.

Kiernan, Kathy, and Retha Power, editors. *This Is My Best: Great Writers Share Their Favorite Work*. San Francisco: Chronicle, 2005.

King, Stephen. *On Writing: A Memoir of the Craft*. New York: Scribner, 2000.

Kovach, Bill, and Tom Rosenstiel. *The Elements of Journalism: What Newspeople Should Know and the Public Should Expect*. New York: Three Rivers Press, 2001, 2007.

Lamott, Anne. *Bird by Bird: Some Instructions on Writing and Life*. New York: Anchor Books, 1995.

Le Guin, Ursula K. *Steering the Craft: A 21st-Century Guide to Sailing the Sea of Story*. Boston: Mariner Books, 2015.

Levine, Amy-Jill. *Short Stories by Jesus: The Enigmatic Parables of a Controversial Rabbi*. New York: HarperOne, 2014.

Lodge, David. *The Art of Fiction: Illustrated from Classic and Modern Texts*. New York: Viking, 1992.

McMorris, Jenny. *The Warden of English: The Life of H.W. Fowler*. Oxford: Oxford University Press, 2001.

McPhee, John. *Draft No. 4: On the Writing Process*. New York: Farrar, Straus and Giroux, 2017.

_____. *The John McPhee Reader*. Edited with an introduction by William L. Howarth. New York: Vintage Books, 1977.

Mencher, Melvin. *News Reporting and Writing*, 9th edition. Boston: McGraw Hill, 2000.

Murray, Donald. *The Essential Don Murray: Lessons from Amer-*

ica's Greatest Writing Teacher. Edited by Thomas Newkirk and Lisa C. Miller. Portsmouth, New Hampshire: Heinemann Boynton/Cook, 2009.

_____. *A Writer Teaches Writing*, 2nd edition. Boston: Houghton Mifflin, 1985.

_____. *Writing to Deadline: The Journalist at Work*. Portsmouth, N.H.: Heinemann, 2000.

Murrow, Edward R. *In Search of Light: The Broadcasts of Edward R. Murrow, 1938–1961*. Edited with an introduction by Edward Bliss, Jr. New York: Knopf, 1967.

Orwell, George. *The Collected Essays, Journalism and Letters of George Orwell*. Edited by Sonia Orwell and Ian Angus. New York and London: Harcourt, Brace Jovanovich, 1968.

Paglia, Camille. *Break, Blow, Burn: Camille Paglia Reads Forty-Three of the World's Best Poems*. New York: Pantheon, 2005.

Perkins, Maxwell. *Editor to Author: The Letters of Maxwell E. Perkins*. Compiled by John Hall Wheelock. New York: Charles Scribner's Sons, 1991.

Pinker, Steven. *The Sense of Style: The Thinking Person's Guide to Writing in the 21st Century*. New York: Viking, 2014.

Plato. *The Republic*. Translated by Robin Waterfield. Oxford: Oxford University Press, 1993.

Plimpton, George. *The Writer's Chapbook: A Compendium of Fact, Opinion, Wit, and Advice from the Twentieth Century's Preeminent Writers*. Edited from the *Paris Review* interviews. New York: Modern Library Edition, 1999. (Published in 1989 by Viking Penguin.)

Posner, Richard A. *The Little Book of Plagiarism*. New York: Pantheon, 2007.

Postman, Neil. *Amusing Ourselves to Death: Public Discourse in the Age of Show Business*. New York: Penguin, 1985.

Prose, Francine. *Reading Like a Writer*. New York: Harper Perennial, 2006.

Provost, Gary. *100 Ways to Improve Your Writing*. New York: Mentor, 1985.

Quiller-Couch, Sir Arthur. *On the Art of Writing*. New York: G. P. Putnam's Sons, 1916.

Quintilian. *Quintilian: On the Teaching of Speaking and Writing: Translations from Books One, Two, and Ten of the Institutio oratoria*. Edited by James J. Murphy. Carbondale: Southern Illinois University Press, 1987.

Rosenblatt, Louise M. *Literature as Exploration*, 5th edition. Foreword by Wayne Booth. New York: The Modern Language Association of America, 1995. (Original edition 1938.)

_____. *The Reader, the Text, the Poem: The Transactional Theory of the Literary Work*. Carbondale: Southern Illinois University Press, 1978.

Scutts, Joanna. "Fascist Sympathies: On Dorothea Brande," in *The Nation*, August 13, 2013.

Shakespeare, William. *Hamlet*. Edited by Harold Jenkins. London: The Arden Shakespeare, Methuen, 1982.

Sidney, Sir Philip. *Defence of Poesy*. English Literature Series, London: Macmillan, 1963. New York: St. Martin's, 1963.

Smith, Frank. *Writing and the Writer*. Hillsdale, N.J.: Lawrence Erlbaum Associates, 1982.

Snyder, Louis L., and Richard B. Morris, Editors. *A Treasury of Great Reporting: "Literature under Pressure" from the Sixteenth Century to Our Own Time*. New York: Simon and Schuster, 1949.

Spector, Stephen. *The Quotable Guide to Punctuation*. New York: Oxford University Press, 2017.

Spencer, Herbert. *The Philosophy of Style.* And Edgar Allan Poe. *The Philosophy of Composition.* New York: Pageant Press, 1959.

Sternburg, Janet, editor. *The Writer on Her Work* (essays by seventeen women). New York: W. W. Norton, 1980.

Strunk, William, Jr. *The Elements of Style: The Original Edition.* Mineola, New York: Dover Publications, Inc., 2006.

_____ and E. B. White. *The Elements of Style with Revisions, an Introduction, and a Chapter on Writing.* New York: The Macmillan Company, 1959. (With several subsequent editions.)

Sweet, Melissa. *Some Writer! The Story of E. B. White.* Boston and New York: Houghton Mifflin Harcourt, 2016.

Sword, Helen. *The Writer's Diet: A Guide to Fit Prose.* Chicago: University of Chicago Press, 2016.

Talese, Gay. *Frank Sinatra Has a Cold and Other Essays.* New York: Penguin, 2011.

Taylor, Robert H., and Herman W. Liebert. *Authors at Work* (manuscripts of famous writers). New York: Grolier Club, 1957.

Thomas, Francis-Noel, and Mark Turner. *Clear and Simple as the Truth: Writing Classic Prose.* Princeton and Oxford: Princeton University Press, 2011.

Tierno, Michael. *Aristotle's Poetics for Screenwriters: Storytelling Secrets from the Greatest Mind in Western Civilizations.* New York: Hyperion, 2002.

Tompkins, Al. *Aim for the Heart: Write, Shoot, Report and Produce for TV and Multimedia.* Washington, D.C.: CQ Press, 2012.

Truss, Lynne. *Eats, Shoots & Leaves: The Zero Tolerance Approach to Punctuation.* New York: Gotham Books, 2004.

Tufte, Virginia. *Artful Sentences: Syntax as Style.* Cheshire, Conn.: Graphics Press, 2006.

Ueland, Brenda. *If You Want to Write: A Book about Art, Independence, and Spirit.* New York: G. P. Putnam's Sons, 1938. (Reissued: St. Paul: Graywolf Press, 1987.)

Vonnegut, Kurt. *Bagombo Snuff Box: Uncollected Short Fiction.* New York: Berkley Books, 1999.

_____ and Lee Stringer. *Like Shaking Hands with God: A Conversation about Writing.* New York: Washington Square Press, 1999.

Wallace, David Foster. "Authority and American Usage," in *Consider the Lobster and Other Essays.* New York: Little, Brown, 2005.

Wolfe, Tom, and E. W. Johnson, *The New Journalism.* London: Picador (published by Pan Books), 1973.

Wood, James. *The Broken Estate: Essays on Literature and Belief.* New York: Picador, 1999.

_____. *How Fiction Works.* New York: Farrar, Straus and Giroux, 2008.

Woolf, Virginia. *A Room of One's Own.* New York: Harcourt, 2005.

Yagoda, Ben. *The Sound on the Page: Great Writers Talk about Style and Voice in Writing.* New York: Harper, 2004.

Zinsser, William. *On Writing Well: The Classic Guide to Writing Nonfiction,* 30th-anniversary edition. New York: HarperCollins, 1976 to 2008.

INDEX

Index

Index

religion and, 302–3
"Three Little Words," 233
Trash Baby, 119–20
Vietnam War and, 266–67, 269
as a writing teacher and coach, 9,
   24–25, 27–28, 76, 100–101, 199,
   215, 240, 246, 249, 300
Writing Tools, 4, 21, 62, 245–46
zero drafting used by, 121, 195
Clark, Shirley (mother), 17–18, 19, 126
Clark, Ted (brother), 19
Clark, Ted (father), 125–26
Clark, Vincent (brother), 19
Clinton, Hillary, 258
clutter, cutting, 20, 22–26, 274
Collins, Seward, 5, 128–29
Communist "witch hunting" by
   McCarthy, 284
comprehensibility of a text, algorithm of,
   204, 239, 240, 242–47, 248–50
confidence, 97–98
   first drafts and, 108, 114–15
   Murray on, 104–7
conflict, as a category of newsworthiness,
   152
Conner, Marc C., 306, 308–9
connotations of words, 27, 30, 33, 255, 295
Conrad, Joseph, 91, 247
Cordelia (in *King Lear*), 223, 225
Coughlin, Charles, 128
Cowley, Malcolm, 240
Craft of Revision, The (Murray), 101
craft of writing, 11–12, 109
   Chaucer on, 103
   first drafts, 97, 108, 112–13, 114–15, 124
   freewriting, 97, 116, 117, 118–21, 124
   incorporating an associated craft
      into, 299, 301, 302–8
   King on, 139, 143
   Lamott on, 97, 108, 109, 111, 112–14
   Le Guin on, 64
   Murray on, 101, 102–7, 274
   planning process and, 41–46
   Quiller-Couch on, 13–15, 16–17, 214
   sentence structure in, 34, 36–40
   subzero drafts, 120, 121, 124
   Vonnegut on, 269, 270, 271
   zero drafts, 112–15, 116, 120–23, 124,
      195
   Zinsser on, 22–26, 274

Cratchit, Bob, 189
creativity, 74, 118, 138, 218, 307
critical thinking, 118, 138
Cunningham, Merce, 74
currency, as a category of newsworthiness, 152

Dante, 154, 175
darling, OED's definition of, 15
Darwin, Charles, 147, 155
Dawkins, Richard, 80
Day, Fred, 269
Dead Zone, The (King), 140
"Defence of Poesy" (Sidney), 276
derivative voice, 90
description, King on, 143
descriptive grammar, 217, 219
Devin, Eddie, 106
Dewey, John, 206
dialogue in nonfiction, 200
Diana, Princess, 87
Dickens, Charles, 71, 187, 188, 189,
   190
Dickinson, Emily, 144, 171
Didion, Joan, 198
digital age
   language and forms of delivery in, 78,
      79–80, 85
   news judgment in, 278–79
   voice in, developing, 81–83, 85, 86
   disadvantage as advantage, 265, 270–72
Divine Comedy (Dante), 154
Dowd, Maureen, 87
Draft No. 4 (McPhee), 41, 42–43
drafts
   first, 97, 108, 112–13, 114–15, 124
   revision of. *See* revisions
   subzero, 120, 121, 124
   zero, 112–15, 116, 120–23, 124, 195
Dreiser, Theodore, 232
Dyer, Geoff, 121

efferent texts, 203, 207–8, 209–10
Egri, Lajos, 148, 178, 179–81, 183, 184
Elbow, Peter, 97–98, 116, 118, 119, 120
Elements of Journalism, The (Kovach and
   Rosenstiel), 261–62
Elements of Style, The (Strunk and
   White), 5, 47, 49–52, 130
   criticism of, 22, 50, 53

331

Index

influence and popularity of, 20,
  51–52, 109, 140
on sentence structure, 54
value of, 50–53, 56–57
White's contributions to, 52–53,
  54–56, 140
Eliot, T. S., 109, 163
Elizabeth II, 187
Elton John, 87
Emigrants, The (Sebald), 166, 167
emphatic word order, 214–15, 219
Epistles of Horace, The (Horace), 273,
  275–76
Esquire, 194, 196
Essential Don Murray, The (Newkirk and
  Miller), 99, 101–2
*Essentials of Composition and Rhetoric,
  The* (Espenshade), 34
Euripides, 223
evolution, 155–56, 266
exclamation points, overuse of, 6, 61–62
experimental frames, voice modulation
  and, 90
experimental writing, 90, 106, 172
eyewitness reporting, 211, 254, 284,
  285–88, 312

Fables of Identity (Frye), 170–73, 174–76
fact-checking, 260, 284
"False Color in Verbs" lesson (Hall),
  31–32
fascism, American, 126–27, 128, 129
"Fascist Sympathies" (Scutts), 126
Father and Son (Gosse), 232
Felshman, Neil, 186–87
Ferry, David, 273, 275–76
fictional truth, 167
Fiedler, Leslie, 163
Finkel, David, 116–17, 118
first drafts, 97, 108, 112–13, 114–15, 124
first-person narrators, 162, 164
flat characters, 148, 185, 187–88, 189–91
Flaubert, Gustave, 190
Fleming, Ian, 173
Flesch, Rudolf, 243, 247–48, 250
  The Art of Plain Talk, 243
  The Art of Readable Writing, 239, 243
  "Readability Formula" of, 204, 240,
    242–47
  White's essay on, 240–41

*Why Johnny Can't Read—and What
  You Can Do about It,* 243
Flesch Test, 204, 240, 242–47
focus, 176, 177
Fog Index, 204, 242, 243, 248–50
Forster, E. M., 148, 185–88, 189–90
Frank Sinatra Has a Cold (Talese),
  193–94, 195–97, 200
free indirect style, 147, 160, 164, 165–69
Free to Write (Clark), 44–46
freewriting, 97, 116, 124
  Clark's use of, 119–20
  differences between zero drafting
    and, 120–21
  Elbow on, 118–19, 120
  Scanlan's use of, 117
French, Thomas, 72, 153, 234
Freud, Sigmund, 129, 135, 179, 223
Frey, James, 235
Fry, Don, 6, 48, 88, 173
Frye, Northrop, 178
  Anatomy of Criticism, 171
  on experience of narrative, 147–48
  Fables of Identity, 170–73, 174–76

Galbraith, John Kenneth, 240
Gardner, John, 308
Garner, Bryan, 4, 242
Garvey, Mark, 50
"Getting at the Truth" (Chute), 240
Glamour of Grammar, The (Clark), 69,
  300
Globe and Mail, The, 90, 91
Gloucester (in *King Lear*), 224
Goldberg, Natalie, 254, 302, 306, 309
  Wild Mind, 299, 301, 302, 303–5
  Writing Down the Bones, 8, 302, 303
Goldfinger, 173–74
Gopnik, Adam, 50
Gornick, Vivian, 204, 229, 232–35, 237,
  238
Gosse, Edmund, 232
Goucher College, 234
grammar
  descriptive, 217, 219
  prescriptive, 217, 219
  rhetorical, 215, 219
Grand Central Winter (Stringer), 270
Graves, Don, 6
Great Gatsby, The (Fitzgerald), 162

Index

Gunning, Robert, 204, 239, 242, 243, 248–50

Hale, Constance "Connie," 6, 78, 87
background of, 84
Sin and Syntax, 79
Vex, Hex, Smash, Smooch, 79
Wired Style, 48, 79–81, 83
Hall, Donald, 6, 27, 28–33
A Carnival of Losses, 28, 29
death of, 28, 30
"False Color in Verbs" lesson of, 31–32
on language, 11, 28, 30–31
Writing Well, 27, 28, 29, 30–32
Hall, Radclyffe, 186–87
Hamilton (Miranda), 189, 223, 224
Hamilton, Alexander, 189, 224, 247
Hamilton, Eliza, 223
Hamlet (Shakespeare), 190, 227, 277
Harcourt, Brace and Howe, 51
Harold, Bloom, 163
Harrington, Walt, 234
Harvest of Shame, 284
Haslam's Bookstore, 59, 248
Hayakawa, S. I., 295
intellectual and political life of, 257–58
Language in Action, 253, 255–56, 295
Language in Thought and Action, 255–56, 257, 259, 260–61, 262–63
on Nazi propagandists, 253, 256, 295
on reliability and credibility of reports, 259, 260–61, 262–63
Hazlitt, William, 301
Heath, Shirley Brice, 216
Heinemann Educational Books, 46
Heller, Joseph, 268
Help! For Writers (Clark), 119
Hemingway, Ernest, 93–94, 95
Hersey, John, 201
Hitchens, Christopher, 292, 293
Hitler, Adolf, 129, 253, 256, 296
Hoffman, Dustin, 122
Hokusai, 103
Holocaust, 127, 257, 286–87, 288
Homer, 155, 269
Horace, 253, 274, 279, 281

"Ars Poetica" (or "Art of Poetry"), 273, 276–77
The Epistles of Horace, 273, 275–76
Horton Hears a Who! (Seuss), 155
How Fiction Works (Wood), 147, 160, 163–65, 187
How to Take the Fog Out of Writing (Gunning), 239, 248–50
Howarth, William L. "Bill," 6, 11, 41–42, 44, 46
Huxley, Aldous, 295–96
Brave New World, 254, 257, 292, 293, 294, 296–97
Brave New World Revisited, 256–57, 291, 292, 293–94
on propaganda, 294–97

identity (as a writer), 125, 130–31, 138
books on, overview on, 109
King on, 98
Lamott on, 109
Stringer on, 271
Ueland on, 130, 131–35, 136, 138
If You Want to Write (Ueland), 125, 130, 131–35, 136
immersive reporting, 201–2
New Journalism on, 198–200
Talese and, 193, 195–97
imposter's syndrome, 97, 113
In Search of Light (Murrow), 254, 282, 283, 285–88, 290
"In the Waiting Room" (Bishop), 232
Inferno (Dante), 154
Institutio Oratoria (Quintilian), 215–18
internet, 79, 85, 278. *See also* digital age
introduction. *See* lead, story
ISIS, 193

Jackson, Shirley, 176
James, Henry, 71
Janko, Richard, 224–25
Jenkins, Bob, 278
Jerome, John, 105
Jesus, 153, 154, 175
Jocasta, 223
John McPhee Reader, The (Howarth), 41–42, 44, 46
John-Steiner, Vera, 48, 68, 74–76
Johnson, Charles, 254, 299, 301, 305–9
Johnson, E. W., 193, 197–98

Index

Index

Index

Index

Index

Index

Index

Westheimer, Ruth, 92
White, E. B., 250
  "Calculating Machine," 240–41, 242
  Charlotte's Web, 50, 88, 239
  The Elements of Style, 6, 20, 35, 47,
    48, 49–51, 52–53, 54–56, 88, 109,
    140, 240–41, 242–43, 250, 312
  Stuart Little, 50
  voice of, 88
white space, 61, 249–50, 251
*Why Johnny Can't Read—and What You
  Can Do about It* (Flesch), 243
Wild Boars (Thai soccer team rescued
  from cave), 149–50, 151–54, 157–58
Wild Mind (Goldberg), 299, 301, 302,
  303–5
Will, George, 87–88
Wills, Garry, 198
Wilson, Mike, 192
Winfrey, Oprah, 235
Wired Style (Hale and Scanlon), 48,
  79–81, 83, 84
Wolfe, Tom, 62, 197–99, 201
  The New Journalism, 5, 148, 193,
    197–99
  on status details, 196
  on very short sentences, 288
  writing style of, 6, 61, 62
Wood, James, 168–69
  The Broken Estate, 163, 166–68
  How Fiction Works, 147, 160, 163–65,
    187
Woolf, Virginia, 75–76
word length. *See* syllable count
word order, emphatic, 214–15, 219
World War II
  Murrow's radio dispatches during,
    254, 283, 284, 285–88
  Orwell on language during, 217
  Vonnegut and, 267–69
  See also Nazi Germany
Write to Learn (Murray), 101

Writer and Psychoanalysis, The (Bergler),
  271
"Writer in the Newsroom" (Murray),
  102–7
Writer Teaches Writing, A (Murray), 101
Writer's Digest, 60
writing books
  overview on selection of, 4–6
  types of, 109
Writing Down the Bones (Goldberg), 8,
  302, 303
Writing for Your Readers (Murray), 101
Writing News for Broadcast (Bliss), 21
writing process. *See* craft of writing
Writing Tools (Clark), 4, 21, 62, 245–46
Writing Well (Hall), 27, 28, 29, 30–32
Writing with Power (Elbow), 116, 118–19
Writing Without Teachers (Elbow), 116,
  118, 119

X-ray reading, 4

Yagoda, Ben, 86
  The Art of Fact, 91–92
  The Sound on the Page, 86, 92–95
  on voice and style, 47, 92–95
Yeats, William Butler, 171, 176

Zen Buddhism, 301, 303, 304, 305
zero drafts, 112–15, 120–23, 124
  Clark's use of, 121, 195
  definition of, 121
  differences between freewriting and,
    120–21
Zinsser, William "Bill," 6, 11, 24–25, 42,
  221
  death of, 21, 311
  on language, 20, 22–24, 274
  On Writing Well, 20, 21–24, 109, 274,
    302

ABOUT THE AUTHOR

By some accounts, Roy Peter Clark is America's writing coach, devoted to creating a nation of writers. A PhD in medieval literature, he is widely considered the most influential writing teacher in the rough-and-tumble world of newspaper journalism. With a deep background in traditional media, Clark has illuminated the discussion of writing on the internet. He has gained fame by teaching writing to children and has nurtured Pulitzer Prize–winning authors such as Thomas French and Diana K. Sugg. He is a teacher who writes and a writer who teaches.

For more than three decades, Clark has taught writing at the Poynter Institute, a school for journalists in St. Petersburg, Florida, considered among the most prominent such teaching institutions in the world. He graduated from Providence College with a degree in English and earned his PhD from Stony Brook University.

In 1977 he was hired by the *St. Petersburg Times* (now the

Tampa Bay Times) as one of America's first writing coaches and worked with the American Society of Newspaper Editors to improve newspaper writing nationwide. He has taught writing at news organizations, schools, businesses, nonprofits, and government agencies in more than forty states and on five continents.

Among his clients at Poynter: the *New York Times,* the *Washington Post,* National Public Radio, *USA Today,* CNN, Gannett, Microsoft, IBM, the U.S. Department of Health and Human Services, Disney, AAA, the World Bank, and countless colleges and universities. He has appeared on *Today* and *The Oprah Winfrey Show.*

Clark has authored or edited nineteen books about writing, reading, language, and journalism. Humorist Dave Barry has said of him: "Roy Peter Clark knows more about writing than anybody I know who is not currently dead." He plays keyboard in a rock band. He lives with his family in St. Petersburg, Florida.